CREATIVE
GARDEN
PLANNING

CREATIVE
GARDEN
PLANNING

TIGER BOOKS INTERNATIONAL
LONDON

A QUINTET BOOK

This edition first published 1989 by
Tiger Books International Ltd.,
London.

Copyright © Quarto 1984
Copyright © This edition 1989 Quintet Publishing Ltd.
ISBN 1 85501 019 4

This book was designed and produced by
Quintet Publishing Limited
6 Blundell Street
London N7 9BH

Coordinating Editor: Geoff Rogers
Senior Editor: Jim Miles
Copy Editor: Mike Darton
Design: Patrick Burton, David Papworth
Editorial Director: Christopher Fagg
Art Director: Alastair Campbell

Typeset in Great Britain by
QV Typesetting Limited
Manufactured in Hong Kong
by Regent Publishing Services Limited
Printed in Hong Kong by Leefung-Asco Printers Limited

All statements in this book giving information or advice are
believed to be true and accurate at the time of going to press
but neither the author nor the publishers can accept any legal
liability for errors or omissions.

The material in this publication
previously appeared in
THE GARDEN ADVISER

Contributors
Richard Gorer
Arthur Hellyer
Peter McHoy
Jim Mather
Yvonne Rees
Alan Toogood
Jack Wilson

Photographs
Gillian Becket
Eric Crichton
Daansmit
Bob Gibbons Photography
Richard and Sally Greenhill
Jerry Harpur
Neill Holmes
Arthur Hellyer
Ian Howes
Patrick Johns
Tom Leighton
National Vegetable Research Station
Photobank
The Plant Photo Library (Susan Roth)
Harry Smith Photography Collection
Photos Horticultural (Michael Warren)
Dennis Woodland

Illustrations
Norman Bancroft-Hunt
Sally Launder
David Papworth
John Woodcock

CONTENTS

INTRODUCTION

Garden design is a branch of art that is especially suitable for amateurs. It is a notable fact that many of the world's most admired gardens were planned by their owners with little or no advice from professional designers. Part of the explanation is that, unlike buildings, most gardens are in a constant process of change as plants grow too large, or prove unsuitable, for the purpose they were chosen for. As a result, successful garden-making usually demands varying degrees of change and adjustment over a period of years, and this is of course true even of professionally-designed gardens,which may require considerable planting alterations as they develop.

Garden planning and design

Professional garden designers invariably prepare accurate plans in order to show their clients what is proposed and to guide the workforce in construction and planting. For a garden that is to be made and planted by the owner-designer such detailed plans are unnecessary — after all, it is far easier to do much of the planning on the ground with sticks, string or powdered lime trickled out of a bag to mark the suggested outlines of paths, lawns, beds, borders and so on. It may indeed save some time and crystallize ideas if a rough sketch plan is prepared before marking out the ground, but such a preliminary sketch is entirely flexible and may be considerably modified as the plan is transferred to actuality. That a plan like this must in any case be regarded as totally tentative, subject to alteration, is inevitable,in that without considerable experience of planning it is difficult to relate the areas shown on a sheet of paper the actual areas on the ground, and in that garden designing is a three-dimensional art whereas plans are only two-dimensional. A perspective sketch gives a three-dimensional effect but is much more difficult to draw. Out on the ground, with the aid of canes to indicate key features such as trees, arches, pergolas or buildings, it is much easier to visualize what the garden is really going to look like as it matures and to ensure that there will be enough tall objects to give the composition height and solidity, to screen parts that need to be hidden and give privacy.

In all but the smallest gardens it is usually wise for a plan not to allow the whole area to be seen at once but to unfold progressively as it is explored. The best preparation for garden-making is to look at as many mature gardens as possible, picking up one idea here, another there, until the whole design begins to shape itself in the mind. This can then be sketched out on paper and finally transferred to the ground. Perhaps only at that stage will it be possible to view the garden properly from different angles, from each creating a mental picture of what the effects will be once the constructional features have been made and the plants have grown up. Even after all this foresight it is probable that adjustments will seem necessary as garden-making proceeds, and maybe years later, when the plants are at last making their full contribution to the scene, still more alterations will appear necessary.

Formal and informal gardens

Gardens may be roughly classified as formal or informal: the formal based mainly on regular, geometric patterns, the informal on much more flowing and irregular shapes. The extreme example of informality is the 'natural' or 'wild' garden which superficially seems to owe little to any art of the designer although in fact it probably depends greatly for its effect on the skill with which it has been put together and kept in balance by pruning, thinning and replanting. Regrettably, nature left to herself nearly always finishes up by producing a wilderness of weeds and tangled growth.

In practice there is no reason for formal and informal designs not to be combined. A very common, and usually effective, formula is to plan the area close to the house formally and break into increasing informality the further away from this starting point. In tiny gardens, however, there may well be room for only one style, usually formal, its shape and architectural features chosen to match the building it accompanies.

Specialist gardens

There is one type of gardening that is hardly ever mentioned in books, and is anathema to professional garden designers, and that is specialization in some particular group of plants. Rose lovers, for example, devote most of their gardens to roses irrespective of what this does to the design; alpine plant enthusiasts make raised beds with unmortared retaining walls, or grow their choicest plants in frames; lovers of dwarf conifers plant minipinetums; and those who love full-scale trees (and have the space to grow them) make arboretums. These are all perfectly sensible ways of making gardens if that is what the owners require — but the results owe little to the rules of aesthetics.

The garden environment

Choice of plants is regulated by soil, temperature, rainfall and availability of light. Soils may be rich or poor, light or heavy, acid or alkaline, and plants have individual preferences for combinations. Fortunately, most of these characteristics are not too difficult to alter. Soils that are poor can be fed with manures and fertilizers. Those that are too light and porous can be improved by manuring and by forking in moisture-holding materials such as peat, leaf mould, decayed garden refuse, spent hop manure and other bulky organic materials. It may seem a little odd that these same dressings should also improve heavy soils, but they do — partly because they are spongy and help to keep soil open, and also because as they decompose they produce humus, which has a great effect on the texture of soil, improving it by binding tiny particles into larger granules with bigger air spaces between them.

Lime improves soil texture in a similar way, but it can also introduce new problems; some plants object to it, and only grow satisfactorily in soils that are acid and contain no free lime. Other plants prefer alkaline soil, and for these lime can do no harm, providing a simple and safe way of reducing soil acidity. It is, however, more difficult to make alkaline soils acid, although prolonged manuring and the use of sulphate of ammonia as a fertilizer eventually achieves this effect over a period of years.

Another way of catering for plants that do not like the soil-type of the garden is to make special beds for them filled with the soil-type that does suit their needs. All the same, beds of acid soil on an alkaline site need to be raised above the natural ground level, or alkaline water is likely to seep into them.

Temperatures may be either too high or too low for the needs of the plants desired in the garden. There are some plants that survive in very cold places and in the wild may be covered with snow in winter; they may suffer when transferred to even slightly warmer places that have little or no snow in winter. Another potential problem is that plants that are quite safe if they remain dormant throughout the cold season may be at risk if set in a place where winter temperatures vary a lot, for then they may start to grow too soon and the tender young growth may be killed by frost. At the other extreme, gardens in the tropics or sub-tropics may encourage plants to go on growing all year when by nature they should have a resting period; this can be just as fatal to success as too much cold.

Gardeners are often heard to talk of 'hardy' and 'tender' plants as if there were some hard and fast divisions between them — it is not so. There is a huge range of variability, from plants that begin to suffer when the temperature falls below 15°C (59°F) to those that are unlikely to be damaged until the temperature falls to -18°C (0°F) or even lower.

Many plant encyclopaedias divide countries, or even continents, into zones of hardiness, giving the plants zone numbers to indicate where they can survive. The system can be very helpful — but there can of course be great differences in temperature within a single zone, and sometimes even within a garden, so it is always wise to get local advice about exactly what does grow, or to observe in the locality what is thriving in other gardens.

Rainfall can vary tremendously, from the minimal amount of the great deserts to the constant wetness of the rainforests. Plants that have adapted themselves to dry conditions can be killed if planted in wet places and vice versa. Fortunately, one can again usually do something about this, watering plants that require more moisture than the district normally supplies, or protecting in some way those that would otherwise be too wet. Such protection is usually most necessary in winter for the many plants that then suffer from a combination of wet and cold for which they are not adapted.

Finally, there is the light factor. Some plants need a great deal of light to make them flower, others are scorched by too much direct sunlight and much prefer to be in the shade. Books and nursery catalogues usually give reliable advice on these matters. One point they may overlook, however, is that many plants with yellow or yellow-variegated leaves only develop their full colour when exposed to fairly strong light: in the shade the colour may be dull or lacking.

Evergreen or deciduous?

All plants with foliage can be classified as either evergreen or deciduous. These terms are usually applied to trees and shrubs, but there are also some herbaceous (soft-stemmed) plants that retain their leaves in winter, kniphofias and some irises for example, and many that grow in winter and die down in summer.

There is a tendency for beginners to suppose that evergreens must be superior to deciduous plants in terms of garden decoration, but this is not so. Each class has its uses, and part of the charm of a well-planted garden can be the constant change of foliage colours, mainly in the deciduous trees and shrubs, and the emergence in winter of entirely new patterns of branch and leaf. A garden filled entirely with evergreens can seem heavy and depressing, and the lack of change can become boring.

Trees and shrubs

Trees and the larger shrubs, whether evergreen or deciduous, play an important role in giving height to the overall garden composition. One well-placed tree may become a vital focal point in a vista or, in large gardens, groups of trees may perform a similar function. Landscape gardens depend mainly on trees for their shape and for the contrast between light and shade, open spaces and solid masses, on which all composition is based. The great English landscape gardens of the eighteenth century were made entirely with trees, grass, water and occasional buildings (which might be classical or romantic, Roman temples, gothic ruins or oriental pavilions, according to the taste of the designer and the fashion of the period).

Trees vary in shape, branch pattern and density. Some are wide-spreading, others tall; the overall shape may be rounded, billowy, weeping, conical or columnar. Some trees produce mutations, or sports, that are different in shape from the norm. In the wild these would not be perpetuated but gardeners may see value in them and maintain them by vegetative propagation.

Weeping and columnar (fastigiate) forms have been particularly welcome. The golden weeping willow is a tree of uncertain origin, in which the secondary branches are completely pendulous and the young bark yellow. The common silver birch is called *Betula pendula* because the ends of its branches hang downwards — this is exaggerated in such varieties as "Dalecarlica", "Tristis" and "Youngii". There are weeping forms of both green-leaved and purple-leaved beech, a beautiful weeping form of the spring cherry, *Prunus subhirtella* "Pendula Rosea", and many more grown in gardens for their pendulous habit.

At the opposite extreme are forms that hold all their branches erect. The most famous of these is the Lombardy poplar, a fastigiate sport of the black poplar which has transformed the landscape of parts of France and Italy but is not a good garden tree because of its wide-spreading thirsty roots. There are many other columnar trees that are far more suitable, particularly among the evergreen cypresses and also less well known trees such as the Dawyck beech and the cypress oak (*Quercus robur* "Fastigata"). The Irish yew and the golden-leaved variety named "Standishii" are both columnar sports of the common yew; the Irish juniper is a narrowly erect form of the common juniper; and *Prunus* "Amanogawa" is a Japanese flowering cherry so narrowly erect that it is sometimes called the flagpole cherry.

These narrow trees can be used as eye-catchers, especially — and valuably — in small gardens because they take up little space. As a contrast with these strong vertical lines, the garden designer may use wide-spreading, even horizontally-branched shrubs such as the two forms of yew known as "Dovastoniana" and

'Dovastonii Aurea', the first dark green, the second green and gold. Equally impressive, horizontally, are the wide forms of juniper such as *Juniperus X media* 'Pfitzerana' and *J. sabina tamariscifolia*, and the horizontally-branched cherry laurels *(Prunus laurocerasus)* such as 'Shipkaensis' and 'Zabeliana'.

Herbaceous perennials

Trees and shrubs are more or less permanent occupants of the garden. They provide the firm 'skeleton' of plant design around or within which less permanent plants can be displayed. These are classified as herbaceous perennials, bulbs (which are really herbaceous perennials that have a special kind of food and moisture storage organ but are always listed separately), biennials and monocarpic plants, and annuals. The longevity of herbaceous perennials varies greatly, from quite short-term plants such as lupins and perennial verbascums to very long-lived plants such as golden rod *(Solidago)* and Michaelmas daisies *(Aster)*. All get larger and larger with age and tend to starve themselves out. In gardens it is wise to lift most of them every three or four years, split them up into smaller pieces if that is possible (it is not for plants such as lupins and verbascums which make a single solid crown or tap root), and replant after digging and feeding the soil. Exceptions are peonies, eryngiums, hellebores and a few others which dislike disturbance and are best left alone until there is clear indication that they are deteriorating.

Because of their semi-permanence, these herbaceous perennials are the second-rank plants in the garden designer's stock. They make their full effect more rapidly than trees and shrubs and so can be used to fill in while the latter are growing but not yet occupying the full space allocated to them. They are also useful to maintain a continuity of colour and to provide a greater diversity of foliage shapes and colours. They can also be moved and rearranged readily when faults in the original planting are revealed.

Annuals and biennials

At the bottom of the time-scale come annuals and biennials, ephemeral plants which are nevertheless extremely useful for temporary displays, to fill gaps which occur through losses, or because the more permanent plants are not yet fully grown. True annuals live for one year only and, when they have flowered and ripened their seed, they die and decay. Their flowering season is often quite brief but spectacular. The hardy kinds can be sown where they are to flower, the half-hardies raised in some protected place and planted out when there is little further risk of frost.

Biennials resemble annuals in dying after flowering and ripening their seed but they require two years to complete the cycle. Note, however, that they must be resown every year to maintain a continuity of flower. Monocarpics die after flowering and seeding but take an indefinite number of years to complete this cycle. In the main they are plants to be grown for their own interest or beauty, not to fit into a general pattern of display because it is uncertain when they will bloom.

Many plants that are actually perennial are grown as annuals or biennials because this is the simplest and most satisfactory way to treat them. This is true of antirrhinums, *Begonia semperflorens* and *Salvia splendens*, which in temperate climates are generally grown as annuals, and of wallflowers, double daisies *(Bellis)* and Brompton or East Lothian stocks *(Matthiola)* which are grown as biennials. It is becoming true of other plants including zonal pelargoniums (zonal-leaved geraniums) and penstemons, which used to be renewed from cuttings but are increasingly being raised from seed in places where it is too cold in winter for them to survive outdoors. This is due in part to the increase in cost of fuel to heat greenhouses or frames, in part to the great improvement of seed varieties. Such plants as these, used temporarily for display and then destroyed or over-wintered in a protected place, are usually referred to as 'bedding plants'.

Plants growing in the wild segregate themselves into species which are fairly uniform in character. They have adapted to the particular environment in which they live and any departures from this norm that are not positively useful tend to drop out after a generation or so. If gardeners decide that these variations suit their purpose they can perpetuate them either by increasing them by vegetative means — cuttings, layers, divisions or grafts — or by growing them in isolation from others of their kind in the hope that, when fertilized with their own pollen, they will reproduce the desirable features for which they have been selected. There have been great improvements in producing such true-breeding varieties and, in particular, in developing hybrids which, in their first generation, breed extremely true to type. In seed catalogues these are distinguished as F^1 hybrids (first filial hybrids). Seed of these is always much more expensive than that of ordinary varieties, and the extra cost can perhaps only be justified if it is really necessary to have plants that are very uniform in habit and flower colour.

Climbers

One type of plant which has not yet been mentioned (because it spans several of the groupings already discussed) comprises the climbers. These may be woody or herbaceous, perennial or annual. Climbers also differ widely in the manner in which they climb. The simplest, such as the climbing roses, are thrusters which push quite stiff but long stems through the branches of trees and shrubs and hang on with their thorns. Next in simplicity of means are the twiners, such as honeysuckles and wisteria, which wind themselves around any firm object they meet whether it be the trunk of a tree or the laths in a trellis.

More sophisticated are the tendril climbers, such as sweet peas which are annuals, or vines which are perennials. These have slender, spiralling appendages which wind around any suitably slender object, be it twig or netting, wire or trellis. Clematis uses a similar method but it is the leaf stalks that do the twining.

Lastly, there are the self-clingers which, either with aerial roots (ivy and climbing hydrangea) or with little adhesive pads (*Parthenocissus tricuspidata*, the Boston ivy), cling to any firm object, even a smooth vertical wall.

Climbers are of great value to the garden designer because they enable walls, fences and other solid objects to be clothed, pergolas and arches covered, and otherwise uninteresting trees made to burst out in cascades of beautiful bloom or decorative foliage. They may be thought of as fulfilling much the same purpose as the wallpapers and drapes used by interior decorators, and in fact, there is a great deal of similarity between the use of many plants in gardens, especially those chosen for their flower colour or leaf shape, and the use of fabrics and paints indoors. Both garden makers and interior decorators are trying to make harmonies or striking colour schemes, and each must maintain a satisfactory balance of scale and a pleasing disposition of objects. It is no accident that some of the most successful garden makers have also been distinguished interior decorators.

Here, then, is the cast which the garden maker can dispose according to inclination. It numbers many thousands of varieties and it is small wonder that the plant population of most gardens is in constant change as owners experiment with one thing and another to see if it is an improvement or just for the pleasure of enjoying something different. It is the design of the garden and the architectural features it contains — buildings, walls, terraces, pergolas, statues, fountains and so forth — plus trees and shrubs that give the garden a more or less permanent character of its own. All else may be regarded as embellishment, rather like the furnishings and decorations of a house, which is subject to easy change according to the whim of its owner.

Cost and maintenance

Finally there are two matters to be considered which have nothing to do with aesthetics but everything to do with economics and mechanics. How much will it cost, and how much energy will it take to maintain the garden once it has been made? Here we meet the old paradox: gardens that cost a lot to make are often the easiest and cheapest to run. Paving costs more than grass, and architectural features are usually more expensive than plants, but neither requires much maintenance. When it comes to the plants themselves, trees and shrubs generally cost more than herbaceous perennials and annuals, but are usually easier and cheaper to look after. Bedding plants and bulbs can be fairly costly and time-consuming, although a good deal depends on the way in which they are grown. Daffodils or crocuses naturalized in grass can be left alone for years, but tulips and hyacinths in beds may need to be lifted and replanted every year, especially if used to maintain colour for a long time in a sequence of flowers.

Science and technology have lightened many gardening tasks. Herbicides take the backache out of weeding, and light electric or petrol-engined lawnmowers make short work of lawn mowing. In large gardens, ride-on mowers or garden tractors can save a great deal of time and labour. But machines themselves require maintenance, and repairs can be expensive.

So, to sum up, if you are short of money and of time or strength, go easy on lawns, herbaceous borders and bedding out and concentrate instead on a few well-chosen trees and shrubs and ground covered with paving or gravel or maybe a mixture of the two. Plants can be grown in gravel if there is soil not far below, and gravel beds, or even complete gravel gardens, are becoming increasingly popular as a means of saving time and labour.

Difficult sites
Suggestions on those problems that confront most gardeners, such as shaded areas under large trees and unsightly sheds.

The healthy garden
Basic advice on general care and hygiene in the garden plus information on the prevention, recognition and treatment of pests and diseases. Propagation techniques to keep your garden stocked with new plants.

Trees and shrubs
Suggestions on using the form and colour of a wide range of trees and shrubs.

Backdrops and boundaries
Advice on deciding on garden screens whether they are walls, hedges or fences. Information on construction, cultivation and maintenance.

Plants for special purposes
Ideas on choosing plants to achieve a specific effect or perform a particular function.

Color in the garden
The ground rules of effective color planning with tables to help you to select a color scheme for your garden.

Garden features
Advice and suggestions on a wide range of garden architecture and patio areas.

GARDEN FEATURES

Planning your garden

The secret of a successful garden is to plan it carefully before beginning to build or to plant. Every site has its limitations — maybe size, shape, soil or orientation — which have to be taken into account in order to get the best results.

Begin by making a scaled plan of the garden on graph paper, marking in accurately any existing large features such as sheds, trees, mature shrubs, paths and patios, and working out their orientation: whether they face north, south, east or west, thus also showing which areas receive most sunshine.

Now make a detailed list of what you and your family want from the garden, remembering to think at least a few years ahead to when your needs may possibly have changed. (If you have very small children, for example, it is safer not to include any pond or water features in your plan. A sunken sand-pit included in the original design can easily be converted into a pool when the children are older.)

Decide how much of the garden should be devoted to sitting and sunbathing in, to having room to eat and to entertain friends, and possibly to having a permanent built-in barbecue. Do you want an area for growing vegetables or soft fruit? Have you always yearned after herbaceous borders and beds of bright annuals? Must you leave space for pets or the storage of bikes and large outdoor toys? If there is no room for a full-scale tennis court, perhaps it would be possible to fit in a net for badminton or a small *boules* pitch.

When your list is complete, place the items in order of importance, remembering that some features require far more time and effort to maintain than others. Try not to be over-ambitious: avoid leaving yourself more mowing, digging or sowing than you can face once the initial enthusiasm has worn off.

Calculate how much space is needed to accommodate each feature, making a note of any that can double up: a Wendy house makes a good bike store, for example, or a putting pitch a fine lawn; make a paper cut-out to the same scale as your plan for each one, and move them around on the plan to see how they fit together. Try not to be influenced too much by existing features that seem not to fit into the scheme of things; remember, many can be moved or disguised later.

A shed or an ugly view at the end of the garden can be hidden behind screening, a trellis, pergolas or hedges, planted with quick-growing climbers such as *Polygonum baldschuanicum*, wisteria and ivy, or sweet-scented flowering climbers for spring and summer such as roses, honeysuckles and clematis.

Paths and paving can be moved from one area to another without too much upheaval, and even established shrubs and small trees can often be safely transplanted if tackled at the right time of year and moved with plenty of soil around their roots.

Many patio and seating areas are for convenience sited close to the house, which is fine if it happens to receive plenty of sun. If, however, your house partly shades the garden, you would do better to create a special area at the other end of the garden, with adequate paved access to prevent wet feet after showers. The inconvenience of carrying food, drinks and seating across the garden is generally far outweighed by the advantages of a sunny site. On the other hand, children's play areas should be positioned near the house where they can be more easily supervised.

When planning features in the garden, take note of its overall shape. Whether the garden is long, wide or small, it is possible to adjust the basic contents to create the optical illusion of planning and space. A long, thin plot can be broken up across its width with staggered beds or hedging, or the eye distracted by trees or large shrubs planted along the sides. Vistas can be created in short, wide gardens by directing the eye along its length to a focal point at the end of the garden: a fountain or statue, an urn, perhaps, or a specimen shrub.

In a small or awkwardly shaped garden consider a change of levels using terracing, steps and raised beds to create immediate, ground-level interest which prevents the eye straying too far afield. Alternatively, beds in the centre — rather than along the sides — always offer the opportunity to walk round in several directions rather than simply up and down.

It is important to make a garden genuinely interesting. However small the plot, try not to let it all be seen at once. Create hidden areas using steps, hedges and sunken gardens, and make sure there is some focal point to catch the attention. Large areas can be broken up using paving or a similar change of material. And in every garden, there should be a good variety of plants chosen for their leaf-shape, colour and habit, with some variation in height from ground cover to trees, trellis and pergolas.

Make sure also that there is something interesting to look at all year round by planting a strong background of evergreens and berried shrubs for autumn and winter, bulbs for spring, and a few favourite summer flowering perennials in case the annuals are late. Plants should be chosen with care and placed according to their own preferences; a shade-loving plant can hardly flourish in full sunlight, nor can an ericaceous species thrive in a chalky soil. Test the soil in the garden in several places, using a pH meter or test kit, before choosing the plants; selected specimens can of course be grown under controlled conditions, using plastic sheeting or tubs.

Plants are best placed in groups (rather than dotted around singly), each clump complementing or contrasting with the next for impact. A variety of shapes, colours and heights stimulates the eye. The best features should be sited to make the most of them, allowing surrounding plants to provide a frame that sets them off. Never forget the obvious rule: tall plants to the back, short to the fore.

Variety of shape, height and colour can be used to add interest to the garden and create perspective. Here the eye is drawn to a fine urn against a background of tall hedging by a clever arrangement of staggered flower beds and a framework of different shrubs and trees.

The seating area should always be positioned where it receives maximum sunshine, with adequate paths to keep feet dry if it is not near the house. Roses, clematis, ivy and other climbing plants entwined round a trellis create a pleasant outlook and help break up the length of the garden.

Clipped hedges in staggered breaks add an air of mystery and the illusion of width to a long garden. Choose warm-coloured varieties with gold or dark green leaves, and space them further apart near to the house, using closer-planted, paler shades into the distance for extra feeling of depth.

Containers

Pots and tubs are an excellent way to brighten a plain expanse of concrete or paving on patio or terrace, and are flexible enough to be planted for year-round interest with small evergreen shrubs and plants, spring bulbs and summer annuals.

There is available a wide range of plain and decorated containers, from wood, metal and concrete to stone, glass-fibre, plastic and terra-cotta scaled-up versions of ordinary flower pots. Earthenware strawberry-pots with holes (and possibly cups) up the sides, are ideal for alpine plants and bulbs as well as strawberries; urns and pedestal vases are particularly suited to framing steps and archways.

Do not be afraid to mix different styles of container: arrange them in groups, and try to vary heights and shapes for interest — some planted with a single tree or shrub, others containing a mixture of varying foliage and flowering plants. Take special care when securely fixing window or balustrade boxes; floor-standing containers should be raised on bricks or wood blocks to aid drainage.

When finally satisfied with the arrangement, fill each container with a good level of crocks or stones before topping up with a quality potting mixture. If a container does not already have holes at the bottom, it may be worth drilling them yourself to improve drainage.

Container-grown plants need more attention than your garden planted varieties. In such restricted space, weed seedlings should be pulled out the instant you spot them; as soon as the plants themselves grow too big or begin to die down, they too should be pulled out and replaced. Spring bulbs which have finished flowering should be lifted and stored until the next season. The soil is of course prone to drying out, so keep it well watered during the summer and feed it regularly while plants are growing. Well sheltered containers may need watering in winter too.

Choice of plants is crucial in such a limited space: aim at a good balance of tall and trailing plants, of colours, shapes and textures. Small shrubs, trees and evergreens are useful for providing a permanent background to other plants — almost any slow-growing or dwarf species can be grown in a tub. If the situation is shady and the soil lime-free, you can grow camellias and rhododendrons, or a selection of the wide-ranging heather family: varieties of *Erica carnea (herbacea)* for winter and early spring flowering, bell heather *(Erica cinerea)* and ling *(Calluna vulgaris)* for summer.

Hollies and oleanders make good tub plants with a fine variety of foliage or flowers. For a more formal look, consider the clipped shapes of box *(Buxus)*, bay *(Laurus nobilis)* or yew *(Taxus)*. Other shrubs worth considering are prickly barberry *(Berberis)*, blue-flowered *Caryopteris*, bush or standard fuchsias, the slow-growing dwarf conifers, sweet-scented *Skimmia japonica*, and spiky lavender.

Seasonal plants should be chosen with equal care to create the most impact. Silver and green trailing foliage is the perfect foil for other plants and helps 'soften' the edges of containers: try silver senecio, lobelia, tiny green creeping Jenny *(Lysimachia)*, or one of the variegated ivies.

Summer annuals are wonderful for creating a riot of colour for very little cost, and it is worth spending some thought on which combinations work best. White alyssum and marguerites set off most colours well but tend to disappear against a white wall or container. Combine with the blues of lobelias, campanulas or violas against red brick and save the brilliant scarlets of geraniums *(Pelargonium)*, cinerarias and salvias to team with golden marigolds, calceolarias and marigolds *(Tagetes)*.

For spring set off miniature tulips and narcissi with forget-me-nots, saxifrage, candytuft and wallflowers; and for autumn keep the show going with dwarf dahlias and chrysanthemums, ornamental peppers and winter cherry *(Solanum)*.

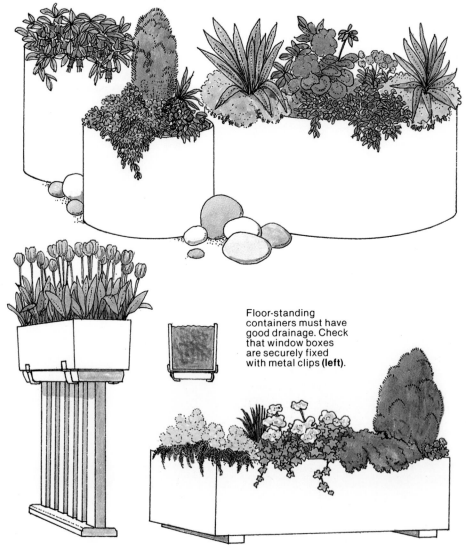

Floor-standing containers must have good drainage. Check that window boxes are securely fixed with metal clips **(left)**.

Contrasting foliage and flowering plants provide a fine display of shapes and colours in large single containers. Lobelia, alyssum, trailing fuchsia and ivy are all useful creeping plants to 'soften' the edges of your tubs and boxes. Marigolds, petunias and pelargoniums are traditional for bright summer colour. Add a couple of dwarf conifers for a change of height, and don't forget to plant some spring bulbs for an early show of blooms.

Plant containers are available in a wide range of shapes and sizes, from ornate stone urns and wooden Versailles baskets to more simple plastic or concrete tubs and boxes. Make the most of the fancier and more expensive styles by planting with a single specimen plant, such as a bushy purple hydrangea or a shaped bay tree; use plainer, cheaper containers for arranging in pairs or groups on the patio. Tub shrubs and small trees need a fair amount of space, so they may have to be planted singly, and their tubs interspersed with boxes of lower-growing plants and flowers. Evergreen varieties are ideal for providing a background to more sensational plants

and for keeping the arrangement looking good throughout the winter. Dwarf conifers are particularly useful in that they are slow-growing and available in a range of colours, from the bluish grey *Chamaecyparis* 'Columnaris' to the deep green *C. l.* 'Ellwoodii' and the golden leaved *C. l.* 'Minima Aurea'. Barberry (Berberis) can be both deciduous and evergreen, with glossy red or green leaves and golden flowers sometimes followed by red, black or blue currant-like fruits. Eucalyptus is valuable for its silver leaves. Mixed plant containers can include a selection of variegated foliage such as ivies, euonymous and herbs like thyme and

marjoram to set off the green leaves of spring bulbs and summer annuals. Aim for a good variety of blooms, from tiny trailing white and yellow alyssum or blue lobelia to the vivid mauves and pinks of petunia. Experiment with the arrangements of containers before filling with soil and plants.

Gravel (**left**) forms an ideal patio surface, here decorated with planted containers. The clean lines of a modern french window (**left**) are softened by a crazy paving patio and colourful tubs.

A sheltered seating area (**above**) can be created anywhere in the garden by surrounding a paved area with evergreens to provide protection from winds and draughts. A selection of conifers, hollies,

rhododendrons, *Fatsia japonica* and *Choisya ternata* are hardy enough to make good informal screening; a well-clipped hedge of privet, box, or other evergreen hedging looks more formal. A

few matching paving slabs extending across the lawn from the seating area links it to the rest of the garden and keeps feet dry.

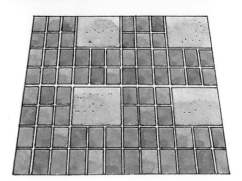

Paving slabs mixed with brick (**above**), a mellow effect for informal patios.

Plain bricks (**below**) laid end-to-end weather into subtle variations of colour.

Varying the gaps between plain paving slabs (**above**) adds interest and variety.

Bricks or blocks laid on sand in a herringbone pattern (**below**) for a patio.

A crazy-paving effect in pastel shades (**above**), in different sizes and styles.

Square grey tiles (**below**) give a discreet, traditional feel to a patio.

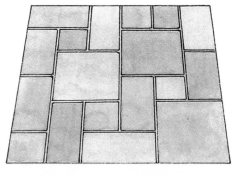
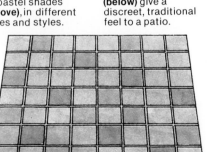

PATIOS: PAVING

Patios are no longer extravagantly paved terraces overlooking acres of garden nor limited to wealthy land-owners. Today even the most modest garden can aspire to a small area, easy to maintain and relatively dry underfoot, in which a few chairs can be placed in the sun, and meals eaten straight after being cooked on a small outdoor barbecue.

A patio can be as large or as small as you wish, depending, for example, on how many you want it to seat and whether you need room for a built-in barbecue, pool, or other integrated feature. It is important, however, to position it where it receives maximum sunshine — even at some distance from the house — for a cold, draughty patio will be poorly used.

Cold winds can be screened using a trellis, hedges of privet, box or other evergreens, or with an informal planting of evergreen shrubs such as conifers, hollies or rhododendrons.

Paving materials depend on personal preference and finances. Gravel is the cheapest and probably the easiest to install: simply level the site and firm the soil before spreading with a 2.5cm (1in) layer of washed pea shingle. Because gravel offers excellent drainage, log slices can be bedded in it (to add interest and a change of texture) without becoming damp and slimy underneath.

Paving slabs are most people's idea of a conventional patio surface; they are readily available both in 100 per cent natural stone and in a reconstituted form which works out considerably cheaper. Variety of shape and colour — from grey and sand to pastel pinks — provides unlimited scope for pattern and design, but simplicity is a good guideline: anything too elaborate may ruin the overall effect. A simple pattern of different sizes, or even a slight variation in the spacing between conventional slabs, can turn out just right.

Bricks are quite expensive new, but second-hand they can work out much cheaper and look more mellow too, laid end-to-end for a conventional design, or herringbone fashion if you are looking for something more elaborate. They also look very effective combined with paving slabs; try leaving some of the spaces empty for planting sweet-scented herbs, shrubs or even a small tree.

If you fancy the old traditional cobbled surface, concrete or granite cobbles are available singly or in blocks to make installation easier.

Slabs and bricks need to be laid on an 8cm (3¼in) bed of sand spread over firmed and levelled soil. Use a straight-edge or spirit level to make sure the surface is flat but sloped slightly to allow the rain to run away easily, away from the house if it is near by. Grout the slabs or bricks with a dry mortar mix, taking care not to get any on the surface of the paving — it's very difficult to remove later. If mortar does get on to the paving slabs or bricks,

remove it immediately with dry sand and a good stiff broom.

You could experiment with several types of paving within the patio area. As an alternative to the bricks and paving stone combination mentioned previously, you could divide the patio into large, distinct areas of gravel, pebbles or cobbled surface and create a paving slab surround. In this way, other features could be integrated with a similar border: a formal pool with a few fish and a fountain, or an area for plants perhaps.

If your patio is well sheltered yet catches plenty of sun, it may get rather too hot. In any case, some form of shade is a good idea for more comfortable eating and reading, using maybe a tree to fend off the sun at its hottest or one of those large umbrellas which fit into a picnic table. Prettiest is a pergola construction that can be intertwined with a quick-growing vine, such as *Vitis coignetiae* (the glory vine), or with other climbers.

The patio (**below**) is shaded by a pergola entwined with a hardy vine, and features a variety of paving effects. Log slices have been set in gravel for good drainage and surrounded by a more formal path of conventional paving slabs. Also enclosed by the paving is a small formal pool and fountain and an interesting scree garden using stone chippings.

Patios: terraces

An elegant raised terrace can be simple or elaborate, traditional — with formal paving and a stone balustrade — or use the natural warmth of wood to create a smart, timber decked surface. Whatever you choose, you can follow the theme through with steps constructed from matching brick, stone or timber and provide shelter from winds and draughts with stone or timber screening and hardy evergreen shrubs and climbers.

The traditional terrace has a dominant formal pattern of paving in stone or brick with shallow steps and ornate urns flanking an elegant stone balustrade. Elements of these can be bought in pre-cast sections and constructed on site quite easily. Plant containers should be carefully chosen to match the style of this type of terrace: highly decorated urns and tubs or smart Versailles baskets.

If you prefer a warmer, more informal look, timber decking is easy to make and maintain; second-hand wood costs a lot less than stone or brick. Any rough-textured splinter-free timber (such as old railway sleepers or split oak) is ideal; simply cut it to shape and treat with a suitable wood preservative before laying in your chosen pattern or design. To help it last longer, first lay a bed of sand over a polythene sheet punched with holes; water can then drain through it although damp is prevented from coming up from below. Alternatively, support the deck on wooden joists to allow air to flow freely underneath.

Timber can be laid in a variety of designs: straight, on the diagonal, or in square sections at right angles. It is advisable to work out your design on paper in order to calculate how much wood you need. Pot plants are essential to add height and interest, either planted in spaces left in the decking or arranged in simple tubs and boxes, and sheltered using matching timber or bamboo screens. The deck surface should be brushed regularly with a wire brush to keep the surface rough and moss-free, or it becomes slippery.

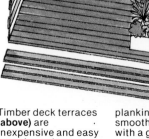

Timber deck terraces **(above)** are inexpensive and easy to make, using second-hand planking rubbed smooth and treated with a good wood preservative.

The combination of a rock garden and terrace **(above)** is a particularly effective design feature. The neat form of the terrace contrasts with the random nature of the rockery. The inclusion of a fountain and statues in a small terraced garden **(right)** adds an element of tranquil formality. Many different styles of fountains are widely available to create a variety of effects in the garden.

Steps

Steps are not as difficult to install as they may seem at first, provided that you take care when making your initial calculations. After you have decided on the materials to use, estimate from their dimensions the number of steps needed, dividing the slope as evenly as possible. Bear in mind that steep steps are not suitable for young children or elderly people in the household. Any step more than 30cm (1ft) high is generally uncomfortable for most people to negotiate. Treads should be slightly sloped to the front or side to prevent puddles forming after rain.

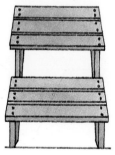

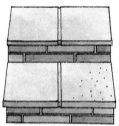

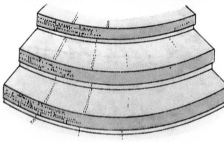

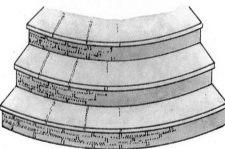

Steps can be constructed from a variety of materials and laid in different ways to create varying effects: brick **(above left)**, paving slabs with brick risers **(above)**, or simple wooden steps **(left)** are only a few of the options. Curved steps **(right)** look grand.

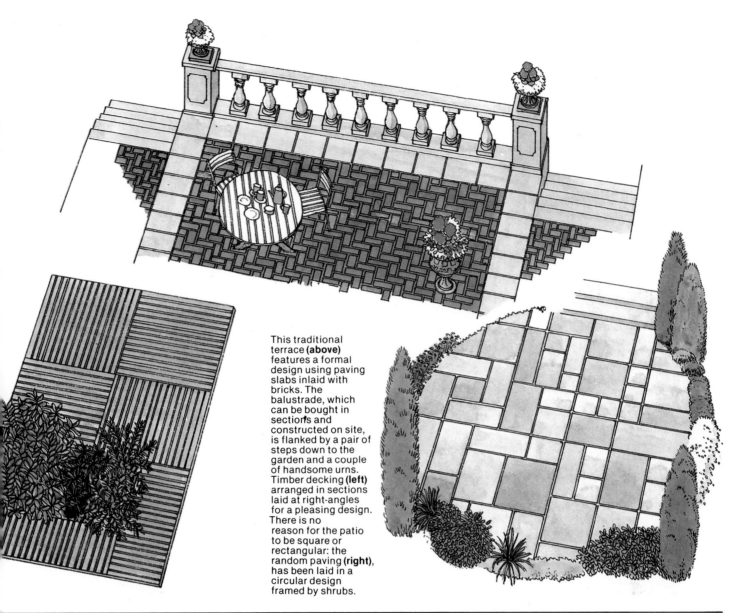

This traditional terrace **(above)** features a formal design using paving slabs inlaid with bricks. The balustrade, which can be bought in sections and constructed on site, is flanked by a pair of steps down to the garden and a couple of handsome urns. Timber decking **(left)** arranged in sections laid at right-angles for a pleasing design. There is no reason for the patio to be square or rectangular: the random paving **(right)**, has been laid in a circular design framed by shrubs.

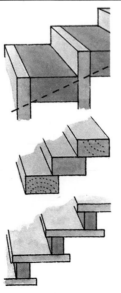

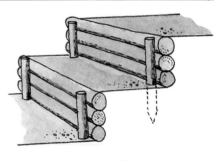

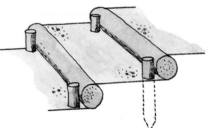

The bright blooms of annuals blend well with garden steps **(above)**. When planting near steps ensure that over-hanging leaves do not become a hazard.

There are many ways in which steps can be constructed; shown here in profile are brick steps with paving risers **(top left)**, simple wooden steps made using old railway timbers **(centre left)**, paving steps with brick risers **(bottom left)**, and logs held in place with wooden stakes **(right)** to create both steep and shallow steps depending on how many logs are used. Take care not to make them too steep, especially if they are to be used by young children, the elderly or the handicapped.

Summerhouses

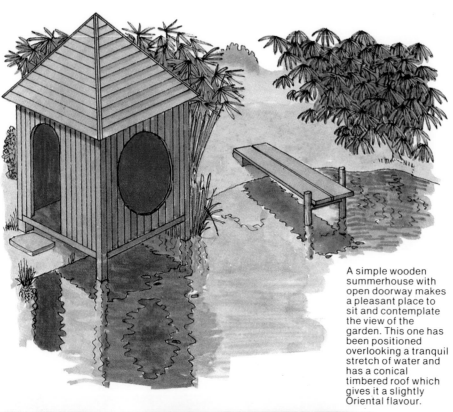

A simple wooden summerhouse with open doorway makes a pleasant place to sit and contemplate the view of the garden. This one has been positioned overlooking a tranquil stretch of water and has a conical timbered roof which gives it a slightly Oriental flavour.

If there is room for one in your garden, a summerhouse is a marvellous combination of sheltered seating area and useful store for chairs, tables and other garden paraphernalia. Its primary purpose is generally to provide somewhere to sit and enjoy the sun, out of the wind and sheltered from the occasional shower, so your main concern must be to position it so that it obtains the maximum sunshine. In exposed situations, screening can be provided using shrubs, hedging or evergreens, bamboo screens or timber fencing, all of which help to 'soften' the lines of the building.

Ideally, a summerhouse should also face a pleasant view — a stretch of water is ideal, especially if it is possible to position the structure on the edge, or even raised on stilts over the water. If it is elegant enough, alternatively, the summerhouse can be used as the focal point within the main plan of the garden.

There is a wide range of sizes and styles available, either to buy ready-made or to build yourself. The very basic type comprises a simple roofed structure which, depending on how exposed its position is, can have glazed or open sides. The standard summerhouse, however, is a timber-built building big enough to store sunloungers, chairs, and maybe a fold-away patio table, with folding or double doors that open out to enable you to sit out, or just inside, depending on the weather. Some styles feature an additional verandah with half-timbered sides, which extends the seating area into the garden and provides some extra internal protection from draughts.

When choosing a summerhouse, be careful to select both size and style appropriate to your requirements and the garden's appearance.

In front of your summerhouse it is a good idea to build some sort of paved area to provide a dry, stable surface for tables and chairs when the weather is especially fine. This might be constructed of concrete paving slabs, brick or crazy paving (according to taste) — but a timber decked area, raised on joists, always looks particularly good alongside a wood-built building. Judicious planting of evergreens and tubs of bright annuals help to soften any hard edges and to blend the area into the garden.

Of course, if you are blessed with a house that faces more or less due south, a lean-to sunroom extension makes an excellent part-conservatory part-summerhouse, that you don't even have to go out of the house to use. With either folding or patio doors, the room can be opened out on to a paved area in summer for sitting out.

An ornamental hexagonal greenhouse makes a very elegant summerhouse if you are short of space or want to make a feature of it. Offering all-year-round shelter, specially made blinds are available to screen the glass from hot sun in summer.

The standard pavilion-type summerhouse **(above left)** often features folding doors and a matching veranda, which can be extended with concrete paving.

A wooden summerhouse **(above right)**, more simply styled and positioned to open directly onto a matching timber-decked patio area.

A simple shelter **(above left)** is perfect for enjoying the sunshine. A lean-to sunroom extension **(left)** makes an excellent part-conservatory part-summerhouse.

This octagonal greenhouse has been boxed in with conifers for privacy and doubles as an all-year-round shelter. Blinds are available to screen the glass in very hot weather.

Greenhouses

A greenhouse offers the keen gardener freedom from the restrictions of climate and soil, so that almost any plant can be grown or propagated from seeds or cuttings.

Basically, the greenhouse is a wooden or aluminium frame infilled with glass panels to catch maximum light and warmth; it should also have its own controllable system of heating, screening and ventilation.

A lean-to is ideal for gardens with restricted space or where the garden side of the house faces maximum sunshine; painting the wall white reflects and can amplify the light and warmth. A free-standing structure, alternatively, can be positioned anywhere in the garden of course, but should be placed to receive maximum light and sunshine and so provide more scope and better results.

The traditional greenhouse has an apex roof and glass half-way or right down to the ground. Newer designs are smart enough themselves to constitute garden features, and to be allowed therefore to remain visible and distinct from the rest of the garden. Some are made up of small hexagonal shapes fitted together to create a honeycomb complex or a futuristic geodesic shape which, although not very economical on space inside, looks suitably presentable in the right setting. The Victorian-style conservatories now produced by a few companies are expensive but create a wonderful environment for growing plants like palms and ferns among colonial-style chairs and tables.

A glasshouse naturally attracts and stores heat during the day when the sun is shining,

The standard, ornate conservatory is perfect for Victorian-style plants.

but cools quite considerably at night. There are various forms of internal heating available with which to control the temperature and help to ensure the success of your plants, particularly the tender varieties.

Paraffin (kerosene) heaters are the cheapest to buy — although they can be expensive to run and the fumes are damaging to some plants. Oil-fuelled heating can be very effective, using a system of heated pipes, but again is expensive to run. Electricity is clean and has the advantage of being thermostatically controlled. But probably the most economical form of heating is a portable natural gas stove.

Control of the temperature and humidity

within the greenhouse is essential if plants are not to suffer from scorching or shrivelling. Some models come complete with vents that open thermostatically according to the temperature of the air inside; with manually-operated forms of heat control, however, it is advisable in summer to open vents first thing in the morning and close them again about an hour before sunset.

The glass panes can be shaded against too much heat in summer by spraying with limewash or a proprietary shading compound in late spring or early summer, and washing off in early to mid-autumn. Alternatively, the panes can be fitted with blinds that can be lowered as and when needed.

Sheds

Sheds are useful for storing garden equipment in and, if large enough, for providing a bench area suitable for propagating cuttings and sowing seeds. If there is room in the garden for a fairly large structure, the building can also double as a workshop or hobby-room, containing possibly a work-bench, table and tools.

Sheds are usually constructed of concrete or timber, and have either an apex or a pent (single sloping) roof. Wood generally blends better with the rest of the garden, but needs a coat of preservative every year or so to keep it in good condition. Concrete, on the other hand, is expensive but needs very little maintenance. Both types can be covered with trellis and smothered with evergreen climbers to conceal them if their position makes that desirable; grape vine, ivy, honeysuckle and climbing roses all make good attractive cover, and the hardy Morello cherry is particularly fine for a north-facing wall.

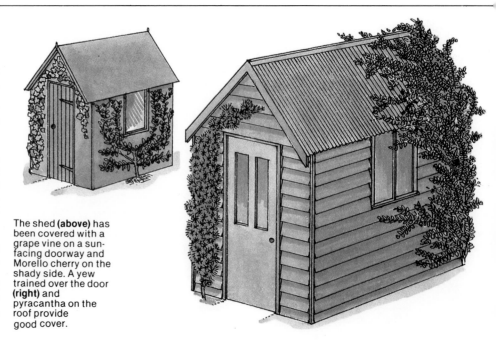

The shed (above) has been covered with a grape vine on a sun-facing doorway and Morello cherry on the shady side. A yew trained over the door (right) and pyracantha on the roof provide good cover.

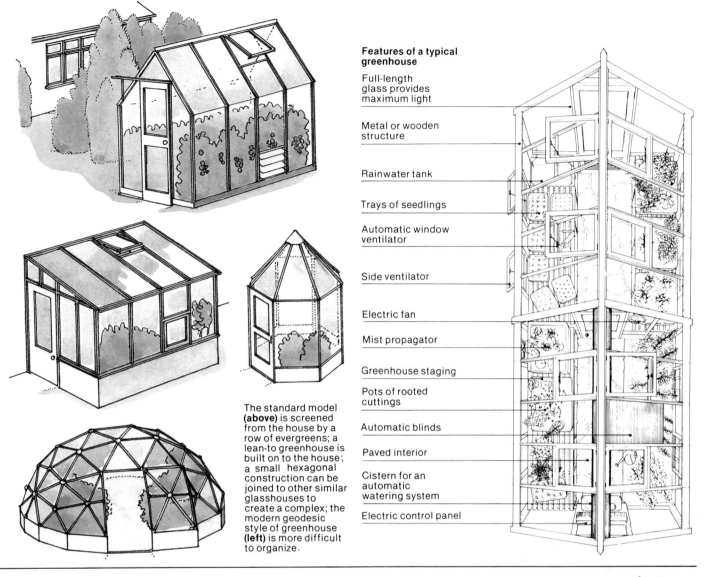

Features of a typical greenhouse

Full-length glass provides maximum light

Metal or wooden structure

Rainwater tank

Trays of seedlings

Automatic window ventilator

Side ventilator

Electric fan

Mist propagator

Greenhouse staging

Pots of rooted cuttings

Automatic blinds

Paved interior

Cistern for an automatic watering system

Electric control panel

The standard model **(above)** is screened from the house by a row of evergreens; a lean-to greenhouse is built on to the house; a small hexagonal construction can be joined to other similar glasshouses to create a complex; the modern geodesic style of greenhouse **(left)** is more difficult to organize.

Most sheds come with optional extras to suit further needs — such as fitted floors, windows or a locking door — and are delivered flat-packed to be erected on site over a stable concrete base.

You may, however, prefer to build your own shed from bricks or timber. The simplest home-made construction is the tiny sentry-box shed commonly seen on allotments. They have a single locking door, and are usually big enough only to store basic tools in, so they can be completely disguised by smothering in an attractive evergreen such as laurel, bay, rhododendron or *Magnolia grandiflora* (leaving only the door free for access).

This pent-roofed shed **(left)** has been covered with a trellis, latticed on the diagonal and grown with rambling red rose and ivy. The tiny shed **(above)** has been smothered with an evergreen.

Herb gardens

Herb gardens were invariably included in the grounds of stately homes and manor houses, not only to provide seasonings and fragrances for the kitchen and parlour, but also as decorative features in their own right. These two examples (**left**) show the variety of colour and form that traditional herb gardens display.

The large formal herb garden (**below**) contains a selection of mainly culinary herbs, arranged in well-clipped blocks linked by low hedges of box (*Buxus*).

Herbs offer such a variety of shape, texture, scent and colour, their culinary uses seem almost a mere bonus. Even the smallest garden should be able to dedicate a few square metres of soil, or a couple of pots on the patio, to growing a selection of herbs. But if there is a larger space to spare, there is tremendous scope for creating wild sweeps or formal patterns of colour and shape.

Most herbs like good drainage and a sunny situation, and are vigorous growers — too vigorous, even, in the case of mints and lemon balm which it is advisable to plant in containers that stand on the patio or are sunk into the soil, to limit their growth. Many herbs attract bees and butterflies to the garden too, especially meadow saffron *(Colchicum autumnale)*, catmint *(Nepeta mussinii)*, santolina, hyssop, bergamot *(Monarda didyma)* and borage *(Borago officinalis)*.

With their subtle shading and variety of foliage and flowers, herbs create many different effects. The informal garden, with plants spilling over each other in a profusion of shapes and colours, aims to look partly overgrown. In fact, each plant has to be chosen

carefully to maintain a good contrast of colour, height and texture without being swamped by its neighbour.

Formal gardens use the wide variety of herbs to create a very different effect. They are then arranged in very definite geometric shapes, such as curves, rectangles, triangles and circles, defined with neatly clipped hedges of box *(Buxus)*. Herbs are usually kept well spaced and cropped to maintain their shape, so it is best to choose upright, compact varieties or to prune the roots as well as the branches of fast-growing herbs. Among formal designs using herbs are the traditional knots, which take quite a lot of care and maintenance; wheel effects, using brick or concrete to divide the plants; and chequerboard designs in which the herbs are planted in a series of squares. Raised beds are particularly suited to formal herb gardens as they help contain the plants and offer excellent drainage.

Another way to use herbs is in order to provide scented, creeping cover for paths, seats and lawns. Creeping thyme *(Thymus serpyllum)* and Roman chamomile *(Chamaemelum nobile)* soften the edges of stone paths in sunny situations if introduced into the cracks between the slabs; pennyroyal *(Mentha pulegium)* and the tiny *Mentha requienii* do well in shady sites. These herbs can

also be used to make herb seats: simply build up a low bank of earth, lay slabs of paving or timber planks along the top, and plant creeping herbs in the gaps between. The seat should be covered with a sweet-scented living cushion by the following year.

Herbs also grow well on a patio or outside the kitchen door — where culinary varieties are easily accessible for adding to soups, grills and stuffings. Remember to provide good drainage with a generous level of crocks or pebbles, and position them where they receive plenty of sunlight.

However you want to display your herbs, aim for a good contrast of leaf shape and colour. For pale and silver foliage, choose rue *(Ruta graveolens)*, woolly thyme *(Thymus pseudolanuginosus)* or wormwood *(Artemisia absinthium)*. For dark leaves, black horehound *(Balluta niger)*, purple basil *(Ocimum basilicum* 'Dark Opal')* and bronze fennel *(Foeniculum vulgare)* are all suitable. Herbs with variegated leaves include pineapple mint *(Mentha suaveolens* 'Variegata')*, golden sage *(Salvia officinalis* 'Icterina')* and variegated lemon balm *(Melissa officinalis* 'Aurea')*. And for bright flowers, choose between: red bergamot *(Monarda didyma)*, blue borage *(Borago officinalis)* and yellow elecampane *(Inula helenium)*.

If there is no room for herbs in the garden, they can be grown successfully in well-drained tubs and containers (**above**) on a patio or near the kitchen door. Place them where they receive plenty of light and sunshine — few herbs thrive in the shade — and spread a good layer of crocks or pebbles in the bottom of the pots to prevent the roots becoming waterlogged.

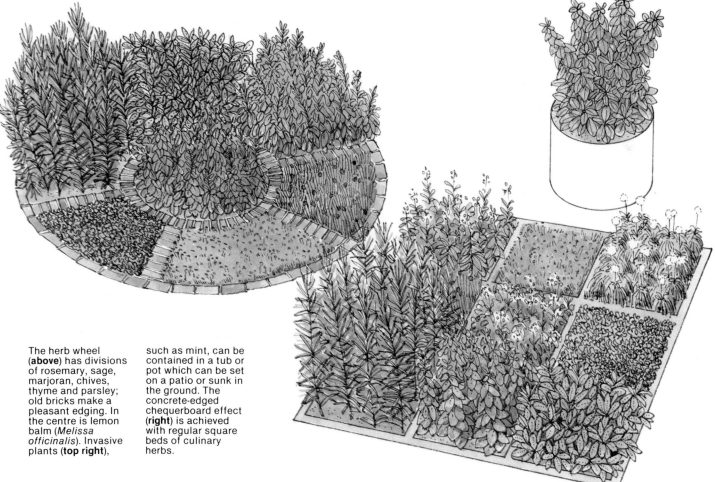

The herb wheel (**above**) has divisions of rosemary, sage, marjoram, chives, thyme and parsley; old bricks make a pleasant edging. In the centre is lemon balm (*Melissa officinalis*). Invasive plants (**top right**), such as mint, can be contained in a tub or pot which can be set on a patio or sunk in the ground. The concrete-edged chequerboard effect (**right**) is achieved with regular square beds of culinary herbs.

Island beds

Island beds are a valuable feature in garden design, both for small gardens in which narrow borders only add emphasis to the overall lack of space, and in larger plots where they can be used to break up large areas of lawn. They can be any shape or size to suit their location — formal geometric shapes or natural irregular sweeps, provided that they do not look out of place or create narrow strips of grass that are then difficult to mow. On the whole, they are easier to maintain than the traditional border because they are accessible from all sides and do not have as many tall plants, thus reducing the need for staking.

It is essential to mark the chosen shape accurately before beginning — there is nothing worse than a meandering line that should be straight or an off-square corner. Informal shapes are of course easiest, but should fit the

natural contours of the garden if they are not to look out of place. Experiment, using a length of hosepipe as a marker, so that you can stand back and view the shape easily from all angles. Once decided on a design, mark out using a pointed stick or a thin trickle of lime.

To mark out a square or rectangular bed, first make a large set-square out of lengths of wood and use it to make the right-angled corners. This done, mark the shape with pegs and lines, checking the accuracy of the resultant shape by measuring the diagonals to see if they are of the same length.

Circular beds are easily drawn by driving a peg into the ground at the approximate centre of the proposed bed. Tie to this a length of twine that is the radius of the required bed, and using it as a pivot, scribe a circle with a sharp stick on the other end of the twine.

Oval beds are marked in a similar fashion but using two pegs with a length of twine approximately three times as long as the distance between them. Knot the twine into a loop,

place over the pegs, and using a sharp stick to take up the slack, draw the shape; the closer together the two pegs are, the more circular the oval.

A regular hexagonal shape is easily achieved by drawing a circle using the peg and twine method mentioned above, then using the same radius to mark off six equally-spaced points around the circumference. Joining up the points with pegs and twine gives the hexagonal shape.

When planning the planting of island beds, remember that they can be seen from all sides, and that plants have to be more or less self-supporting, so do not choose anything that grows too tall. Small shrubs and trees are useful for adding height and perennial interest in informal beds, and can also provide the focal point in a more formal arrangement: a bay tree in the centre of a circular herbal bed, for example, or the holly in the ericaceous bed of heathers and rhododendrons shown here.

An irregularly shaped bed can be planted

Aim at a good variety of shape and colour when planning island beds. This informally-shaped bed (**below right**) has been planted with perennials: delphiniums, lupins, pampus grass and the giant pom-poms of *Allium gigantum* rise out of a sea of contrasting leaves and flowers.

with perennials rather like the traditional herbaceous borders; taller flowering plants, such as lupins, foxgloves, delphiniums or red-hot pokers *(Kniphofia)* should be placed towards the centre. The rest of the bed may contain all your personal favourites, positioned according to colour, shape and texture for a good balance of different leaves and flowers: primula, *Gypsophila*, *Anchusa angustifolia*, thrift *(Armeria)*, elephant's ears *(Bergenia)*, astilbe, *Dianthus*, *Salvia*, phlox, *Sedum*, aster, campanula, *Rudbeckia*, *Geum* and pansies are but a few.

The more formal beds are perfect for creating geometric shapes of living colour using seasonal plants like those seen and admired in amenity gardens. Mark out your design on the bed first, using pegs and twine or a trail of lime, then plant with areas of single coloured bulbs or bright wallflowers for spring, annuals for summer. Low-growing compact annuals with masses of flowers are the most successful and are easier to conform to a shape: *Alyssum*, lobelia, marigolds *(Tagetes)*, verbena, begonias, *Matricara*, petunias and asters all blend together well.

Formal beds of brightly coloured annuals grown in neat, geometric shapes are fun to make and provide a glorious show of summer colour.

The circular bed (**above**) combines four different heathers and four types of rhododendron round a central holly tree. Heathers can be chosen to provide colour all year round, with a wide variety of flowers and foliage from dark green, golden and red tinged needle-like leaves to bronze, red, pink, white and dark purple flowers.

The circular bed (**above**) has been planted with *Salvia*, petunias, marigolds, lobelias, asters, *Matricaria* and *Pyrethrum* to create a mass of reds, golds, blues, yellows and mauves. The large bed (**left**) is more informal, with a variety of different shrubs ranged round a flowering cherry. Here, it is the shape and colour of the flowers and foliage that has been balanced to provide a series of contrasting and complementary patterns.

Raised beds

Raised beds can be formal or informal as appropriate to the style of the garden. Dry stone walling, bricks, peat blocks or even old railway sleepers are the usual means of constructing the retaining walls. Providing not only an excellent opportunity to control soil-type and drainage — particularly important in a problem garden — raised beds also offer easier access to plants for the handicapped gardener, and protection for the plants from toys and bicycles when children stray from the paths.

Brick retaining walls look the most formal. They should be at least two to three bricks thick, upon proper concrete foundations. It is a good idea to stake out the site beforehand, using pegs and string to check that corners are square, and to ensure that the size suits your garden, then to leave the foundations 24 hours to make sure it is level. Lay one of the corner bricks first and start working towards the centre, making sure that the mortar used is not as solid as the bricks themselves. This ensures that in heavy frost it is the mortar that gives and not the bricks.

Raised beds need careful drainage, depending on their size, the soil character and the local climate. Intermittent gaps left in the brick joints are sufficient in some cases; alternatively, insert small pipes of clay, asbestos, concrete or plastic at 1m (39in) intervals from the bottom to a height about a third of the way up the wall. The pipes should be between 5cm (2in) and 7.5cm (3in) in diameter, and extend the full depth of the wall — and about 30cm (12in) into the soil beneath. If they drain on to a patio or other paved area, remember to provide a gulley to allow the water to run away.

Small trees and shrubs add height and weight to raised beds; but otherwise fill with your favourite annuals for a blaze of colour and scent in summer, bulbs for spring and a few evergreens to maintain interest over winter. Always include a selection of good creeping and trailing plants to 'soften' the edges.

For a more natural effect, use dry stone walling to construct your retaining walls, and leave out the occasional stone for interplanting with appropriate plants. This type of bed is ideal for growing alpines, which thrive in a free-draining, rocky setting and can provide colour and interest all year round.

Dry stone walls can be laid on sand, hardcore or concrete foundations, and to stand firm should be built with the width of their base equal to half their height, and tapered slightly from bottom to top, yet leaning slightly backwards. The actual stones of the wall can be interplanted with alpines for an even softer, more natural effect.

If your garden is on very chalky soil but you wish to grow some of the beautiful lime-hating plants such as rhododendron and magnolia, it is possible to create a lime-free setting for them using raised beds. In this instance, use pre-formed peat blocks 30 x 10 x 10cm (12 x 4 x 4in), soaked for 24 hours and laid as you would bricks, for your retaining walls. Line the bottom of the bed with a sheet of strong plastic; top with a good layer of crocks and pebbles for drainage; then fill with a mixture of loam, sand and peat.

There are many dwarf rhododendrons available which are ideal for raised beds — varieties such as *R. yakushimanum* which provide good dense foliage as well as a mass of compact blooms. Camellias, too, offer a fine display of glossy green leaves especially when in flower, which tends to be late winter to mid-spring — a welcome mass of pink, white or deep red flowers. For winter colour, witch hazel enjoys an acid soil, and the popular *Hamamelis mollis* brightens the garden with yellow flowers and a distinctive sweet scent.

Informal beds enclosed by dry stone walling (**left**) are ideal for making rock gardens where standard alpines can be grown.

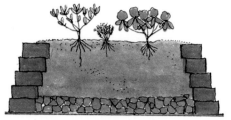

Cross-section of the acid bed retained by peat blocks (**above** and **right**) shows how a sheet of plastic topped with a good layer of crocks for drainage and suitable compost enables lime-hating plants to be grown in a garden with chalky soil. This bed includes a selection of suitable ericaceous plants.

Beds retained by brick walls tend to look more formal but are perfect if you have children, who all too often ride their bicycles over the flower beds. Some proper system of drainage is important, either by means of drainage pipes built into the brickwork (**above**), or by leaving occasional gaps in the brick joints (**right**) to allow water to drain away.

The small compact bed (**above**) has a small birch as centrepiece, surrounded by colourful summer planting; and the larger arrangement (**right**) a blaze of annuals with a sweet-scented mock orange (*Choisya ternata*): orange *Calendula*, mauve petunias, pink *Dianthus* and the dwarf poppy *Eschscholzia*.

Sunken beds

One of the best ways to treat a deep hollow or a very uneven site is to create a sunken garden out of it, saving a lot of levelling and possibly creating a fascinating feature into the bargain. The soil tends to be poorly drained in such sunken areas, so it is advisable to base any plan around moisture-loving plants, such as roses, or even bog plants, depending on how bad the problem is.

Roses are perfect for making a formal garden, which can be paved with brick or stone and designed to include raised or inset beds of different varieties. Some form of screening adds to the attraction and helps to ward off draughts: a hedge of lavender makes a sweet-smelling and effective wind-break; alternatively, erect a trellis all round on which to grow climbing or rambling roses such as the scarlet 'Danse du Feu', white 'Climbing Iceberg', or yellow 'Albéric Barbier'.

The main beds can be planted with a selection of standard and bush roses designed to bloom at different times with a complementary range of colours and scents. The large flowered roses (formerly hybrid tea) are particularly useful in that they produce fat blooms from early summer until the first frosts. 'Whisky Mac' has the advantage of a coppery-orange colour and a good scent; the popular 'Peace' produces huge pink-edged pale yellow blooms.

Miniature roses grow to about 45cm (18in) high and are perfect for raised beds where they can be seen and smelt more easily. Scented varieties include the pink 'Baby Faurax', white 'Snow Carpet' and orange-yellow 'Darling Flame'.

A more informal-style sunken garden can be constructed using crazy paving and a palisade of old railway sleepers. A circular design looks most attractive planted with evergreen shrubs round the top for extra protection and to 'soften' the timber edging; steps down can be made from timber to match. If the soil tends to be rather soggy and poorly drained, create a special bog garden with moisture-lovers such as ferns, hostas and lilies.

For spring flowering, choose the lovely yellow globe flower *(Trollius europaeus)*, or bell-flowered plantain lily *(Hosta)*, and for summer you can enjoy blue monkshood *(Aconitum napellus)*, spiraea *(Astilbe)* which has pink, white and red blooms, scarlet monkey flower *(Mimulus)*, yellow ligularia *(Ligularia przewalskii)*, or the striking giant rhubarb *(Rheum palmata)* which produces huge leaves up to 1.5m (5ft) tall and large red flowers.

For late summer and autumn, plant loosestrife *(Lythrum salicaria)*, which produces red, purple and pink flowers, and waxbells *(Kirengeshoma palmata)*.

Roses flourish in a moist soil, making them ideal for sunken gardens. In the rose garden (**below**) a central bed of standards is surrounded by large-flowered bush roses, while ramblers smother the trellis and provide screening all round. Miniatures in raised beds of brick or stone are easier to see and smell than at ground level.

Bog plants grow well in a sunken area with poor drainage. The circular garden (**above**) is made using vertical railway sleepers and crazy paving and features moisture-lovers such as ferns, hostas, iris, lilies and astilbe.

Low growing rockery plants flourish on the scant soil between millstone steps (**left**). Informal steps, framed by dwarf conifers, lead naturally into a sunken garden (**below**).

PLANTS
FOR
SPECIAL
PURPOSES

Ground cover plants

The most commercially planted ground cover plant is no doubt *Hypericum calycinum* (the St John's wort often called rose of Sharon). It is effective as ground cover but it is not a very interesting plant; it has large golden yellow flowers in summer but does not flower continuously. There are other ground cover plants which grow just as well and can be used to give shades of green, red, grey and variegated foliage.

Hedera canariensis (**below**) provides effective ground cover and is particularly useful for shady areas. It grows quickly in any type of soil. The creamy flowers of *Symphytum grandiflorum* (**bottom**) are a short-lived spring bonus on an excellent ground cover plant that spreads rapidly in sun or shade.

GROUND COVER PLANTS

Botanical name	Common name	Height
Ajuga reptans (Perennial)	Bugle	10–30cm (4–12in)
Alchemilla mollis (Perennial)	Lady's mantle	30–45cm (12–18in)
Berberis candidula (Shrub)	Barberry	60cm (2ft)
Bergenia, various (Perennial)	Saxifrage	30cm (12in)
Calluna vulgaris (Shrub)	Ling, Heather	30–45cm (12–18in)
Cotoneaster dammeri (Shrub)		Prostrate
Epimedium, various (Perennial)	Barrenwort; Bishop's hat	30cm (12in)
Erica carnea (herbacea) (Shrub)	Heather	Up to 30cm (12in)
Euonymus fortunei radicans variegatus (Shrub)		40cm (16in)
Euphorbia, various (Perennial)	Spurge	45cm (18in)
Gaultheria (Shrub)	Partridge berry	G.procumbens Prostrate G.shallon 1.8m (6ft)
Geranium, various (Perennial)	Cranesbill	20–60cm (8–24in)
Hebe pinquifolia 'Pagei' (Shrub)	Veronica	15–23cm (6–9in)
Hedera, various (Shrub)	Ivy	Spreading
Hosta, various (Perennial)	Plantain lily	38–90cm (15–36in)
Hyperium calycinum (Shrub)	Rose of Sharon	30–45cm 12–18in)
Lavandula (Shrub)	Lavender	30–80cm (12–32in)
Lysimachia nummularia (Perennial)	Creeping Jenny	Prostrate
Mahonia aquifolium (Shrub)	Oregon grape	90–120cm (3–4ft)
Nepeta mussinii (Perennial)	Catmint	30–45cm (12–18in)
Pachysandra terminalis (Perennial)		20–30cm (8–12in)
Polygonum affine (Perennial)	Knotweed	15–23cm (6–9in)
Potentilla 'Mandschurica' (Shrub)	Cinquefoil	30cm (12in)
Prunus laurocerasus 'Zabeliana' (Shrub)		1.2m (4ft)
Pulmonaria angustifolia (Perennial)	Lungwort	30cm (12in)
Santolina chamaecyparissus (incana) (Shrub)	Lavender cotton	45–60cm (18–24in)
Sarcococca humilis (Shrub)	Christmas box; Sweet box	60cm (2ft)
Sedum, various (Perennial)	Stonecrop	30cm (12in)
Symphytum grandiflorum (Perennial)	Russian comfrey	20cm (8in)
Tiarella cordifolia (Perennial)	Foam flower	15–30cm (6–12in)
Thymus serpyllum (Perennial)	Thyme	2.5–10cm (1–4in)
Vinca major (Shrub)	Periwinkle	15–30cm (6–12in)
Vinca minor (Shrub)	Periwinkle	5–10cm (2–4in)

Flower	Foliage	Season	Suitable sites
Blue	Multicoloured and variegated forms	Mid summer	Heavy clay; shady; chalky
Yellow-green calyces	Light green, hairy palmate leaves	Early to late summer	Heavy clay; chalky; industrial; shady; coastal
Yellow	Evergreen, spiny	Late spring	Heavy clay; chalky; shade; industrial; coastal
Shades of pink, purple and white	Autumn colour	Spring and autumn	Heavy clay; coastal. Tolerates dryness and deep shade
White, pink, purple and white	Coloured foliage	Mid summer to late autumn	Lime-free; coastal
White, red berries	Evergreen	Summer autumn	Shady; industrial; heavy clay; chalky; coastal
Wide range	Autumn tints	All year	Chalky; heavy clay; industrial
White, pink, purple	Light or dark green bronze, yellow	Late autumn to late spring	Coastal; lime-free
Green-white	Grey-green and variegated white and pink	All year	Chalky; heavy clay; coastal; industrial
Yellow, red bracts	Evergreen	Mid to late spring	Dry sunny
Pinkish white flowers, red or black berries	Evergreen	All year	Lime-free soil
Shades of blue, pink or white	Dense leaves some with autumn tints	Early summer to early autumn	Coastal; heavy clay; industrial
White	Grey-green, evergreen	Early summer	Coastal; dry sunny; industrial
	Variegated forms	All year	Heavy clay; industrial
White, purple	Wide colour range including variegated forms	Summer	Heavy clay; shady
Yellow	Bright green; variegated forms	Summer	Heavy clay; dry sunny; industrial
Shades of blue and purple, fragrant	Evergreen, aromatic	Summer	Dry sunny
Yellow	Mid-green and golden	Summer	Shady
Yellow fragrant flowers, blue-black berries	Evergreen	Spring	Industrial
Lavender blue, fragrant	Grey-green aromatic	Late spring to early autumn	Industrial; heavy clay
White, fragrant	Mid green; variegated form available	All year	Lime-free
Deep pink, rose red	Bright green becoming darker	Summer	Industrial; shady
White	Silver-grey foliage on purple stems	Late spring to early autumn	Industrial; shady
White; dark red fruits, finally black	Willow-like leaves	Evergreen	Industrial; clay
Pink or purple changing to blue	White spotted form available	Spring	Shady; clay
Yellow flowers	Silver-grey aromatic	Summer	Dry sunny
White flowers fragrant	Evergreen	Late winter	Chalk; heavy clay
Pink, yellow, white	Fleshy	Late summer	Dry sunny
White/pink shades	Rough, mid-green	Spring	Heavy clay
Cream white	Turning bronze – red in winter	All year	Shady; heavy clay
White, shades of pink and lilac	Aromatic	Summer	Dry sunny
Blue	Evergreen; variegated forms available	Spring to autumn	Industrial; heavy clay
Blue	Evergreen; variegated forms available	Spring to autumn	Industrial; heavy clay

The periwinkle *(Vinca)* provides many reliable and easy ground cover plants which do well in shade and can be planted under hedges. They send out creeping stems that root very easily and, when established, rapidly cover a fair area. The best known are *V. major* with blue flowers (there is a creamy white and green variegated form *V. major* 'Variegata') and *V. minor* 'Bowles' Variety', which has larger, deeper blue flowers. The following are also recommended: *V. minor* 'Alba', white; *V. minor* 'Azurea Flore Pleno', double, sky blue; *V. minor* 'Gertrude Jekyll', glistening white; *V. minor* 'Variegata', leaves variegated creamy white. The greater periwinkles, *Vinca major*, are approximately 35cm (14in) in height, whereas the lesser periwinkles, *Vinca minor*, are about 15cm (6in) high.

Symphytum grandiflorum (Russian comfrey) is a very good ground cover plant. It is like the wild comfrey but grows only to a height of 30cm (1ft). It has evergreen hairy foliage, and small tubular flowers which rise above the foliage in the spring; they are cream with red tips. It can be an invasive plant and should not be planted in confined areas.

Pachysandra terminalis is a glossy-leaved plant growing up to 30cm (1ft) in height. It is difficult to establish but, once started, forms a thick and pleasant low mass. The fragrant early spring flowers are white but inconspicuous. The silver variegated form, 'Variegata', is more attractive but takes even longer to establish than the type plant. *Pachysandra* spreads by underground stolons and should not be planted in small areas adjacent to lawns.

Cotoneaster horizontalis (**above**) is one of several cotoneasters that can be grown as ground cover plants.

Once established, *Pachysandra terminalis* (**right**) spreads vigorously by underground stems to form a dense mass of weed-proof growth. The glossy foliage is evergreen and adorned in spring with small white fragrant flowers. A variegated form is also available.

Attractive foliage and fresh yellow-green flowers make *Alchemilla mollis* (**right**) a highly desirable ground cover plant. It will flourish in any moist well-drained soil and seeds itself so readily that it very quickly fills its allotted space.

Ajuga reptans 'Burgundy Glow' (**right**) forms a carpet of bronze foliage dotted with small blue flowers throughout the summer months. An ideal gound cover plant for moist shady locations. It spreads rapidly by vigorous stems that radiate across the surface of the soil.

Planting ground cover

If the area to be covered is overgrown with difficult weeds such as couch-grass, nettles, ground elder, docks or bindweed, treat it all with a suitable weedkiller — avoiding all the plants that are to stay — at least four weeks before planting; check the manufacturer's recommendations. This should kill off the weeds and leave no harmful residue in the soil. Ground cover plants usually spread roughly in a proportion equal to their height and, if required to interlock, the initial planting distance should be 15-25cm (6-10in) or less. The mat type of plants require a planting distance of 30-45cm (12-18in). The very dwarf mat-forming plants such as *Ajuga*, *Sedum* and thyme require spacing at 15-30cm (6-12in).

All weeds must be removed by hoe or by

hand until the plants have grown together and become established. This should not be too difficult; the site should have been well cleared before planting.

Replace any plants that die, and remove all dead wood and any rubbish that accumulates in and around the plants. All large tree leaves should be removed to the compost heap; the smaller leaves can be left to help as a natural mulch. In addition, apply a good mulch of well-rotted compost either in the spring or autumn. When planting on a steep bank make sure that the plants are secure and then protect the root area with stones above them. These can be removed when the plants have become established. Replace any soil that has been washed down a bank planting.

The late winter or early spring fragrant flowers of *Sarcococca humilis* (**above**) are borne amid glossy evergreen foliage. This densely branched shrub grows up to 60cm (2ft) tall and provides good ground cover in moist shady places. One of the most popular ground cover plants is *Vinca minor* 'Bowles' Variety' (**left**). It bears lovely blue flowers all summer long. Several euphorbias can be grown as ground cover. *E. myrsinites* (**top right**) produces plantlets on long spreading stems, and *E. epithymoides* (**centre right**) forms dense evergreen bushes that suppress weeds effectively. Both these euphorbias produce bright yellow 'flowers' (really bracts) in spring. For superb fragrance and ground cover too, choose *Lavandula* 'Hidcote' (**right**).

Fragrant plants

It is difficult to define fragrance because it is so subjective; what is fragrant to one person may be uninteresting — or even objectionable — to others. Books on botany tend to ignore fragrance, referring to it instead as 'odour'. Botanically, odour is really all it is: it attracts insects that collect the nectar and pollen and at the same time pollinate the flowers. The fragrance thus helps flowers to carry out their primary function — to produce seeds. Unfortunately, because the modern hybridist works towards bigger and more colourful flowers, fragrance has to some extent diminished in many kinds of cultivated flowers. A special case is the musk *Mimulus moschatus*, which is now almost scentless although its presentday hybrids have many large bright flowers.

Many flower shows have a class for fragrant roses, which are sometimes judged by a blind person who is able to distinguish the scent quality or intensity much better than a sighted judge. The pleasure that fragrant plants bring to blind and partially sighted people is evident from the many public gardens planted especially for their enjoyment.

Fragrant roses

Of all the fragrant cultivated plants, roses stand supreme. The scent from roses can vary from a heavy musk perfume to a light lemony fragrance. At one time it was thought that all deep red roses were fragrant, but today many of them are scentless, and indeed some of the bicolours and pale soft colours are heavily scented.

In general, it is the old-fashioned shrub roses which have the most intense perfume. Many of the modern cultivars actually have little or none at all, although there are exceptions. Yet the old roses, although they may have the advantage of perfume, do have some disadvantages: with some exceptions, they only flower once a year, usually in early to midsummer; they tend to be susceptible to black spot and mildew; the flowers are large, with cabbage-like open centres that are easily damaged by rain; many are too large for the small modern garden; and although most are strong-growing, some tend to have a straggly habit.

Old-fashioned roses look their best planted in a shrub border, where they require little attention except that given to other shrubs plus, if necessary, routine spraying against black spot and mildew.

During the last 40 years a new group of shrub roses has been developed, the modern shrub roses, several of which carry a delightful fragrance. The very popular cluster-flowered (or *floribunda*) roses and the large-flowered (or hybrid tea) roses also contain a number of superbly fragrant varieties. There are also several climbing roses with an agreeable scent. Selected fragrant examples of all these types of roses are described in the table.

Fragrant shrubs

Garden shrubs can provide fragrance in all seasons, including winter. This selection includes the most widely available shrubs prized for their scented flowers and, in some cases, for their aromatic foliage too.

Buddleia: Butterfly bush
The cultivars of *Buddleia davidii*, justifiably popular for their graceful flower clusters in shades of red, purple, pink and white, also bring superb fragrance to the summer garden. Bushes grow to about 2.4m (8ft) in height and spread.

Chimonanthes: Winter sweet
This is one of several shrubs that provide sweetly-scented flowers during the winter. *Chimonanthes praecox*, which takes several years to establish has pale yellow flowers with a purplish centre; *C. p.* 'Luteus' has all-yellow blooms. Both reach a height of about 3m (10ft).

Daphne cneorum (**top left**) and *Daphne odora* 'Aureomarginata' (**centre left**) are both prized for their sweet-smelling flowers. *Nicotiana alata* 'Lime Green' (**left**) is also heavily scented.

Choisya ternata: Mexican orange blossom
The common name aptly describes the heady fragrance this shrub offers in spring. Both the white flowers and the glossy, evergreen leaves (when crushed) are fragrant. A superb shrub for a sunny sheltered spot, *Choisya ternata* grows to a height of 2-3m (6½-10ft).

Clethra alnifolia: Sweet pepper bush
Late summer sees the emergence of slender clusters of creamy white scented 'flowers' on this deciduous shrub, which requires a lime-free soil. Grow *C. a.* 'Paniculata' for the most abundant bloom; up to 2.1m (7ft) tall.

Corylopsis
This easily-grown deciduous shrub provides cowslip-scented, pale yellow flowers in early spring. Best grown on acid or neutral soils, *Corylopsis* generally reach a height of 1.5-2.1m (5-7ft). Recommended species are *C. pauciflora*, *C. spicata*, *C. veitchiana* and *C. willmottiae* (up to 3m/10ft tall).

Cytisus battandieri: Moroccan broom
For a tang of pineapple, grow this fast-growing tall shrub, preferably against a warm wall. The cone-shaped yellow flowers appear in midsummer.

Daphne

The daphnes are among the most fragrant of shrubs. From late winter until early spring the bare stems of the most popular daphne, *Daphne mezereum*, are clothed in sweetly scented blooms of white, pink or purplish red depending on variety. Also in bloom during winter and early spring is *Daphne odora*

Of the floribunda roses 'Arthur Bell' (**above**) is a favourite for its heavy fragrance. Frühlingsgold (**below**) blooms briefly but with a delicious scent.

'Aureomarginata', and as spring turns to summer *D. cneorum*, *D. X burkwoodii* 'Somerset' and *D. retusa* add their scent to the garden air.

Daphnes range in size from 30cm to 1.5m (1-5ft), and thrive in a moist but well-drained acid soil.

Genista cinerea

This lovely member of the pea family has profuse clusters of fragrant yellow pea flowers in early to mid summer. It forms a bush up to 3m (10ft) tall and 2.4m (8ft) across.

Hamamelis: Witch hazel

For fascinating flowers in the depths of winter it is hard to beat this shrub. Its spidery yellow or reddish-yellow blooms are delicately scented, their strap-like petals able to withstand the severest weather. Choose from *H. X intermedia* 'Jelena' ('Copper Beauty'), yellow-suffused coppery red; *H. mollis*, golden yellow; *H. m.* 'Goldcrest', golden yellow and claret; and *H. m.* 'Pallida', sulphur yellow. All grow slowly to about 3m (10ft) tall.

Jasminum officinale

In a warm, sheltered site the climber jasmine and its variety 'Affine' ('Grandiflorum') can be relied upon for a crop of sweet-smelling white flowers throughout the summer.

OLD ROSES

Botanical name	Height	Flower Colour	Flowering season	Notes
Rosa alba 'Königin von Dänemarck'	180cm (6ft)	Soft pink	Mid summer	Specimen bushes reach 180cm (6ft)
Rosa bourboniana 'Boule de Neige'	150cm (5ft)	Rich cream	All summer	Suitable for hedging
Rosa bourboniana 'Madame Isaac de Pereire'	180cm (6ft)	Purple crimson	All summer	Suitable for hedging
Rosa centifolia 'De Meaux'	90cm (3ft)	Pink	Mid summer	Slender growth, light green foliage
Rosa centifolia 'Tour de Malakoff'	210cm (7ft)	Lilac pink	Mid summer	Very vigorous
Rosa chinensis 'Cramoisie Superieure'	90cm (3ft)	Crimson	All summer	Moderately vigorous
Rosa damascena 'Madam Hardy'	150cm (5ft)	Pure white	All summer	Vigorous
Rosa gallica 'Belle de Crecy'	120cm (4ft)	Deep pink	Mid summer	Untidy habit, very few thorns, low growth
Rosa gallica 'Rosa Mundi'	90cm (3ft)	Striped pink, crimson, white	Mid summer	Vigorous
Rosa rugosa 'Blanc Double de Coubert'	150cm (5ft)	Pure white	All summer	Suitable for hedging
Rosa rugosa 'Mrs Anthony Waterer'	120cm (4ft)	Deep crimson	All summer	Suitable for hedging, vigorous

MODERN SHRUB ROSES

Botanical name	Height	Flower Colour	Flowering season	Notes
R. 'Chinatown'	180cm (6ft)	Bright yellow	Repeat flowering	Suitable for hedging
R. 'Frühlingsgold'	180cm (6ft)	Primrose	Early summer	
R. 'Penelope'	180cm (6ft)	Light pink	Repeat flowering	Suitable for hedging

FLORIBUNDA

Botanical name	Height	Flower Colour	Flowering season	Notes
R. 'Arthur Bell'	1m (3.3ft)	Yellow to cream	All summer	Vigorous upright growth
R. 'Elizabeth of Glamis'	75cm (30in)	Light salmon shaded orange	Early to mid summer	
R. 'Escapade'	90cm (3ft)	Rosy violet with a white eye	All summer	Disease resistant
R. 'Fragrant Delight'	75cm (30in)	Orange salmon	All summer	Very vigorous
R. 'Korresia'	90cm (3ft)	Bright yellow	All summer	
R. 'Margaret Merril'	90cm (3ft)	Pearl white	Repeat flowering	
R. 'Southampton'	105cm (3.5ft)	Apricot orange	Repeat flowering	Suitable for hedging

HYBRID TEA

Botanical name	Height	Flower Colour	Flowering season	Notes
R. 'Admiral Rodney'	105cm (3.5ft)	Light rose pink	Early summer to mid autumn	
R. 'Fragrant Cloud'	90cm (3ft)	Coral red	Early summer to mid autumn	Vigorous and upright
R. 'Prima Ballerina'	105cm (3.5ft)	Deep rose pink	Early summer to mid autumn	Very vigorous
R. 'Red Devil'	105cm (3.5ft)	Light red	Early summer to mid autumn	Vigorous and upright
R. 'Wendy Cussons'	1m (3.3ft)	Rose red to deep pink	Early summer to mid autumn	Vigorous and bushy
R. 'Whisky Mac'	75cm (2.5ft)	Amber yellow	Early summer to mid autumn	

CLIMBING ROSES

Botanical name	Height	Flower Colour	Flowering season	Notes
R. 'Compassion'	3m (10ft)	Pink to apricot-pink	Repeat flowering	
R. 'Maigold'	3.4m (11ft)	Apricot yellow	Early summer	Vigorous pillar or wall rose
R. 'New Dawn'	2.7m (9ft)	Light pearl pink	Repeat flowering	Bushy pillar rose
R. 'Rosy Mantle'	2.5-3.5m (8-10ft)	Rose pink	Repeat flowering	
R. 'Zephirine Drouhin'	2.7m (9ft)	Deep pink	Repeat flowering	Thornless, vigorous.

Plants for cutting

The range of plants which can be used as cut flowers is much wider than is generally supposed, for the market growers commonly restrict their variety to the minumum that is commercial so as to maximize the use of space, packaging and transport. This inevitably results in a reduced selection for the purchaser. But the amateur gardener need not be concerned by such problems, and can grow whichever plants may be thought suitable for house decoration.

The average garden today is small, and becoming smaller. If flowers are to be cut from display borders, the resultant gaps left may be unsightly. So it is a good idea, if cut flowers are to be a continuing requirement, to allocate a space somewhere in the garden specifically to the growing of flowers to be cut — a cut flower area. Allotments are often used for this purpose, and generally provide good growing conditions; cut flower allotments also brighten up what otherwise are predominantly vegetable-growing zones.

Cut flowers are on the whole annuals or biennials and perennials; some cut flowers are provided by shrubs and trees (like lilac) but they are distinctly in the minority. The cutting of some flowers from several shrubs is actually beneficial to the health of the plants; the flowers can be lovely too. But keen floral arrangers use all kinds of plants for flowers, foliage and seed-heads.

This selection of flowers to cut is intended as a starter list.

Camellias (*Camellia* species), when established, have lovely sprays of large, colourful flowers with deep green glossy foliage; they last well in water. Spring is their time for flowering. Daphne flowers (*Daphne* species) are very fragrant: one stem can scent a room. They do not really like being cut, but one or two stems' loss do no harm to the plant, which flowers in spring and summer. The forsythias (species of the shrub *Forsythia*) genuinely benefit from cutting. A harbinger of spring, the plant's golden-yellow flowers can be cut in bud to open indoors. The 'Hortensia' hybrids of the hydrangeas add body to a flower arrangement in mid-summer; *Hydrangea paniculata* produces large spikes of flowers in the late summer. The winter-flowering jasmine *(Jasminum nudiflorum)* is invaluable during late winter and early spring; *J. revolutum* produces lovely golden-yellow flowers in summer.

The rose genus *(Rosa)* provides cut flowers from mid-summer until mid-autumn in so many colours that the choice is almost endless. The end of each cut stem should be split to allow it to take up water. From late spring to autumn the various forms of the shrub *Spiraea* give colour and elegance; the bridal wreath *(S. arguta)* has white flowers, and *S. X bumalda* 'Anthony Waterer' has crimson flowers throughout the summer. The lovely heads of the flowers of the lilac (*Syringa* species) vary in colour from white through to deep purple in spring and early summer. The leaves should be removed from cut stems or the flowers tend to droop. Viburnums (*Viburnum* species) can be used as cut flowers but should not be cut back too much. *V. X burkwoodii* has fragrant pink budded white flowers in early spring; *V. carlesii* produces rounded clusters of pure white flowers with a daphne-like fragrance.

The cutting of flowers from shrubs should be carried out with great care, leaving no snags, and maintaining the overall shape of the bush. All shrub flower stems should be split to enable the stem to take up water.

Annuals and perennials

Annuals, and some perennials grown as biennials, are a fruitful source of cut flowers. Grown from seed in one year they are very rewarding, although the sowing, the pricking out (with half-hardy annuals also the hardening off) and the planting out are all time-consuming. Hardy annuals can be sown where they are to flower, of course, either in the autumn or in the early spring.

The following selection includes many of the best.

The annual asters (*Callistephus* species) make lovely flowers all summer, with colours from white through to deep purple. Half-hardy annuals, they tend to suffer from wilt, but the many types available are all well worth growing. The pot marigold (*Calendula* species), a hardy annual, repeats bloom all summer, bearing masses of orange and yellow-orange flowers. All spent flower heads should be removed to prolong the display. The hardy annual cornflower *(Centaurea cyanus)* has flowers in many colours from white to purple in countless shades. Wallflowers (*Cheiranthus* species) are perennials but are usually grown as biennials; they provide many lovely colours, with pastel shades from lemon yellow to deep, rich reds. The Siberian wallflower *C. X allionii* has attractive flowers in yellow and orange.

The hardy annual chrysanthemums are better known for the autumn-flowering types than the annual ones; *C. carinatum* has fern-like foliage and bright daisy-like flowers, yellow through to deep red, most with a zonal eye of yellow. *Clarkia elegans*, another hardy annual, bears masses of double flowers on slender stems and in colours of white, pink and cerise. The same colours may be found on the half-hardy annual *Cosmea*, sometimes called cosmos; it has pretty fern-like foliage. A hardy annual always available from a florist is the rocket larkspur, *Delphinium ajacis* — and rightly so. It has slender stems of stock-like flowers in white, pink, red and deep blue, and many intermediate colours. The flowers of the blanket flower *Gaillardia* — a plant that may be hardy or half-hardy annual or perennial — are single or double, mostly yellow, flame and red, often edged in contrasting shades. They make splendid summer border displays. Of the hardy annual *Godetia*, the single and double flowers, some frilled, are in many shades of white, pink and red. *Gypsophila*, also known as baby's breath, is a hardy annual which has a delicate froth of tiny white flowers on a widely branching stem, ideal for use in combination with sweet peas (see below). The mallow (*Lavatera* species) is a superb flower for cutting: the rose-pink, silver-pink and white flowers are borne on strong stems; the best are *L. trimestris* 'Mont Blanc', *L.* 'Loveliness' and *L.* 'Silver Cup'.

Another first-class flower for cutting is the sweet pea *(Lathyrus odoratus)*; available in many shades from white to deep purple, this hardy annual is fragrant and can be grown to many heights between 30cm (12in) and 1.8m (6ft). Also a hardy annual, Love-in-a-mist *(Nigella damascena)* has pretty blue flowers much like those of the cornflower, followed by decorative seed-heads. *Rudbeckia* makes an excellent cut flower, in colours from yellow to mahogany, some possibly bicoloured. Among the best of these hardy and half-hardy annuals are *R.* 'Marmalade', golden orange; *R.* 'Rustic Dwarfs', mahogany-tipped and variegated orange; *R.* 'Irish Eyes', golden yellow with a bright yellow centre — all of these varieties of *R. hirta*, the black-eyed Susan. The sweet

These plants provide excellent cut flowers: from left to right, *Gladiolus* 'Extremist', dusty mauve; *Lavatera trimestris* 'Silver Cup', pink; *Crocosmia masonorum*, vivid orange; *Aconitum napellus* 'Bicolor', blue-and-white hooded flowers.

scabious (*Scabiosa* species) also gives a fine selection of colours, from white to purple. A new cultivar of this hardy annual called 'Paper Moon' has soft lavender flowers which eventually shed their petals to leave papery spheres with a blue eye. And finally, the half-hardy annual zinnias (*Zinnia* species) provide gaily-coloured flowers of substance in white, gold, bronze, cerise, red, and many intermediate shades.

Perennials

A herbaceous border can give a good supply of cut flowers during the summer months. Perennials are generally taller than annuals, have stiffer stems, and produce their best flowers when they are well established, after three years, despite commonly being left very much to their own devices after the first year in many gardens. They appreciate a yearly mulching and a dressing of a good general fertilizer in the spring to give of their best. The flower stems need some support against wind damage, for which twiggy branches are ideal. To maintain the quality of the flowers and to prevent overcrowding, they should be dug out and split up at least once every five years — although to this rule there are one or two exceptions such as *Aster amellus* cultivars, *Eryngium* and peonies.

Once a border has been emptied, dig it over thoroughly and incorporate plenty of well-rotted manure or compost before sprinkling in some general fertilizer at a rate of 60gm per m² (2oz per sq yd) and forking it in lightly. Prior to replanting, divide the plants into three or four pieces and use only one outside piece for replanting; discard the rest.

There are many perennials to choose from; the following selection includes many of the best.

Achillea

A long-lasting cut flower on tall 1.2m (4ft) stems, its flowers are golden yellow from midsummer until early autumn, borne in large, flat heads; the foliage is deeply cut and aromatic. The best cultivars are 'Gold Plate' and 'Parker's Variety'.

Aconitum: Monkshood

The blue and white or violet-blue flowers are carried on stems 120 to 135cm (4 to 4½ft) tall from mid-summer until early autumn. Supports are required if grown in open positions.

All parts of this plant are poisonous — flowers, stems and roots: wash hands thoroughly after handling. The two best cultivars are 'Spark's Variety' and 'Bressingham Spire'.

Aster amellus

This is a superb border plant, of which the best varieties are *A.* 'King George', deep blue, 60cm (2ft) tall; *A.* 'Jacqueline Genebrier', pink, 90cm (3ft); and *A.* 'Violet Queen', 45cm (1½ft). *Aster X frikartii*, a hybrid between *A. amellus* and *A. thomsonii*, bears lovely orange-centred blue flowers on stout stems up to 75cm (30in) tall. All flower in late summer and early autumn.

Astrantia: Masterwort

Astrantias make good cut flowers, with grey and white or pink and white intricate flowers decorated with a mass of stamens. Height: 40-75cm (15-30in). Flowering periods vary throughout the summer.

Campanula: Bellflower

The *Campanula* genus is a large and diverse one. Most of them are blue in many shades, light pink and white. *C. lactiflora* offers many good cultivars, 1.2m (4ft) in height. *C. latifolia*, 100cm (3½ft), and *C. persicifolia*, 90cm (3ft), also have many cultivars. They flower from early summer to early autumn.

Chrysanthemum maximum: Shasta daisy

This flower and its cultivars are also advantageous to the flower arranger; their white or pale cream single, semi-double, double or fimbriated flowers are held on stiff stems 75-90cm (2½-3ft) in height. The flowering period is mid- to late summer.

Crocosmia and Curtonus: Montbretia

These bulbous plants commonly grow to be so crowded in an average garden that their true worth goes unrecognized. *Crocosmia masonorum* is the best of the genus: it has graceful, arching stems carrying vivid orange flowers at a height of 75cm (2½ft). There are several cultivars in all, with slight variations in colour, flowering from mid-summer to early autumn.

Dahlia

A large and diverse genus, dahlias are available in many colours, some mixed, from white through red to the deepest purple. The single varieties are the best for floral ar-

rangements. Height: 45-120cm (1½-4ft). The flowering period is mid-summer until early autumn.

Dianthus: Pink, Border carnation

These are lovely — and common — cut flowers in white, pink, red and intermediate shades, and have pleasant fragrance. Height: 15-30cm (6-12in). They flower in mid-summer.

Eryngium: Sea holly

Very eye-catching, very prickly plants with blue flowering heads, these grow to a height of 45-90cm (1½-3ft) and flower in mid-summer.

Gypsophila

G. paniculata is the perennial form; *G.* 'Bristol Fairy' and *G.* 'Flamingo' are white and double pink respectively. Height: 120cm (4ft). The flowering period is mid-summer until early autumn.

Helenium: Sneezewort

A sun-loving and very free-flowering plant, the sneezewort has yellow, orange or mahogany flowers. Recommended cultivars are *H.* 'Moerheim Beauty', *H.* 'Gold Fox' and *H.* 'Bressingham Gold'. Height: 60-110cm (2½-3ft). It is in flower from early summer until mid-autumn.

Scabiosa: Scabious, Pincushion flower

One of the well-known flowers at florists', the colours of the scabious vary from white to light and dark blue. The best ones are *S.* 'Clive Greaves', deep blue; *S.* 'Moonstone', light blue; and *S.* 'Miss Willmott', white. Height: 75cm (2½ft). The flowering period lasts from early autumn, but the plant does not do well in clayey soils.

All of these plants are good garden plants and amply repay care and attention.

Bulbous plants suitable for cutting comprise another elite group. Daffodils, including narcissi, are perhaps the most commonly available at the florists'. Gladioli should be planted in sequence from early spring onwards to prolong the flowering times; doing this, the season can be extended for flowers from mid-summer to early autumn. Tulips come into flower in spring in many colours.

Rudbeckia hirta 'Marmalade' (**far right**) produces 10cm (4in) golden blooms that are excellent for indoor decoration. Daffodil 'Fortune' (**centre right**), one of many daffodils well-loved for their spring blooms. *Syringa* flowers (**right**) last well in water.

Plants for drying

There are many plants that can be dried or otherwise preserved for ornamental purposes and used in virtually permanent flower arrangements. Many plants — particularly the herbs, for example — are also dried for use in the kitchen. Preserved ornamental plants were great favourites of the Victorians who dried, pressed and oiled all manner of plant material. Today this method of prolonging the beauty of plants is experiencing a comeback.

Dried flowers and leaves provide long-lasting decorative arrangements; moreover — and much more than is generally the case at present — they can be used to complement the cut flowers which in winter are so expensive to buy. Requiring little attention, they have only to be dusted from time to time. Dried flowers and leaves can be used in containers, for pictures and plaques, and in swags (three-dimensional arrangements which can be hung up on a wall without a frame).

Suitable plants

The Table features a wide range of plants suitable for drying or preserving. Many of the flowering plants can be sown and gathered in one season: the hardy and half-hardy annuals.

The half-hardy annuals should be sown in gentle heat during the early spring in seed pans, and after germination should be pricked out in seed trays when the first true leaves have appeared. Grow them on until late spring, and harden them off in a cold frame before planting them in a border in early summer.

The hardy annuals can be sown where they are to flower in mid-spring, when weather conditions are suitable and the soil is warm; sow thinly. After their germination, thin out to 23cm (9in) apart. All these annuals thrive in well prepared soil in a sunny position and require little attention.

The two hardy biennials in the Table, *Dipsacus* (teasel) and *Lunaria* (honesty), should be planted as seed in early summer for flowering the same time the following year.

The parts of the plants that are suitable for preserving include the flowers, the seed-heads, the foliage and the fruit. Some of the most fascinating plants for preservation are the ornamental gourds, which can be grown in the same way as marrows. Sow the seeds in pots or boxes in a frame or greenhouse in spring. Plant out early in summer, depending on the weather, and water freely, giving liquid fertilizer as necessary. Train the stems on to a trellis or similar support in order to avoid slug damage and soil splashes. Cut the inedible fruits when they are large enough to handle, wash them and lay them out in a well ventilated room out of the sun for about eight weeks. Many colours and patterns of gourds can be grown from one packet of mixed seed.

The stately flower spires of *Verbascum* (**above**) grace the perennial border during mid-summer. The seed-heads that follow are excellent subjects for drying.

Drying technique

The method used for drying plant material uses the fact that when a plant dies, a change takes place which leaves it a facsimile of itself when alive, but brown where once it was green. When the life of a plant comes to an end, it stops taking up water, which is not replaced as it evaporates; the plant then shrivels and dies. The ones to dry, therefore, are those that die back gracefully, retaining their shape. They tend to have a finely branching, strong, rigid structure, able by itself to support the dead tissue and so retain the shape even when completely dehydrated. This retention is particularly good if the final water evaporation is gradual.

It is far better to dry plants indoors. Some plants do dry naturally out of doors, but they can be damaged by weather conditions. Other plants tend to shrivel when drying and instead, for good results, require pressing.

Drying is most successfully effected by bunching and hanging. Cut the flowers and seed-heads for hanging up to dry. Flowers must be in good condition — avoid misshapen heads or any that have been damaged — and should be neither moist nor yet fully open. Seed-heads should be cut when they are beginning to dry on the plant. Care must be taken when gathering thistles, pampas grass and bulrushes for these all break readily and should be cut when half developed. Tie the stems of the plant material in small bunches, with a hanging loop, and ensure that the flowers or seed-heads do not rub each other. Remove any leaves — without special measures (see below) they do not dry successfully and commonly become patchy and increase the humidity as the water evaporates.

Hang the plant material up to dry in the dark. The bunches should be hung upside down, which gives a better shape to the flowers and seed-heads, and avoids a drooping appearance. If the drying is too slow the colours may fade. A warm place with a free circulation of air — *not* the airing cupboard — gives the best results.

Store the dried plants for future use where they were dried or in boxes without lids, layering with tissue-paper to avoid crushing. Dried material is fragile, so great care is needed.

Preserving foliage

All foliage to be preserved should be cut when the leaves are fully grown and at their best. The time required to treat the leaves is dependent on the type of leaf.

Foliage is normally better preserved with glycerine than dried. The glycerine is mixed with water in a solution made up of one part of glycerine to two parts of boiling water, but it must be cold when used. Stir the solution well when mixing. It can be used over and over again. The newly-picked stems take up the mixture, and the water evaporates but the glycerine remains in the leaf cells. Because of the water loss, the natural colour is not retained, so the leaves turn brown, dark green or blue-grey, or variations of these colours depending on the plant composition. The results, though, are tough and long-lasting. The plant material must of course be treated while it is still absorbing water, for the solution must be carried to every part of the foliage.

Arranging dried plants

Dried plant material which loses its shape can be 'revived' by holding it over the spout of a steaming kettle for a few seconds and then reshaping quickly. If the material is flat it can be lightly ironed — use a warm iron: this is certainly the best method for large leaves.

When arranging dried plant material, it can be supported with plasticine, dry plastic foam or a pinholder. If natural flowers or foliage are also used, the stem ends of the dried material should be dipped in candle wax to prevent them from taking up water.

The purple flowers of *Lunaria annua* (**below**) are replaced by flat seed-pods.

The prickly flower-heads of *Dipsacus fullonum* (**below**) dry well.

PLANTS FOR DRYING

Botanical name	Common name	Height	Flower colour	Foliage	Decorative feature
Allium, various (Bulb)	Onion (and related plants)	23-120cm (9-48in)	Lilac, blue, gold white, red	Grey-green	Seed-head/fruit
Althaea (Biennial)	Hollyhock	90-180cm (3-6ft)	Many colours but not blue	Grey-green	Seed-head/fruit
Amaranthus caudatus (Half-hardy annual)	Love-lies-bleeding	90cm (3ft)	Red/dark red	Pale green, netted red	Flowers
Ammobium alatum (Half-hardy annual)	Winged everlasting	45-60cm (18-24in)	White and yellow	Grey	Flowers
Angelica archangelica (Perennial)	Holy ghost	1.8-3m (6-10ft)	Yellow-green	Aromatic	Seed-head/fruit
Briza media (Grass)	Quaking grass	30-45cm (12-18in)	Golden nodding flowers	Small heart-shaped purple-brown spikes on thin stalks	Seed-head/fruit
Bromus brizaeformis (Grass)	Ornamental oats	40-120cm (16-48in)	Purplish red panicles	Pale green	Seed-head/fruit
Castanea sativa (Tree)	Sweet chestnut	Up to 21.3m (70ft)	Cream	Shiny, lance-shaped	Foliage
Celosia argentea 'Plumosa' *C.a.* 'Cristata' (Half-hardy annuals)	Prince of Wales' feathers Cockscomb	23-60cm (9-24in)	Red, yellow orange	Light green	Flowers
Clematis vitalba (Climbing shrub)	Travellers joy, Old man's beard	Climber	Greenish white	Glossy green hairless leaves	Seed-head/fruit
Cortaderia, various (Grass)	Pampas grass	1.2-2.1m (4-7ft)	Gold, rose, silver	Bluish green evergreen	Seed-head
Cucurbita pepo (Half-hardy annual)	Ornamental gourd	Climber	Yellow	Large, green	Fruit (gourd)
Dipsacus fullonum (Hardy biennial)	Teasel	45cm-2m (18in-6½ft)	Pink or white	Lance-shaped, green	Seed-head
Fagus, various (Tree)	Beech	Grow as a hedge		Elliptical leaves green, copper and purple	Foliage
Gomphrena, various (Half-hardy annual)	Everlasting globe amaranth	30cm (12in)	Orange, yellow, purple, pink and white	Bright green	Flowers
Helichrysum (Half-hardy annual)	Straw flower	90-120cm (3-4ft)	Many colours available	Pale green	Flowers
Helipterum, various (Hardy annual)	Everlasting	45cm (18in)	Yellow	Woolly, almost white	Flowers turn green after drying
Helleborus corsica (Perennial)	Hellebore	60cm (2ft)	Yellow-green	Thick and spiny	Foliage
Koelaria glauca (Grass)	Blue meadow grass	60cm (2ft)	Intense blue	Blue	Seed-head
Lagarus ovatus (Grass)	Hare's tail grass	45cm (18in)	Fluffy white heads	Pale green	Seed-head
Limonium, various (Half-hardy annual)	Statice, everlasting	30cm (12in)	Many colours	Green	Flowers
Liriodendron tulipifera (Tree)	Tulip tree	over 18m (60ft)	Yellow-green with orange markings	Squarish leaves turn yellow in autumn	Foliage
Lunaria annua (Hardy biennial)	Honesty	75cm (30in)	Silvery seed pods	Dark green	Seed-head
Moluccella laevis (Half-hardy annual)	Bells of Ireland	60cm (2ft)	Spikes of white flowers with pale green calyx	Pale green	Flowers
Nicandra physaloides (Hardy annual)	Shoo-fly plant	Up to 90cm (3ft)	Pale blue	Globular fruits enclosed by green and purple calyces	Fruiting branches Seed-head
Nigella damascena (Hardy annual)	Love-in-a-mist	45cm (18in)	Blue. Multi-coloured form available	Feathery shape, green	Seed-head
Panicum violaceum (Grass)	Millet	90cm (3ft)	Green and violet	Pale green	Seed-head
Papaver orientale (Perennial)	Oriental poppy	60-90cm (2-3ft)	Shades of pink and red, white	Silver-green	Seed-head/fruit
Physalis franchetii (Perennial)	Chinese lantern	60cm (2ft)	Globular orange fruits in a papery calyx	Pale green	Seed-head/fruit
Setaria italica (Grass	Foxtail millet	45cm (18in)	Panicles of reddish gold	Pale green	Seed-head
Triticum spelta (Grass)	Ornamental wheat	60cm (2ft)	Biscuit colour	Biscuit colour when ripe	Seed-head
Verbascum, various (Perennial)	Mullein	90-180cm (3-6ft)	Wide range of colours		Seed-head/fruit
Xeranthemum annuum (Hardy-annual)	Immortelle	60cm (2ft)	Shades of pink, purple-lilac and white	Grey-green	Flowers. They keep their colour after drying
Zinnia, various (Half-hardy annual)		15-75cm (6-30in)	Many colours, flowers round with thick petals	Grey-green	Flowers

Colour
In The
Garden

Introduction

Colour has a strong effect on the emotions. A garden that contains only the various greens of leaves seems restful but may in time become boring. Yet a garden completely filled with bright coloured flowers is certainly exciting — but may equally quickly become tiring. The story is told of a man who, having been taken to admire a bed of particularly bright geraniums, begged to be led away to cool his eyes on the parsley. There seems to be a good scientific reason for that reaction. If one stares for a while at an area of bright red and then closes one's eyes, an image of green appears briefly against the darkness. It is as if the surfeit of red has produced a need for green to complement it; in fact, green is known as the complementary colour for red.

Sunlight is composed of all the colours that appear in a rainbow or when it is split up by a prism: this is direct light. What we actually see when looking at objects around us is the light they reflect. The colours that the eye registers from them can all be made by mixing yellow, red and blue pigments (with the addition of black or white to darken or lighten them and so make the different shades and tints). If the three primary colours are placed around a circle numbered like a clock face, with yellow at the top (12), red at 4 and blue at 8 and the intermediate colours made by mixing any two of these are filled in between, so that orange-yellow is at 1, orange at 2, orange-red at 3, red-violet at 5, violet at 6, blue-violet at 7, blue-green at 9, green at 10 and yellow-green at 11, it will be found that all the complementary colours face one another across the clock. Red is seen to be complementary to green, orange to blue and so on all round the colour circle.

But the colour clock tells us something more. The nearer the colours are on the clock face, the more they harmonize. Broadly speaking all colour associations can be split up into harmonies and contrasts, the former less violent to the senses than the latter. This violence can be reduced by introducing linking colours, shown on the clock face between those that are contrasting too much for satisfaction. The softest harmonies of all are produced by the paled or darkened tints and shades of the full colours.

Armed with such information it is possible to approach colour planning in the garden in a very logical and systematic way. Appreciation of this has grown rapidly among gardeners in recent years thanks to the activities of flower arrangers, particularly at flower shows. The fine floral exhibits that are such an admired feature of many shows demonstrate the effective use of colour and form, and because flower arrangers have been trained, or have trained themselves, in both they usually also make good garden designers.

In borders of flowers there are several ways in which colour can be used. The simplest is to restrict each border to a limited range of colours — for example, to use only white flowers and grey or silver-leaved plants with perhaps just a touch of light yellow, blue, pink and mauve; to go entirely for strong colours in a limited range, such as blue and purple or red, orange and yellow; or to make quiet harmonies with soft blues, pinks and cream. The effects so produced may be lively or sad, stimulating or restful, but they can never jar the senses by dissonance.

Another safe method is to arrange the colours in a border in a progressive sequence, starting with white and pale yellow at one end and gradually working up to the strongest oranges, reds and crimsons at the other end. Alternatively, if there is sufficient length, these strong colours could be set in the centre and the colour sequence appear in reverse, not necessarily with the same flowers, to either end. Such arrangements are sometimes referred to as rainbow borders because they roughly follow the sequence of colours in a rainbow, but usually with marked differences in shade and intensity.

This is another feature of colour that must be considered. Of course, not all colours are fully saturated or intense: in practice they occur in an infinite variety of intensities and gradations which an artist simulates by adding white, black or brown or by diluting the colour with more solvent. Flowers exhibit innumerable gradations of this kind and can thus be chosen to give the precise effect that is sought.

Most flower borders are neither planned for a limited colour range nor for a rainbow effect, but are filled with colours randomly distributed. Unless all the plants are carefully placed in relation to their neighbours, the effect can be insipid or tiresome to the eye. It takes some ingenuity to arrange a border without having any clashes, but one method of sorting out such problems before actually committing oneself to plant is to write the names, colours, heights and flowering times of all the plants to be used on little circles or ovals of cardboard and then move these about on an outline plan of the border until a satisfactory mix is achieved. Flowering time is important, for it is no use planning some fine colour association only to find that the colours do not appear at the same time. Height is also a useful piece of information: comparison shows at a glance whether any plant is likely to be concealed by a taller one growing next to it.

Green, grey, silver and white, whether in flowers or foliage, can be used to break up all the other colours and prevent clashes between them. The advantage of leaves over flowers is that they are usually present for much longer. There are a great many variations of green and grey and even, oddly enough, of white, partly because the latter is often not quite pure, but also because of differences in the surface texture of petals or in the way they are arranged, both of which affect the way in which they reflect light.

Colour can also be used to play tricks with perspective. Some colours (especially the strong ones), are seen more clearly than others (mainly the weak ones), and so they seem to be closer to the eye. If a long border is planted so that the colours range progressively towards the weaker, for example starting with the full-blooded crimsons, purples, reds and oranges at one end and gradually toning down to the pale mauves, pinks, creams and white at the other end (much in the manner already described for a rainbow border), it appears even longer than it really is when viewed from the strong-coloured end and shorter than it is when seen from the weak-coloured end.

There are no unbreakable rules in the use of colour. Some would say that the bluish reds should never be mixed with the yellowish reds because they clash. But that clash may be precisely the effect desired. I remember once asking a very sensitive and clever garden-maker why she had planted orange alstroemeria in the middle of a lot of flowers in the magenta range — and receiving the reply that it was to make fools ask questions. Theatrical designers often get away with the most outrageous colour combinations, using them to stir the senses and create a peak of excitement. Nevertheless, what may be fully justified on the stage for a performance that continues only for an hour or so may be intolerable in a garden that has to be lived with. If in doubt, try the colours you fancy on a sheet of paper, using paints or crayons; place a splodge of each desired colour against another and gradually build up from this.

One difficulty in communicating ideas about colour is the very meagre vocabulary on the subject that most of us have. Colour charts are useful — if the person with whom we are trying to communicate has access to the same colour chart. If not, terms such as Tyrian rose and Turkey red have little meaning. Colour descriptions in nursery and seed catalogues can accordingly be very misleading; often, one catalogue appears completely to contradict another. The ideal is to see the plants flowering before deciding to use them — but that is a counsel of perfection that is rarely practical. In the following lists of some suggested plants arranged according to the colour of their flowers I have tried to use only familiar terms, such as lavender-blue, violet-purple and rose-pink, although I know that again each of these covers a fairly wide range of colour.

The bright pinks of *Phlox paniculata* varieties and roses provide bold splashes of colour in this garden. The large heart-shaped leaves of the tree *Catalpa bignonioides* 'Aurea' provide a refreshing shade of yellow-green to the darker foliage greens. But the balance of colour is never constant; as the seasons change so new plants come into flower as others fade. Timing is therefore an important part of planning colour in the garden. It is also vital to know the mature size and shape of garden plants; subjects chosen carefully for their colour may be overshadowed by taller plants as the garden develops.

Arranging the colours of the rainbow in a circle (**left**) helps to show which ones clash and which ones are complementary. Colours facing each other directly across the circle are complementary and liable to clash. Those that lie close together around the circle harmonize with each other and can be used as links between the contrasting colours.

Borders composed of just one or two colours, such as this pink and silver one (**left**), often produce more effective colouring schemes than those mixing many hues. The cascading mounds of azaleas in full flower (**right**) are effective through the sheer 'weight' of their colour.

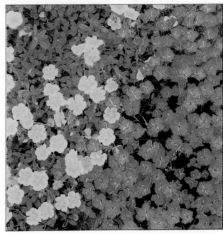

The double pink flowers of *Prunus* 'Kanzan' (**left**) form a restful backdrop to the bright early spring blooms of polyanthus and *Myosotis*. Yellow and pink form a simple yet strikingly effective combination in this mixed planting of *Helianthemum* and *Dianthus* (**above**).

Yellow flowers

Yellow is a colour that raises strong feelings. In its most concentrated form it is a penetrating and dominant colour that some people find unbearable. A colleague of mine complains of the yellow rash that breaks out when the daffodils flower in spring. Letters deploring the acid yellow of rape fields in flower in summer are common in the newspapers. Yet yellow is essential to most garden designers — a cheerful and compelling colour freely available at most seasons, and unsurpassed for making exhilarating displays when combined with red and orange. It can also be used to brighten up blues and purples, especially in its lighter forms, such as primrose, sulphur, lemon and mimosa yellow.

Some gardeners like yellow so much that they plant yellow borders or even yellow

Tagetes 'Lemon Queen' (**left**) forms a bright foreground to this garden border. The yellow pea-like flowers of *Genista aetnensis* (**right**) appear during mid- and late-summer. They are borne in loose clusters on a shrub reaching up to 6m (20ft) in height.

Crocus chrysanthus

Fritillaria imperialis

Laburnum 'Vossii'

Limnanthes douglasii

Kerria japonica 'Pleniflora'

Koelreuteria paniculata

	SPRING					SUMMER
ANNUALS/BEDDING	**Cheiranthus cheiri** (Wallflower) *Height:* 25-45cm (10-18in) *Spread:* 20-25cm (8-10in) *Soil:* Ordinary *Site:* Sunny 'Cloth of Gold' 'Golden Monarch' 'Primrose Monarch	**Limnanthes douglasii** (Poached egg flower) *Height:* 15cm (6in) *Spread:* 23cm (9in) *Soil:* Ordinary *Site:* Open Pale yellow and white	**Pansy** *Height:* 15-23cm (6-9in) *Spread:* 15cm (6in) *Soil:* Ordinary *Site:* Sun or shade 'Clear Crystals', golden yellow 'Coronation Gold', deep golden yellow 'Sunny Boy', yellow and black 'Yellow Bedder', bright yellow	**Polyanthus** *Height:* 20cm (8in) *Spread:* 15cm (6in) *Soil:* Ordinary *Site:* Sun or moderate shade 'Triumph Yellow', deep yellow		**Antirrhinum** (Snapdragon) *Height:* 38-45cm (15-18in) *Spread:* 23cm (9in) *Soil:* Ordinary *Site:* Open 'Regal Yellow' 'Yellow Monarch'
BULBS	**Crocus** *Height:* 10cm (4in) *Spread:* 7.5cm (3in) *Soil:* Ordinary *Site:* Open or light shade 'Large Yellow', daffodil yellow *C.chrysanthus* 'Cream Beauty', cream *C.chrysanthus* 'E.A. Bowles', deep butter yellow	**Fritillaria imperialis** (Crown Imperial) *Height:* 75cm (30in) *Spread:* 25cm (10in) *Soil:* Rich *Site:* Open 'Lutea Maxima', golden yellow	**Hyacinth** *Height:* 25cm (10in) *Spread:* 15cm (6in) *Soil:* Ordinary *Site:* Open 'City of Haarlem', pale yellow	**Narcissus** (Daffodil) *Height:* 30-50cm (12-20in) *Spread:* 15cm (6in) *Soil:* Ordinary *Site:* Sun or light shade 'Carlton', light yellow 'February Gold', deep yellow 'Golden harvest', deep yellow 'Spellbinder', sulphur yellow 'Trevithian', lemon yellow 'Yellow Cheerfulness', light yellow	**Tulip** *Height:* 30-60cm (12-24in) *Spread:* 10cm (4in) *Soil:* Ordinary *Site:* Open 'Beauty of Apeldoorn', creamy yellow flushed orange 'Bellona', daffodil yellow 'Golden Harvest', lemon yellow 'Golden Springtime', deep yellow 'West Point', daffodil yellow	**Allium moly** *Height:* 25cm (10in) *Spread:* 7.5cm (3in) *Soil:* Ordinary *Site:* Sun or partial shade Buttercup yellow
PERENNIALS	**Alyssum saxatile** (Gold dust) *Height:* 23cm (9in) *Spread:* 23cm (9in) *Soil:* Ordinary *Site:* Open 'Golden Queen', bright yellow 'Citrinum', lemon yellow	**Doronicum** (Leopard's bane) *Height:* 20-90cm (8-36in) *Spread:* 20-30cm (8-12in) *Soil:* Ordinary *Site:* Sun or light shade *D.cordatum*, marigold yellow *D.plantagineum*, 'Harpur Crewe', marigold yellow	**Euphorbia** (Spurge) *Height:* 15-45cm (6-18in) *Spread:* 30cm (12in) *Soil:* Ordinary *Site:* Sunny *E.myrsinites*, sulphur yellow *E.polychroma (epithymoides)*, lime yellow	**Trollius** (Globe flower) *Height:* 45-60cm (18-24in) *Spread:* 25cm (10in) *Soil:* Ordinary, moist *Site:* Sun or semi-shade 'Canary Bird', lemon yellow 'Golden Queen', orange yellow		**Achillea filipendulina** *Height:* 90cm (36in) *Spread:* 30cm (12in) *Soil:* Ordinary *Site:* Open 'Coronation Gold', marigold yellow 'Moonshine', canary yellow
SHRUBS/TREES	**Azalea, deciduous** *Height:* 1.5m (5ft) *Spread:* 1.2m (4ft) *Soil:* Acid, no lime *Site:* Open or light shade *Rhododendron luteum*, deep yellow 'Klondyke', orange-yellow	**Cytisus praecox** (Broom) *Height:* 1.2m (4ft) *Spread:* 90cm (3ft) *Soil:* Ordinary *Site:* Open Sulphur yellow	**Forsythia** (Golden bells) *Height:* 2-2.4m (6-8ft) *Spread:* 1-1.2m (3-4ft) *Soil:* Ordinary *Site:* Sun or light shade 'Lynwood', daffodil yellow	**Kerria japonica** (Jew's mallow) *Height:* 1.2-1.8m (4-6ft) *Spread:* 90cm (3ft) *Soil:* Ordinary *Site:* Sun or shade Buttercup yellow	**Laburnum** (Golden chain) *Height:* 4.8-7m (16-23ft) *Spread:* 3-4.5m (10-15ft) *Soil:* Ordinary *Site:* Open 'Vossii', golden yellow	**Cytisus** (Broom) *Height:* 1.8-4m (6-13ft) *Spread:* 1.2-2m (4-6ft) *Soil:* Ordinary *Site:* Open *C.battandieri*, light yellow 'Cornish Cream', cream 'Golden Sunlight', deep yellow

gardens. There is a notable example of the latter at Crathes Castle in Scotland, a garden divided into a number of sections, several of which are devoted to single colours, one of which is yellow. Here, much of the foliage as well as the flowers is yellow or lime green, and white is the only other colour admitted. It is always a centre of interest and also of controversy between the yellow-lovers and the yellow-haters.

Because it is so clearly seen, yellow can be used to define shapes even at a considerable distance. At Dawyck, another Scottish garden (but one that differs greatly from Crathes Castle in being mainly woodland), a great 'river' of golden daffodils flows down a wide grassed ride between the forest trees on a hillside to finish up in a huge 'lake' of daffodils in the

meadow below. Only white would make a similarly clearcut contrast to the green of turf and tree foliage.

Although yellow is such a basic flower colour it almost disappears from trees and shrubs after summer, its place taken by the yellowing foliage of deciduous species and the yellow colour of some ripening fruits. Yellow-flowered bulbs are also lacking in autumn with one notable exception, the sternbergias, which look superficially like golden crocuses though they are totally unrelated. Only the shortage of supply prevents this lovely and easily grown flower from being much more widely used and appreciated.

Potentilla fruticosa · *Solidago 'Goldenmosa'* · *Sternbergia lutea* · *Hypericum calycinum* · *Zinnia 'Pacific Gold'* · *Rudbeckia fulgida 'Goldsturm'*

AUTUMN

Calendula
(Pot marigold)
Height: 30-45cm (12-18in)
Spread: 25cm (10in)
Soil: Ordinary
Site: Open
'Lemon Queen', lemon yellow
'Yellow Gitana', golden yellow

Nasturtium
Height: 30cm (12in)
Spread: 25cm (10in)
Soil: Ordinary
Site: Sunny
'Golden Gleam', golden yellow

Nicotiana
(Sweet tobacco)
Height: 75cm (30in)
Spread: 25cm (10in)
Soil: Ordinary
Site: Sun or shade
'Lime Green', pale yellow-green

Tagetes (Marigold)
Height: 15-90cm (6-36in)
Spread: 15-25cm (6-10in)
Soil: Ordinary
Site: Sunny
'Diamond Jubilee', bright yellow
'First Lady', light yellow
'Gold Lady' golden yellow
'Showboat', deep yellow
T.signata 'Golden Gem'
T.signata 'Lemon Gem'
'Yellow Boy'

Rudbeckia
(Coneflower)
Height: 45cm (18in)
Spread: 30cm (12in)
Soil: Ordinary
Site: Open
'Marmalade', marigold yellow and black

Zinnia
Height: 25-60cm (10-24in)
Spread: 20cm (8in)
Soil: Ordinary
Site: Sunny
'Pacific Yellow', bright yellow
'Peter Pan', golden yellow
'Yellow Ruffles', saffron yellow

Gladiolus
Height: 60-90cm (24-36in)
Spread: 20cm (8in)
Soil: Ordinary
Site: Open
'Flowersong', daffodil yellow
'Green Woodpecker', lime yellow
'Landmark', cream

Iris xiphium
(Dutch iris)
Height: 75cm (30in)
Spread: 10cm (4in)
Soil: Ordinary
Site: Open
'Yellow Queen', deep yellow

Lilium (Lily)
Height: 1-1.5m (3½-5ft)
Spread: 25cm (10in)
Soil: Acid, no lime
Site: Sun or dappled shade
'Connecticut King', daffodil yellow
'Destiny', lemon yellow
'Limelight', chartreuse yellow
L.monadelphum, light yellow
L.pyrenaicum, greenish yellow
L.testaceum, apricot yellow

Dahlia
Height: 30-90cm (24-36in)
Spread: 45-90cm (18-36in)
Soil: Ordinary
Site: Sunny
'Claire de Lune', light sulphur yellow
'Glory of Heemstede', primrose
'Klankstade Kerkrade', sulphur yellow
'Yellow Frank Hornsey', clear yellow

Sternbergia lutea
Height: 10cm (4in)
Spread: 7.5cm (3in)
Soil: Ordinary
Site: Sunny
Buttercup yellow

Anthemis tinctoria
Height: 75cm (30in)
Spread: 45cm (18in)
Soil: Ordinary, well drained
Site: Sunny
'E.C.Buxton', sulphur yellow
'Grallagh Gold', deep yellow

Geum
Height: 60cm (24in)
Spread: 23cm (9in)
Soil: Ordinary
Site: Open
'Lady Stratheden', marigold yellow

Ligularia clivorum
Height: 90cm (36in)
Spread: 60cm (24in)
Soil: Ordinary
Site: Open or light shade
'Gregynog Gold', deep yellow

Lysimachia punctata
(Yellow loosestrife)
Height: 90cm (36in)
Spread: 45cm (18in)
Soil: Ordinary
Site: Open or light shade
Bright yellow

Rudbeckia
(Coneflower)
Height: 60-180cm (2-6ft)
Spread: 45cm (18in)
Soil: Ordinary
Site: Sunny
'Goldquelle', chrome yellow
'Goldsturm', deep yellow and black
'Herbstonne', butter yellow

Solidago
(Golden Rod)
Height: 60-120cm (2-4ft)
Spread: 60cm (2ft)
Soil: Ordinary
Site: Sun or light shade
'Goldenmosa', mimosa yellow
'Golden Wings', sunflower yellow

Genista
(Broom)
Height: 45cm-6m (18in-20ft)
Spread: 60cm-3m (2-10ft)
Soil: Ordinary
Site: Open
G.aetnensis, light yellow
G.hispanica, gorse yellow
G.tenera (*virgata*), bright yellow

Koelreuteria paniculata
(Golden grain tree)
Height: 4.8-7m (16-23ft)
Spread: 4-5.2m (13-17ft)
Soil: Ordinary
Site: Sunny
Light yellow

Potentilla
(Shrubby cinquefoil)
Height: 45-120cm (18in-4ft)
Spread: 90cm (3ft)
Soil: Ordinary
Site: Open
'Elizabeth', soft yellow
'Goldfinger', marigold yellow
'Primrose Beauty', primrose yellow

Senecio
(Shrubby ragwort)
Height: 90cm (3ft)
Spread: 90cm (3ft)
Soil: Ordinary, well drained
Site: Sunny, sheltered
'Sunshine' (*S.greyi*), marigold yellow

Hypericum
(St John's wort)
Height: 1.2m (4ft)
Spread: 90cm (3ft)
Soil: Ordinary
Site: Open or light shade
'Hidcote', buttercup yellow

Spartium junceum
(Spanish broom)
Height: 2.4m (8ft)
Spread: 1.2m (4ft)
Soil: Ordinary
Site: Open
Daffodil yellow

Orange flowers

Because it is a mixture of red and yellow, orange combines the penetrating qualities of both those colours. It is the colour usually chosen for the clothing of those who, while at work, are at risk from fast-moving traffic because it catches the eye at a distance so exceptionally well. In the garden it can be used in a similar way to attract attention, and it is also useful in association with reds and yellows to create explosions of colour. The opposite approach is to contrast orange with blue as, for example, by planting *Lilium bulbiferum* against a background of *Campanula lactiflora* or mixing *Kniphofia galpinii* with the lavender and yellow daisy flowers of *Aster frikartii*.

It is not a colour that covers a very wide range of variations, like pink or purple, nor is it found naturally in a great many species, least of all among temperate-zone trees. But it is a colour that has been brought into many hybrids by deliberate breeding and selection, and so it is among cultivated varieties, rather than those existing in the wild, that it must mainly be sought.

In some species, orange is available only in mixture. For example many beautiful shades of orange exist in Iceland poppies *(Papaver nudicaule)*, but the seed that is commonly offered also gives salmon pink, yellow and pink flowers: a delightful mixture, but not one that could be recommended to those seeking plain orange for a particular colour scheme. The same is true of the delightful little Welsh poppy, *Meconopsis cambrica*, the seed of which usually gives both yellow and orange forms, but because this species is perennial it is possi-

Cheiranthus

Rhododendron (Azalea)

Euphorbia griffithii 'Fireglow'

Berberis darwinii

Tagetes erecta 'Orange Jubilee'

Dahlia

	SPRING					SUMMER
ANNUALS/BEDDING	**Cheiranthus allionii** (Siberian wallflower) *Height:* 30cm (12in) *Spread:* 23cm (9in) *Soil:* Ordinary *Site:* Sunny Bright orange	**Pansy** *Height:* 15-23cm (6-9in) *Spread:* 15cm (6in) *Soil:* Ordinary *Site:* Sun or shade 'Clear Crystals Orange', apricot 'Imperial Orange Prince', deep orange 'Orange Bedder', clear orange	**Polyanthus** *Height:* 20cm (8in) *Spread:* 15cm (6in) *Soil:* Ordinary *Site:* Sun or moderate shade 'Monarch Giant Orange', shades of orange			**Antirrhinum** (Snapdragon) *Height:* 20-40cm (8-16in) *Spread:* 15-25cm (6-10in) *Soil:* Ordinary *Site:* Open 'Regal Apricot', apricot and orange 'Orange Monarch', deep orange and cerise
BULBS	**Crocus** *Height:* 10cm (4in) *Spread:* 7.5cm (3in) *Soil:* Ordinary *Site:* Open or light shade C.ancyrensis, bright orange C.chrysanthus 'Zwanenburg', yellow and red-bronze	**Fritillaria imperialis** (Crown imperial) *Height:* 75cm (30in) *Spread:* 25cm (10in) *Soil:* Rich *Site:* Open 'Aurora', bronzy orange 'Rubra Maxima', tangerine	**Hyacinth** *Height:* 25cm (10in) *Spread:* 15cm (6in) *Soil:* Ordinary *Site:* Open 'Gypsy Queen', yellow and light tangerine	**Narcissus** (Daffodil) *Height:* 30-50cm (12-20in) *Spread:* 15cm (6in) *Soil:* Ordinary *Site:* Sun or shade 'Fortune', yellow and orange 'Sempre Avanti', cream and orange 'Texas', yellow and tangerine	**Tulip** *Height:* 30-60cm (12-24in) *Spread:* 10cm (4in) *Soil:* Ordinary *Site:* Open 'De Wet', golden orange 'Marechal Niel', yellow and light orange 'Orange Nassau', bronzy orange 'Orange Sun', orange and carmine	**Gladiolus** *Height:* 60-90cm (2-3ft) *Spread:* 20cm (8in) *Soil:* Ordinary *Site:* Open 'Albert Schweitzer', tangerine 'Atlantic', tangerine 'Orange Chiffon', orange and salmon 'Prince Bernhardt', vermilion-orange
PERENNIALS	**Euphorbia griffithii** (Spurge) *Height:* 60-75cm (24-30in) *Spread:* 30cm (12in) *Soil:* Ordinary *Site:* Sun or partial shade 'Fireglow', red-orange	**Trollius** (Globe flower) *Height:* 45-60cm (18-24in) *Spread:* 25cm (10in) *Soil:* Ordinary, moist *Site:* Sun or partial shade 'Orange Princess', orange 'Fireglobe', light orange				**Geum** (Avens) *Height:* 30-45cm (12-18in) *Spread:* 23cm (9in) *Soil:* Ordinary *Site:* Open G.borisii, deep orange G. 'Fire Opal', coppery-orange
SHRUBS/TREES	**Azalea, deciduous** *Height:* 1.5m (5ft) *Spread:* 1.2m (4ft) *Soil:* Acid, no lime *Site:* Open or dappled shade 'Gibraltar', red-orange 'Christopher Wren', orange-yellow 'Klondyke', orange-gold	**Berberis** (Barberry) *Height:* 1-3m (3½-10ft) *Spread:* 60-180cm (2-6ft) *Soil:* Ordinary *Site:* Open B.darwinii, orange B.linearifolia, red-orange B.stenophylla 'Coccinea', red buds, orange flowers	**Rhododendron** *Height:* 1.2-3m (4-10ft) *Spread:* 1.2-2.4m (4-8ft) *Soil:* Acid, no lime *Site:* Open or dappled shade 'Goldsworth Orange', light orange and apricot R.dicroanthum, deep orange			**Buddleia globosa** (Orange ball tree) *Height:* 3-4m (10-13ft) *Spread:* 2-2.4m (6-8ft) *Soil:* Ordinary *Site:* Sunny Light orange

ble to select the orange-flowered plants and discard the yellow, a stratagem of little use with the short-lived, if not definitely biennial, Iceland poppies.

Similarly, although there are few orange-flowered selections of polyanthus, it is now usual for this colour to be included in mixtures with yellow, pink and red. With these it is not difficult to select the orange-flowered plants and increase them by division after flowering, for they live for several years.

For beautiful shades of orange in late spring *Cheiranthus X allionii* (**left**) has much to offer. The Siberian wallflower thrives in any well-drained soil in a sunny location and should be planted in autumn for colour the following spring.

The vivid orange of marigolds such as *Tagetes erecta* 'Orange Jubilee' (**left**) is a bold and useful colour for summer bedding schemes and borders.

Crocosmia

Zinnia 'Peter Pan Orange'

Kniphofia galpinii

AUTUMN

Calendula (Pot marigold) *Height*: 30-45cm (12-18in) *Spread*: 25cm (10in) *Soil*: Ordinary *Site*: Open 'Geisha Girl', reddish orange 'Orange King', deep orange 'Radio', deep orange	**Dimorphotheca** (Star of the veldt) *Height*: 30cm (12in) *Spread*: 15cm (6in) *Soil*: Ordinary *Site*: Sunny 'Giant Orange' ('Goliath'), orange	**Tagetes** (Marigold) *Height*: 15-90cm (6-36in) *Spread*: 15-25cm (6-10in) *Soil*: Ordinary *Site*: Sunny 'Apollo', orange 'Orange Lady', deep orange 'Orange Jubilee', light orange *T.signata* 'Tangerine Gem', tangerine	**Rudbeckia hirta** (Coneflower) *Height*: 60cm (24in) *Spread*: 30cm (12in) *Soil*: Ordinary *Site*: Open 'Rustic Dwarf', yellow with bronzy orange	**Tithonia speciosa** (Mexican sunflower) *Height*: 75cm (30in) *Spread*: 25cm (10in) *Soil*: Ordinary *Site*: Sunny Tangerine	**Zinnia** *Height*: 25-60cm (10-24in) *Spread*: 20cm (8in) *Soil*: Ordinary *Site*: Sunny 'Orange Ruffles' 'Peter Pan Orange'
Ixia (African corn lily) *Height*: 40cm (16in) *Spread*: 10cm (4in) *Soil*: Ordinary, well drained *Site*: Sunny, warm 'Afterglow', orange-buff 'Conqueror', orange-red	**Lilium** (Lily) *Height*: 1-1.5m (3½-5ft) *Spread*: 25cm (10in) *Soil*: Ordinary *Site*: Sun or dappled shade *L.bulbiferum*, orange *L.davidii willimotiae*, deep red- orange *L.hansonii*, yellow-orange *L.pardalinum*, deep red-orange		**Dahlia** *Height*: 30-100cm (12-39in) *Spread*: 45-90cm (18-36in) *Soil*: Ordinary *Site*: Open 'Jescot Julie', burnt orange and purple 'Shirley Alliance', soft orange 'Sweitzer's Kirkarde', shades of orange	**Lilium** (Lily) *Height*: 1-1.5m (3½-5ft) *Spread*: 25cm (10in) *Soil*: Acid, no lime *Site*: Sun or dappled shade *L.henryi*, pale orange	
Helenium (Sneezewort) *Height*: 90cm (3ft) *Spread*: 30cm (1ft) *Soil*: Ordinary *Site*: Open 'Coppelia', coppery-orange	**Hemerocallis** (Day lily) *Height*: 90cm (3ft) *Spread*: 60cm (2ft) *Soil*: Ordinary *Site*: Open or light shade 'Cartwheels', light orange 'Doubloons', orange 'Kwanso Plena', buff-orange, double flowers	**Ligularia clivorum** *Height*: 90cm (3ft) *Spread*: 60cm (2ft) *Soil*: Ordinary *Site*: Open or light shade 'Desdemona', orange	**Crocosmia** (Montbretia) *Height*: 60-75cm (24-30in) *Spread*: 25cm (10in) *Soil*: Ordinary *Site*: Sunny, warm 'Jackanapes', yellow and orange *C.masonorum*, tangerine	**Kniphofia** (Red hot poker) *Height*: 75-120cm (30-48in) *Spread*: 30-45cm (12-18in) *Soil*: Ordinary *Site*: Open *K.galpinii*, orange 'Loddon Variety', red-orange	
Helianthemum (Sun rose, rock rose) *Height*: 20-40cm (8-16in) *Spread*: 25-45cm (10-18in) *Soil*: Ordinary, alkaline *Site*: Sunny 'Ben Fhada', orange and yellow 'Ben Nevis', coppery orange 'Firedragon' (Mrs Clay), red- orange	**Potentilla** (Shrubby cinquefoil) *Height*: 90cm (3ft) *Spread*: 90cm (3ft) *Soil*: Ordinary *Site*: Open 'Tangerine', light coppery- orange				

Red flowers

There are many different shades of red, from scarlet and vermilion to crimson and magenta, and their effect on the senses is very different. Someone once said that red burned holes in the landscape, but the reference must surely have been to the reds at the yellow end of the range where the colours that are very difficult to assimilate chiefly occur. The bluer reds, including the much maligned magentas, are often much easier to place and far less strident, especially if they are accompanied by a good deal of green.

Of course, stridency may quite legitimately be an end. It can be used to draw the eye to any spot in the garden. If brilliant reds are associated with yellow or white the effect is even more compelling. At Sissinghurst Castle in Kent the vivid vermilion *Lychnis* *chalcedonica* has been used most effectively against a background of *Achillea* 'Coronation Gold', but this was in an area of the garden where nearly all the colours are in the yellow-orange-red range with the intention of producing a gay and stimulating environment. It is no accident that this compartment of the garden is in front of the cottage in which Sir Harold Nicolson had his study, for he liked bright colours whereas his wife, Vita Sackville-West, who planted it for him, preferred softer, more muted colour schemes.

In gardens a scattering of red here and there can create so many different focal points that the result is restless and confusing. It may be preferable to keep such strong colours together and allow them to drift away quite gently into quieter pinks, blues, mauves, creams and white. But it is always safe to mix greens of any kind with red, except perhaps the sharper lime greens, and this is one very satisfactory way of bringing them into tune with the garden as a whole. It is fortunate that rhododendrons grow best in woodland for there are many intense shades of red among them and these colours are toned down and made acceptable by the dappled shade and also by the predominant greenness of the setting. In Britain it is even more fortunate that the only rhododendron species that has found the climate so congenial that it has leapt the garden fence and naturalized itself extensively in the countryside, is *rhododendron ponticum* with its relatively quiet colour range in the blue-mauves and light purples.

Many plants used in bedding schemes are

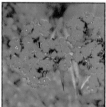
Malus

Tulip

Escallonia

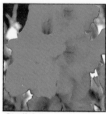
Gladiolus

Embothrium coccineum

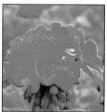
Pelargonium zonale

	SPRING			SUMMER		
ANNUALS/BEDDING	**Dianthus barbatus** (Sweet William) *Height:* 45cm (18in) *Spread:* 25cm (10in) *Soil:* Ordinary *Site:* Open 'Messenger Scarlet' 'Scarlet Beauty'	**Matthiola incana** (East Lothian stocks) *Height:* 45cm (18in) *Spread:* 25cm (10in) *Soil:* Ordinary, well drained *Site:* Sunny, sheltered 'Kelvedon Crimson' 'Kelvedon Scarlet'	**Polyanthus** *Height:* 20cm (8in) *Spread:* 15cm (6in) *Soil:* Ordinary *Site:* Sun, or moderate shade 'Monarch Scarlet'	**Antirrhinum** (Snapdragon) *Height:* 20-40cm (8-16in) *Spread:* 15-25cm (6-10in) *Soil:* Ordinary *Site:* Open 'Regal Bright Scarlet' 'Regal Crimson'	**Begonia semperflorens** *Height:* 25cm (10in) *Spread:* 15cm (6in) *Soil:* Ordinary *Site:* Open 'Danica Rose' 'Danica Scarlet'	**Dianthus caryophyllus** (Carnation) *Height:* 45cm (18in) *Spread:* 25cm (10in) *Soil:* Ordinary with lime *Site:* Open 'Crimson Knight' 'Scarlet Knight'
BULBS	**Anemone blanda** *Height:* 10cm (4in) *Spread:* 10cm (4in) *Soil:* Ordinary *Site:* Sun, or light shade 'Radar', carmine and white	**Hyacinth** *Height:* 25cm (10in) *Spread:* 15cm (6in) *Soil:* Ordinary *Site:* Open 'Jan Bos', carmine 'Tubergen's Scarlet'	**Tulip** *Height:* 30-60cm (1-2ft) *Spread:* 10cm (4in) *Soil:* Ordinary *Site:* Open 'Apeldoorn', scarlet 'Electra', carmine 'Holland's Glory', orange red 'Red Riding Hood', signal red	**Allium sphaerocephalum** *Height:* 60cm (2ft) *Spread:* 10cm (4in) *Soil:* Ordinary *Site:* Open Red, maroon	**Gladiolus** *Height:* 60-90cm (2-3ft) *Spread:* 20cm (8in) *Soil:* Ordinary *Site:* Open 'Firestone', vermilion 'Oscar', crimson	**Lilium** (Lily) *Height:* 75cm (30in) *Spread:* 25cm (10in) *Soil:* Ordinary, with added peat *Site:* Sun or dappled shade 'Cinnabar', deep red 'Enchantment', nasturtium red 'Lilium Tigrinum', orange-red
PERENNIALS	**Bergenia** *Height:* 30cm (12in) *Spread:* 45cm (18in) *Soil:* Ordinary *Site:* Sun or shade 'Abendglut', rosy red 'Ballawley', crimson	**Paeonia officinalis** (Peony) *Height:* 75cm (2½ft) *Spread:* 45cm (18in) *Soil:* Ordinary, rich *Site:* Open 'Rubra Plena', deep crimson	**Viola** *Height:* 10cm (4in) *Spread:* 15cm (6in) *Soil:* Ordinary *Site:* Sun or partial shade 'Arkwright's Ruby', mahogany red and maroon	**Astilbe** *Height:* 45-60cm (18-24in) *Spread:* 30cm (12in) *Soil:* Ordinary, moist *Site:* Sun or light shade 'Fanal', crimson 'Jo Ophorst', ruby-red	**Geum** *Height:* 60cm (2ft) *Spread:* 20cm (10in) *Soil:* Ordinary *Site:* Open 'Mrs Bradshaw', signal red	**Hemerocallis** (Day lily) *Height:* 90cm (3ft) *Spread:* 45cm (18in) *Soil:* Ordinary *Site:* Open or light shade 'Stafford', bright mahogany red
SHRUBS/TREES	**Azalea, deciduous** *Height:* 1.5m (5ft) *Spread:* 1.5m (5ft) *Soil:* Acid, no lime *Site:* Sun, or dappled shade 'Coccinea Speciosa', orange-red 'Dr M. Oosthoek', deep orange-red 'Royal Command', vermilion	**Malus** (Crab apple) *Height:* 4.5-6m (15-20ft) *Spread:* 3.5-4.5m (12-15ft) *Soil:* Ordinary *Site:* Open 'Lemoinei', deep carmine 'Profusion', wine-red	**Ribes sanguineum** (Flowering currant) *Height:* 2-2.5m (6½-8ft) *Soil:* Ordinary *Site:* Sun or shade 'Pulborough Scarlet', light crimson	**Cistus** (Rock rose) *Height:* 60-100cm (2-3½ft) *Spread:* 45-60cm (1½-2ft) *Soil:* Ordinary or alkaline *Site:* Warm, sunny 'Purpureus', carmine and maroon 'Sunset', deep magenta	**Escallonia** *Height:* 2.5-3m (8-10ft) *Spread:* 2-2.5m (6½-8ft) *Soil:* Ordinary *Site:* Sunny, sheltered 'Crimson Spire', crimson 'Donard Brilliance', rose red	**Embothrium coccineum** (Fire bush) *Height:* 4-6m (13-20ft) *Spread:* 2.5-3m (8-10ft) *Soil:* Acid, no lime *Site:* Sunny, sheltered 'Lanceolatum', deep scarlet

red; tulips in the spring, geraniums, begonias, scarlet salvias and numerous others in the summer. Many of these plants come from much warmer countries than the cool temperate regions in which they are planted, and they do bring an exotic warmth that can be welcome in the formal, obviously man-made settings in which bedding plants are commonly used.

Salvia 'Blaze of Fire' (**right**) is an apt name for this extremely popular bedding plant. It bears bright scarlet blooms from mid-summer until autumn on stems 30cm (12in) high. The exquisite flowers of *Tulipa* 'Red Riding Hood' (**left**) are borne in mid-spring above beautifully variegated foliage. This 20cm (8in) tulip is an excellent choice for rockeries. Plant the bulbs in late autumn in well-drained soil. A sunny sheltered spot will suit them.

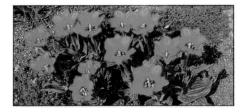

Fuchsia

Lychnis

Weigela

Dahlia

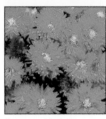

Aster novi-belgii

Schizostylis

AUTUMN

Pelargonium zonale
(Zonal-leaved geranium)
Height: 45cm (18in)
Spread: 30cm (12in)
Soil: Ordinary
Site: Sunny
'Sprinter', scarlet
'Vulcan', dark red

Impatiens sultanii
(Busy Lizzie)
Height: 15-20cm (6-8in)
Spread: 20-25cm (8-10in)
Soil: Ordinary
Site: Sun or shade
'Blitz', orange-scarlet
'Carmine Baby', carmine

Petunia
Height: 23cm (9in)
Spread: 23cm (9in)
Soil: Ordinary
Site: Sunny
'Dwarf Resisto Scarlet'
'Red Cloud', deep scarlet

Callistephus
(Annual aster)
Height: 25-60cm (10-24in)
Spread: 25cm (10in)
Soil: Ordinary
Site: Open or semi-shade
'Milady Rose Red'

Salvia splendens
Height: 30cm (12in)
Spread: 25cm (10in)
Soil: Ordinary
Site: Sunny
'Blaze of Fire', scarlet

Verbena
Height: 15cm (6in)
Spread: 30cm (12in)
Soil: Ordinary
Site: Sunny
'Blaze', scarlet
'Sparkle', scarlet and white

Dahlia
Height: 30-90cm (1-3ft)
Spread: 45-90cm (1½-3ft)
Soil: Ordinary
Site: Open
'Bacchus', blood red
'Majuba', cardinal red

Schizostylis
(Kaffir lily)
Height: 45cm (18in)
Spread: 23cm (9in)
Soil: Ordinary
Site: Sunny, warm
S. *coccinea* 'Major', deep scarlet

Lychnis
Height: 60-90cm (2-3ft)
Spread: 30cm (12in)
Soil: Ordinary
Site: Sunny
L. *chalcedonica*, scarlet
L. *coronaria*, deep magenta

Paeonia lactiflora
(Chinese peony)
Height: 70-90cm (2½-3ft)
Spread: 45cm (18in)
Soil: Ordinary
Site: Sunny
'Felix Crousse', carmine
'Mons. Martin Cahuzac', crimson

Papaver orientale
(Oriental poppy)
Height: 75cm (2½ft)
Spread: 45cm (18in)
Soil: Ordinary
Site: Sunny
'Goliath', light crimson
'Marcus Perry', scarlet and black

Aster novi-belgii
(Michaelmas daisy)
Height: 30-90cm (1-3ft)
Spread: 45-60cm (18-24in)
Soil: Ordinary
Site: Sun or light shade
'Carnival', deep carmine
'Freda Ballard', deep red
'Winston S. Churchill', carmine

Lobelia cardinalis
Height: 60cm (2ft)
Spread: 30cm (12in)
Soil: Ordinary, rather moist
Site: Open or light shade
L. *cardinalis*, grenadier red
'Queen Victoria', light crimson

Phlox
Height: 90cm (3ft)
Spread: 30-40cm (12-16in)
Soil: Ordinary
Site: Sun or light shade
'Brigadier', orange-red
'Starfire', deep red

Fuchsia
Height: 30-100cm (1-3½ft)
Spread: 25-60cm (10-24in)
Soil: Ordinary
Site: Sunny, sheltered
'Margaret', scarlet and violet
'Mrs Popple', signal red and violet
'Rufus', bright red

Spiraea japonica
Height: 1.2m (4ft)
Spread: 1.5m (5ft)
Soil: Ordinary
Site: Open
'Anthony Waterer', carmine

Weigela
Height: 1.5-2.5m (5-8ft)
Spread: 1.2-2m (4-6½ft)
Soil: Ordinary
Site: Open
'Bristol Ruby', deep carmine

Hebe
(Shrubby veronica)
Height: 1-1.5m (3½-5ft)
Spread: 1-1.2m (3½-4ft)
Soil: Ordinary
Site: Sunny, sheltered
'Simon Delaux', crimson

Hydrangea macrophylla
Height: 1.5-2m (5-6½ft)
Spread: 1-1.2m (3½-4ft)
Soil: Alkaline for red flowers
Site: Sun, or semi-shade
'Hamburg', rose-red deepening to crimson
'Westfalen', carmine

Pink flowers

There are a great many plants with pink flowers — yet no one ever seems to make a pink garden or even a pink border. Perhaps it is too miscellaneous a colour for that, scarcely a true colour in its own right but paler versions of red, red-purple and orange-red. The first gives the true pinks, such as that of apple blossom and dog roses; the second the mallow pinks, carmine pinks, lilac pinks and mauve pinks; the third the salmon pinks, peach pinks and shell pinks. All these are essentially link colours, admirable for blending the stronger hues into the overall colour scheme whatever that may be. In general it seems wise to use them either in harmonies with other colours closely related to them — the mauve pinks with the blues and the salmon pinks with the oranges rather than the other way round — or,

alternatively, as strong contrast: soft pink London Pride with blue primroses and polyanthuses or purple tulips, salmon pink roses with the deepest blue delphiniums.

Yet, even after all this, it remains true that most pinks are easy to handle, unaggressive, and so unlikely to produce strong reactions from those who view them. The addition of white makes them even more harmless yet agreeable particularly, for example, when *Lavatera* 'Silver Cup' and *L.* 'Mont Blanc' are planted together. Carpets of pink *Claytonia sibirica* can be made in thin woodland or beneath groups of deciduous trees with white and mauve wood anemones and the fuller blue of bluebells, either British or Spanish, without raising an eyebrow. The worst that could be said of such schemes is that they are pretty

Anemone
'Albert Schweitzer'

Rhododendron
'Pink Pearl'

Camellia x williamsii
'Donation'

Astilbe x arendsii

Escallonia
'Apple Blossom'

Geranium endressii
'Wargrave Pink'

	SPRING				SUMMER	
ANNUALS/BEDDING	**Matthiola incana** (East Lothian stocks) *Height:* 45cm (18in) *Spread:* 25cm (10in) *Soil:* Ordinary, well drained *Site:* Sunny, sheltered 'Kelvedon Exquisite', pink	**Myosotis** (Forget-me-not) *Height:* 25-30cm (10-12in) *Spread:* 20cm (8in) *Soil:* Ordinary *Site:* Sun or shade 'Carmine King', rose-pink	**Polyanthus** *Height:* 25cm (10in) *Spread:* 15cm (6in) *Soil:* Ordinary *Site:* Sun or moderate shade 'Pacific Giants Pink', shades of pink 'Triumph Pink', shades of pink		**Antirrhinum** (Snapdragon) *Height:* 38-45cm (15-18in) *Spread:* 23cm (9in) *Soil:* Ordinary *Site:* Open 'Coral Monarch' coral-pink 'Regal Rose', rose-pink	**Cleome spinosa** (Spider flower) *Height:* 90cm (36in) *Spread:* 25cm (10in) *Soil:* Ordinary *Site:* Open 'Rose Queen', rose-pink
BULBS	**Anemone blanda** (Windflower) *Height:* 10-15cm (4-6in) *Spread:* 10cm (4in) *Soil:* Ordinary *Site:* Sun or partial shade 'Charmer', clear pink	**Hyacinth** *Height:* 25cm (10in) *Spread:* 15cm (6in) *Soil:* Ordinary *Site:* Sunny 'Anna Marie', bright pink 'Lady Derby', rose-pink 'Pink Pearl', carmine-pink	**Scilla campanulata** (Spanish bluebell) *Height:* 38cm (15in) *Spread:* 15cm (6in) *Soil:* Ordinary *Site:* Sun or shade 'Rosea', soft pink	**Tulip** *Height:* 20-60cm (8-24in) *Spread:* 10cm (4in) *Soil:* Ordinary *Site:* Open 'Clara Butt', salmon-rose 'Elizabeth Arden', salmon-pink 'Mariette', bright rose-pink 'Peach Blossom', deep pink	**Allium** *Height:* 20-38cm (8-15in) *Spread:* 10cm (4in) *Soil:* Open *Site:* Open *A.cernuum,* soft rose-pink *A.ostrowskianum,* purplish pink	**Gladiolus** *Height:* 60-90cm (24-36in) *Spread:* 20cm (8in) *Soil:* Ordinary *Site:* Open 'Columbine', soft pink and white 'Delacroix', pink and red 'Miss America', deep pink 'Peter Pears', shrimp-pink
PERENNIALS	**Arabis caucasica** (Rock cress) *Height:* 15cm (6in) *Spread:* 30cm (12in) *Soil:* Ordinary, alkaline *Site:* Open 'Rosabella', soft pink	**Bergenia** *Height:* 30cm (12in) *Spread:* 45cm (18in) *Soil:* Ordinary *Site:* Sun or shade *B.cordifolia,* mauve-pink *B.purpurascens,* deep-pink *B.schmidtii,* light pink	**Paeonia officinalis** (Peony) *Height:* 75cm (30in) *Spread:* 45cm (18in) *Soil:* Ordinary *Site:* Open 'Rosea Superba', rose-pink	**Saxifraga urbium** (London pride) *Height:* 30cm (12in) *Spread:* 25cm (10in) *Soil:* Ordinary *Site:* Open or shady Soft pink	**Astilbe** *Height:* 45-60cm (18-24in) *Spread:* 30cm (12in) *Soil:* Ordinary, moist *Site:* Sun or light shade 'Betsy Cuperus, pale pink 'Bressingham Beauty', warm pink 'Ostrich Plume', coral-pink	**Dianthus plumarius allwoodii** (Pinks) *Height:* 15-30cm (6-12in) *Spread:* 25cm (10in) *Soil:* Ordinary, alkaline *Site:* Open 'Doris', soft salmon-pink and rose 'Excelsior', rose-pink 'Inchmery', pale pink
SHRUBS/TREES	**Azalea, evergreen** *Height:* 1-1.2m (3½-4ft) *Spread:* 1-1.2m (3½-4ft) *Site:* Dappled shade 'Blaauw's Pink', light cerise pink 'Fedora', deep pink 'Hinomayo', soft pink 'Kirin', deep rose 'Rosebud', rose-pink	**Camellia** *Height:* 2-2.4m (6½-8ft) *Spread:* 1.2-1.5m (4-5ft) *Soil:* Moderately acid *Site:* Dappled or half shade 'Anticipation', deep rose 'Debbie', rose-pink 'Donation', orchid-pink 'Elegans', peach-pink	**Prunus** (Cherry) *Height:* 3-6m (10-20ft) *Spread:* 1-6m (3½-20ft) *Soil:* Ordinary *Site:* Open 'Accolade', pale rose-pink 'Amanogawa', shell pink 'Kanzan', purplish pink 'Pink Perfection', bright rose-pink	**Rhododendron** *Height:* 1.2-3m (4-10ft) *Spread:* 1.2-2.5m (4-8ft) *Soil:* Acid, no lime *Site:* Open or dappled shade 'Betty Wormald', deep rose-pink 'Bow Bells', silvery pink 'Cynthia', deep rose 'Mrs G. W. Leak', rose-crimson 'Pink Pearl', lilac-pink	**Cistus** (Rock rose) *Height:* 60-100cm (2-3½ft) *Spread:* 60-100cm (2-3½ft) *Soil:* Ordinary or alkaline *Site:* Sunny *C.albidus,* rose *C.* 'Silver Pink', soft pink *C.skanbergii,* clear pink	**Clematis** (Virgin's bower) *Height:* 2.5-3m (8-10ft) *Spread:* 150cm (5ft) *Soil:* Ordinary, alkaline *Site:* Open 'Comtesse de Bouchard', light rose-pink 'Hagley Hybrid', shell pink

The funnel flowers of *Sidalcea* 'Rose Queen' (**left**) appear from early summer until early autumn on stems 75cm (30in) tall. Colour is used to good effect in this classic garden setting (**right**). Against a bold background of foliage plants of various shapes and hues phlox and roses provide the key colour interest in shades of pink.

rather than exciting, and that the gardener who makes them may be described as playing safe rather than playing to the gallery.

The public reaction to pink flowers is ambiguous. Rose growers report that there is greater demand for red and yellow roses than for pink, although no tulip has ever been more popular than 'Clara Butt' (usually planted with a groundwork of forget-me-nots), which the lovely glowing pink lily-flowered tulip 'Mariette' looks set to rival. Probably the most popular of all Chinese peonies is 'Sarah Bernhardt' which is apple-blossom pink. And everyone rejoices when the pink-flowered Japanese cherries bloom in spring, particularly Kanzan, which has been so freely planted that there is now an élite opposition to it on the grounds that it is too common.

Hemerocallis 'Pink Damask'

Kolkwitzia amabilis 'Pink Cloud'

Petunia 'Resisto Rose'

Calluna vulgaris

Colchicum speciosum

Sedum spectabile 'Autumn Joy'

AUTUMN

Godetia *Height:* 30cm (12in) *Spread:* 15cm (6in) *Soil:* Ordinary *Site:* Sun or light shade 'Sybil Sherwood', salmon-pink	**Lavatera rosea** *Height:* 75cm (30in) *Spread:* 45cm (18in) *Soil:* Ordinary *Site:* Open 'Silver Cup', rose-pink	**Petunia** *Height:* 23-30cm (9-12in) *Spread:* 23cm (9in) *Soil:* Ordinary *Site:* Sunny 'Pink Satin', soft pink 'Resisto Rose', rose-pink	**Aster** *Height:* 25cm (10in) *Spread:* 20cm (8in) *Soil:* Ordinary *Site:* Sun or shade 'Meteor', rose-pink 'Milady Rose' 'Pink Magic', light pink		
			Colchicum speciosum *Height:* 15cm (6in) *Spread:* 15cm (6in) *Soil:* Ordinary *Site:* Open or light shade Lilac-pink	**Dahlia** *Height:* 30-100cm (12-39in) *Spread:* 45-90cm (18-36in) *Soil:* Ordinary *Site:* Open 'Cherrio', deep cerise 'Gerrie Hock', silvery pink 'Piper's Pink', deep pink 'Richard Marc', bright pink and lemon	**Nerine bowdenii** *Height:* 60cm (24in) *Spread:* 25cm (10in) *Soil:* Ordinary, well drained *Site:* Sunny, warm Deep rose-pink
Geranium endressii *Height:* 40cm (16in) *Spread:* 45cm (18in) *Soil:* Ordinary *Site:* Open or light shade 'Wargrave Pink', baby-pink	**Hemerocallis** (Day lily) *Height:* 90cm (3ft) *Spread:* 45cm (18in) *Soil:* Ordinary *Site:* Open 'Pink Damask', buff-pink	**Sidalcea** *Height:* 75-120cm (30-48in) *Spread:* 30cm (12in) *Soil:* Ordinary *Site:* Open 'Loveliness', shell-pink 'Rose Queen', mallow-pink	**Anemone hybrida** (Japanese windflower) *Height:* 60cm (24in) *Spread:* 25cm (10in) *Soil:* Ordinary *Site:* Sun or shade 'Bressingham Glow', deep rose-pink 'Lady Gilmour', light pink	**Aster novae angliae and A.novii belgii** (Michaelmas daisy) *Height:* 30-90cm (12-36in) *Spread:* 25-30cm (10-12in) *Soil:* Ordinary *Site:* Sun or shade 'Alma Potschke', salmon-pink or rose 'Fellowship', mid pink 'Harrington's Pink', baby-pink 'Patricia Ballard', purplish pink	**Sedum spectabile** *Height:* 45cm (18in) *Spread:* 30cm (12in) *Soil:* Ordinary *Site:* Sunny 'Autumn Joy', salmon-rose deepening to coppery rose 'Brilliant', rose-pink
Escallonia *Height:* 2.5-3m (8-10ft) *Spread:* 1.2-2m (4-6½ft) *Soil:* Ordinary *Site:* Sunny, sheltered 'Apple Blossom', pink and white 'Edinensis', pale pink 'Langleyensis', muted rose-pink	**Kolkwitzia amabilis** (Beauty bush) *Height:* 2.4-3m (8-10ft) *Spread:* 120-150cm (4-5ft) *Soil:* Ordinary *Site:* Open Clear pink and cream	**Lavatera olbia** (Tree mallow) *Height:* 1.5-2m (5-6½ft) *Spread:* 1-1.2m (3-4ft) *Soil:* Ordinary, well drained *Site:* Sunny 'Rosea', bright rose-pink	**Calluna vulgaris** (Heather, ling) *Height:* 23-60cm (9-24in) *Spread:* 23-30cm (9-12in) *Soil:* Acid, no lime *Site:* Open 'H. E. Beale', light pink 'Peter Sparkes', deep pink	**Ceanothus delineanus** (Californian lilac, mountain sweet) *Height:* 2m (6½ft) *Spread:* 1m (3½ft) *Soil:* Ordinary *Site:* Sunny, sheltered 'Perle Rose', rose-pink	**Hebe** (Shrubby veronica) *Height:* 90-120cm (3-4ft) *Spread:* 60-90cm (2-3ft) *Soil:* Ordinary *Site:* Sunny, sheltered 'Carnea', light rose-pink 'Great Orme', rose-pink

Violet and purple flowers

The hinterland between blue and red is occupied by the wide range of purples and violets. There is, of course, no hard and fast line drawn at either end of this great band of colours beyond which one can say that one is a blue, not a blue-purple, or that another is a red, not a red-purple. Each of us registers colours in our own individual way, and classifies them accordingly. But it is equally true that all violets and purples contain some elements of both blue and red. They can be made by combining white light of varying intensity passed through red and blue filters, or they can be mixed on an artist's palette with varying proportions of blue and red paint.

But having said that, one has still told only a small part of the story, for violet and purple colours — like all the others — are subject to an infinite number of variations produced by other agencies which dull or brighten the colour or modify it in other ways. There are some flowers that are such a dark purple as to appear almost black; such flowers can be found among both hellebores and tulips, such as the one well named 'Queen of Night'. The iris family is also good at producing these very dark colours; they turn up frequently in the fritillaries. Right at the other end of the scale are the very light violets and purples to which we give such names as mauve, lilac and amethyst.

Deep purple is a rich colour to handle in the garden — one can easily have too much of it — but in moderation it is highly valuable. It is not perceived as sharply as red or yellow, and so can be used to give dark shades to colour compositions and to tone down colours which might otherwise claim too much attention. These dark purples and the lighter shades of purple and violet are blending colours useful in linking more clamorous colours with the greens and browns that almost invariably form the background and carpet of the garden. Light blue irises look even more delightful when planted with mahogany red *Viola* 'Arkwright's Ruby' and lilac purple *Allium christophii*, a combination in which all the colours are muted and the effect is totally restful. Equally harmonious is an association of purple irises with violet-blue hardy geraniums and sulphur yellow *Alchemilla mollis*. There is really no end to the satisfying combinations that can be devised using purple and violet as the unifying colours.

Aubrieta

Magnolia liliiflora 'Nigra'

Erica

Cheiranthus cheiri

Primula denticulata

Syringa

SPRING				SUMMER	
ANNUALS/BEDDING					
Cheiranthus cheiri (Wallflower) *Height:* 25-45cm (10-18in) *Spread:* 20-25m (8-10in) *Soil:* Ordinary *Site:* Sunny 'Ruby Gem', ruby-violet	**Matthiola incana** (East Lothian stocks) *Height:* 45cm (18in) *Spread:* 25cm (10in) *Soil:* Ordinary *Site:* Sunny, sheltered 'Kelvedon Purple'	**Lunaria biennis** (Honesty) *Height:* 90cm (3ft) *Soil:* Ordinary *Site:* Open or light shade Red-purple		**Alyssum maritimum** *Height:* 10cm (4in) *Spread:* 15cm (6in) *Soil:* Ordinary *Site:* Open 'Royal Carpet', deep violet-purple 'Wonderland', red-purple	**Amaranthus caudatus** (Love-lies-bleeding) *Height:* 75cm (30in) *Spread:* 30cm (1ft) *Soil:* Ordinary *Site:* Open Crimson-purple
BULBS					
Allium *Height:* 60-90cm (2-3ft) *Spread:* 10cm (4in) *Soil:* Ordinary *Site:* Sunny A. aflatuenense, deep blue-purple A. christophii, lilac purple	**Crocus** *Height:* 10m (4in) *Spread:* 8cm (3¼in) *Soil:* Ordinary *Site:* Open or light shade 'Pickwick', heliotrope and white 'Remembrance', deep blue-purple	**Tulip** *Height:* 38-71cm (15-28in) *Spread:* 20cm (8in) *Soil:* Ordinary *Site:* Open 'Bleu Aimable', lilac-mauve and violet-purple 'Maytime', lilac-purple 'Purple Star', red-purple 'Queen of the Night', deep maroon-purple		**Brodiaea laxa** *Height:* 45cm (18in) *Spread:* 10cm (4in) *Soil:* Ordinary, well drained *Site:* Sunny, warm Violet-purple	**Gladiolus** *Height:* 60-90cm (2-3ft) *Spread:* 20cm (8in) *Soil:* Ordinary *Site:* Open 'Blue Conqueror', blue-purple 'Blue Isle', petunia purple G. byzantinus, magenta
PERENNIALS					
Aubrieta *Height:* 15cm (6in) *Spread:* 25m (10in) *Soil:* Ordinary, alkaline *Site:* Open 'Dr Mules', deep violet-purple 'Greencourt Purple', violet-purple	**Phlox** *Height:* 10-15cm (4-6in) *Spread:* 15cm (6in) *Soil:* Ordinary *Site:* Open P. douglasii 'Waterloo', red-purple P. subulata 'Temiscaming', red-purple	**Pansy** *Height:* 10cm (4in) *Spread:* 15m (6in) *Soil:* Ordinary *Site:* Sun or shade 'Clear Crystals', violet-blue, deep blue-purple with black blotch 'Prince Henry', violet-purple	**Primula** (Primrose) *Height:* 15cm (6in) *Spread:* 15cm (6in) *Soil:* Ordinary *Site:* Open or light shade P. denticulata, blue-mauve 'Wanda', red-purple	**Aconitum** (Monkshood) *Height:* 90cm (3ft) *Spread:* 30cm (1ft) *Soil:* Ordinary *Site:* Sun or shade 'Bressingham Spire', blue-violet 'Spark's Variety', deep blue-purple	**Agapanthus** (African lily) *Height:* 45-90cm (18-36in) *Spread:* 45cm (18in) *Soil:* Ordinary *Site:* Sunny, sheltered 'Headbourne Hybrid', light to deep violet
SHRUBS/TREES					
Daphne *Height:* 60-90cm (2-3ft) *Spread:* 45-60cm (18-24in) *Soil:* Ordinary with peat *Site:* Open D. collina, blue-purple D. mezereum, red-purple	**Erica** (Heath, heather) *Height:* 15-25cm (6-10in) *Spread:* 25cm (10in) *Soil:* Ordinary *Site:* Open E. carnea 'King George', red-purple E. carnea 'Vivellii', red-purple E. darleyensis, rosy purple E. mediterranea, red-purple	**Magnolia** *Height:* 2.5-4.5m (8-15ft) *Spread:* 2-4m (6½-13ft) *Soil:* Moderately acid *Site:* Open or dappled shade M. liliiflora 'Nigra', deep reddish purple M. soulangeana 'Lennei', rose-purple	**Syringa** (Lilac) *Height:* 1-4m (3¼-13ft) *Spread:* 1-2.5m (4-8ft) *Soil:* Ordinary *Site:* Open 'Charles Joly', deep reddish purple 'Katherine Havemeyer', lavender-purple S. microphylla, blue-lilac	**Abutilon** *Height:* 3-5m (10-16½ft) *Spread:* 1.5m (5ft) *Soil:* Ordinary *Site:* Sunny, sheltered A. suntense, blue-violet A. vitifolium, light mauve	**Buddleia** (Butterfly bush) *Height:* 2.4-3m (8-10ft) *Spread:* 2m (6½ft) *Soil:* Ordinary, alkaline *Site:* Open 'Black Knight', dark violet-purple 'Royal Purple', plum purple

The rich purple blooms of *Clematis* 'Jackmanii Superba' (**left**) appear from mid-summer until early autumn on twining stems that reach over 3m (10ft) high on suitable supports. This is one of the popular large-flowered hybrids. Lavender (**right**) provides a summer harvest of delicate violet flowers with the added bonus of a superb fragrance. Even the grey-green foliage of this charming plant is aromatic.

Abutilon suntense

Amaranthus caudatus

Clematis 'The President'

Clematis 'Barbara Jackman'

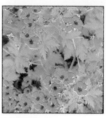

Geranium

Salvia splendens

AUTUMN

Echium plantagineum *Height:* 30cm (12in) *Spread:* 23cm (9in) *Soil:* Ordinary *Site:* Open Blue-purple	**Heliotropium peruvianum** (Heliotrope) *Height:* 38-45cm (15-18in) *Spread:* 25cm (10in) *Soil:* Ordinary *Site:* Open 'Marine', violet-purple	**Petunia** *Height:* 23-30cm (9-12in) *Spread:* 23cm (9in) *Soil:* Ordinary *Site:* Sunny, warm 'Marina', deep blue-violet 'Resisto Blue', deep blue-violet	**Salvia splendens** *Height:* 30cm (1ft) *Spread:* 25cm (10in) *Soil:* Ordinary *Site:* Sunny 'Royal Purple', deep blue-purple		
			Colchicum speciosum *Height:* 15cm (6in) *Spread:* 8cm (3¼in) *Soil:* Ordinary *Site:* Open or light shade 'Lilac Wonder', amethyst	**Dahlia** *Height:* 30-100cm (1-3¼ft) *Spread:* 45-90cm (18-36in) *Soil:* Ordinary *Site:* Open 'Carousel', deep purple 'Hallmark', pink-lavender 'Hamari Girl', pink-lavender 'Lavengro', deep lavender and bronze 'Reveille', red-maroon and white	
Delphinium (Larkspur) *Height:* 90-180cm (3-6ft) *Spread:* 45cm (18in) *Soil:* Ordinary *Site:* Open 'Black Knight', deep blue-purple 'Nimrod', royal purple 'Strawberry Fair', mulberry purple	**Erigeron** (Fleabane) *Height:* 45-60m (18-24in) *Spread:* 30-45cm (12-18in) *Soil:* Ordinary *Site:* Open 'Darkest of All', deep violet 'Foerster's Liebling', red-purple	**Geranium** *Height:* 25-30cm (10-12in) *Spread:* 30cm (12in) *Soil:* Ordinary, alkaline *Site:* Sun or partial shade G. *himalayense* (*grandiflorum*), deep violet-blue G. *pratense* 'Plenum Coeruleum', lavender, double flowers	**Aster novi-belgii** (Michaelmas daisy) *Height:* 30-90cm (1-3ft) *Spread:* 25-30cm (10-12in) *Soil:* Ordinary *Site:* Sun or light shade 'Coombe Rosemary', violet-purple 'Gayborder Royal', crimson-purple 'Jenny', violet-purple	**Liriope muscari** *Height:* 30cm (1ft) *Spread:* 25cm (10in) *Soil:* Ordinary *Site:* Sunny Violet-mauve	**Phlox** *Height:* 60-90cm (2-3ft) *Spread:* 30cm (1ft) *Soil:* Ordinary *Site:* Sun or shade 'Aida', crimson-purple 'Hampton Court', heliotrope 'Vintage Wine', red-purple
Clematis (Virgin's bower) *Height:* 2.5-3m (8-10ft) *Spread:* 1.5m (5ft) *Soil:* Ordinary, alkaline *Site:* Open 'Barbara Jackman', blue and petunia purple 'Jackmanii Superba', deep blue-purple 'The President', deep blue-purple			**Calluna vulgaris** (Heather, ling) *Height:* 20-60cm (8-24in) *Spread:* 23-30cm (9-12in) *Soil:* Acid, no lime *Site:* Open 'Mullion', light purple 'Robert Chapman', light purple	**Clematis** (Virgin's bower) *Height:* 2.5-3m (8-10ft) *Spread:* 1.5m (5ft) *Soil:* Ordinary, alkaline *Site:* Open 'Kermesina', red-purple 'Royal Velours', deep purple	**Hebe** (Shrubby veronica) *Height:* 60-180cm (2-6ft) *Spread:* 60-90cm (2-3ft) *Soil:* Ordinary *Site:* Sunny, sheltered 'Autumn Glory', violet-purple 'Carl Teschner', deep violet-purple 'Midsummer Beauty', lavender purple

Blue flowers

Blue is sometimes described as a 'depressing' colour, but 'relaxing' would be both kinder and nearer to the truth. Borders devoted almost entirely to blue are nearly as common as white borders or white gardens. But almost invariably the description is interpreted broadly to include related colours in the violet-purple range, and possibly some grey, silver and white as well.

Both yellow and white liven up blue in a striking but quite different way, as may be seen by comparing flowers which actually combine them, for example blue polyanthus and *Chionodoxa luciliae*. The polyanthuses almost always have a yellow eye, which both warms and brightens the flowers, whereas the chionodoxa has a white centre which makes it even cooler than it would be without it. It is

In late winter and early spring the charming blue, white-centred flowers of *Chionodoxa luciliae* (**left**) brighten the garden with their colour. Growing only 15cm (6in) high, this bulbous plant is excellent for growing at the front of the border. *Meconopsis betonicifolia* (**right**) bears these striking blue flowers up to 7.5cm (3in) across in mid-summer. Grow in a semi-shaded sheltered spot. Water freely in summer.

Anemone blanda 'Blue Pearl'

Rhododendron 'Susan'

Hyacinthus orientalis 'Ostara'

Veronica gentianoides

Wisteria floribunda 'Macrobotrys'

Muscari armeniacum 'Heavenly Blue'

	SPRING				SUMMER	
ANNUALS/BEDDING	**Myosotis** (Forget-me-not) *Height:* 25-30cm (10-12in) *Spread:* 20cm (8in) *Soil:* Ordinary *Site:* Sun or shade 'Royal Blue', deep blue	**Pansy** *Height:* 15-23cm (6-9in) *Spread:* 15cm (6in) *Soil:* Ordinary *Site:* Sun or moderate shade 'Azure Blue', sky blue 'Blue Bedder', dark blue 'Clear Crystals'	**Polyanthus** *Height:* 15-25cm (6-10in) *Spread:* 15cm (6in) *Soil:* Ordinary *Site:* Sun or moderate shade 'Pacific Giant', blue shades		**Ageratum** *Height:* 10-45cm (4-18in) *Spread:* 15cm (6in) *Soil:* Ordinary *Site:* Open *A.houstianum*, soft blue 'Blue Danube', violet-blue 'Blue Mink', soft blue	**Anchusa cápensis** *Height:* 23cm (9in) *Spread:* 23cm (9in) *Soil:* Ordinary *Site:* Open 'Blue Angel', ultramarine
BULBS	**Anemone blanda** *Height:* 10-15cm (4-6in) *Spread:* 10cm (4in) *Soil:* Ordinary *Site:* Sun or light shade *Atrocoerulea*, deep blue	**Chionodoxa** (Glory of the snow) *Height:* 10-15cm (4-6in) *Spread:* 10-15cm (4-6in) *Soil:* Ordinary *Site:* Open *C.gigantea*, pale blue *C.luciliae*, sky blue and white	**Hyacinth** *Height:* 25cm (10in) *Spread:* 15cm (6in) *Soil:* Ordinary *Site:* Open 'Delft Blue', light blue 'King of the Blues', mid-blue 'Ostara', deep blue	**Muscari** (Grape hyacinth) *Height:* 15cm (6in) *Spread:* 8cm (3¼in) *Soil:* Ordinary *Site:* Open or light shade 'Blue Spike', light blue 'Heavenly Blue', gentian blue *M. tubergeniana*, dark and light blue	**Allium coeruleum** *Height:* 60cm (2ft) *Spread:* 10cm (4in) *Soil:* Ordinary *Site:* Sun Deep cornflower blue	**Iris xiphium** (Dutch iris) *Height:* 75cm (30in) *Spread:* 10cm (4in) *Soil:* Ordinary *Site:* Open 'Purple Sensation', violet blue 'Wedgwood', wedgwood blue
PERENNIALS	**Aquilegia glandulosa** (Altai mountain columbine) *Height:* 38cm (15in) *Spread:* 23cm (9in) *Soil:* Ordinary, well drained *Site:* Open Sky blue and white	**Omphalodès verna** *Height:* 15cm (6in) *Spread:* 15cm (6in) *Soil:* Ordinary *Site:* Open Forget-me-not blue	**Pulmonaria angustifolia** (Lungwort) *Height:* 20cm (8in) *Spread:* 20cm (8in) */Soil:* Ordinary *Site:* Sun or shade 'Azurea', gentian blue	**Veronica gentianoides** *Height:* 45cm (18in) *Spread:* 25cm (10in) *Soil:* Ordinary *Site:* Open Pale blue	**Anchusa** (Alkanet) *Height:* 90cm (3ft) *Spread:* 30cm (1ft) *Soil:* Ordinary, well drained *Site:* Open 'Loddon Royalist', Oxford blue	**Campanula** (Bellflower) *Height:* 25-150cm (10in-5ft) *Spread:* 20-30cm (8-12in) *Soil:* Ordinary *Site:* Sunny *C.carpatica* 'Isobel', deep blue *C.glomerata* 'Superba', deep violet blue *C.latiloba* 'Percy Piper', deep lavender blue *C.persicifolia* 'Telham Beauty', light lavender blue
SHRUBS/TREES	**Ceanothus, evergreen** (Californian lilac, mountain sweet) *Height:* 30cm-6m (1-20ft) *Spread:* 2-3m (6½-10ft) *Soil:* Ordinary *Site:* Sunny, warm *C.* 'Cascade', light blue *C.impressus*, deep blue	**Rhododendron.** *Height:* 1.2-3m (4-10ft) *Spread:* 1.2-2.5m (4-8ft) *Soil:* Acid, no lime *Site:* Open or dappled shade 'Blue Bird', lavender blue 'Blue Peter', lavender blue *R.augustinii*, violet blue 'Susan', light heliotrope	**Rosmarinus** (Rosemary) *Height:* 60-90cm (2-3ft) *Spread:* 45-60cm (18-24in) *Soil:* Ordinary, well drained *Site:* Sunny, warm 'Miss Jessup's Upright' (Pyramidalis), violet blue 'Severn Seas', deep violet blue	**Wisteria** ((Wistaria) *Height:* 3-15m (10-50ft) *Spread:* 2-4m (6½-13ft) *Soil:* Ordinary *Site:* Sunny *W. floribunda*, violet blue *W. sinensis*, mauve blue	**Abutilon** *Height:* 3-5m (10-16½ft) *Spread:* 1.5m (5ft) *Soil:* Ordinary *Site:* Sunny, sheltered *A.suntense*, blue-violet *A.vitifolium*, pale blue	**Ceanothus delineanus** (Californian lilac, mountain sweet) *Height:* 2m (6½ft) *Spread:* 90cm (3ft) *Soil:* Ordinary *Site:* Sunny, sheltered 'Gloire de Plantières', deep blue 'Gloire de Versailles', light blue 'Topaz', medium blue

strange that some people actually object to the yellow eye of the polyanthus and have succeeded in removing it by prolonged breeding and selection. The result is a much drabber flower: most people prefer the normal combination of blue and yellow.

These flowers give a practical lesson in the way in which blue can be best used in the garden in association with yellow or white. Many species actually occur in two or even all three colours. There are all yellow and all white primroses and polyanthuses as well as blue ones, white and cream delphiniums to go with the blue varieties, both blue and white campanulas, and many more such examples.

Blue also blends well with the related purples, but too much of this, unrelieved by any brighter colours, can produce too sombre

an effect. Blue and red can be a dangerously clashing combination, yet it is traditional to mix scarlet geraniums with blue lobelia and, although the result may make colour-sensitive viewers shudder, there is no doubt that most people find it stimulating.

There is a close chemical relationship between the dyes that produce blue, purple, red and pink flowers, which is strikingly exemplified by the behaviour of the manifold varieties of the common mop-headed and lacecap hydrangeas. In acid soils all the colours are in the blue and blue-purple range; remove these same plants to alkaline soil and the flowers change to pink, red or red-purple. White-flowered hydrangeas, having no pigment to be worked on, are immune to this colour change caused by soil chemistry.

Muscari tubergeniana

Anchusa azurea

Hydrangea macrophylla 'Blue Wave'

Campanula carpatica

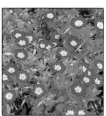

Convolvulus 'Blue Flash'

Lobelia erinus 'Crystal Palace'

				AUTUMN	
Convolvulus minor *Height:* 30cm (12in) *Spread:* 30cm (12in) *Soil:* Ordinary *Site:* Open 'Blue Flash', deep blue, white and yellow 'Royal Ensign', ultramarine and yellow	**Centaurea cyanus** (Cornflower) *Height:* 30-90cm (1-3ft) *Spread:* 20cm (8in) *Soil:* Ordinary *Site:* Open 'Blue Diadem', Oxford blue 'Jubilee Gem' (dwarf), Oxford blue	**Lobelia** *Height:* 10-15cm (4-6in) *Spread:* 15-20cm (6-8in) *Soil:* Ordinary *Site:* Open 'Crystal Palace', dark blue 'Mrs Clibran', mid-blue and white	**Nigella damascena** (Love-in-a-mist) *Height:* 45cm (18in) *Spread:* 23cm (9in) *Soil:* Ordinary *Site:* Open . 'Miss Jekyll', cornflower blue	**Aster** *Height:* 25cm (10in) *Spread:* 20cm (8in) *Soil:* Ordinary *Site:* Sun or shade 'Blue Magic' 'Milady Blue'	**Salvia patens** *Height:* 60cm (2ft) *Spread:* 45cm (18in) *Soil:* Ordinary, well drained *Site:* Sunny, warm Gentian blue
Ixiolirion pallasii *Height:* 45cm (18in) *Spread:* 10cm (4in) *Soil:* Ordinary *Site:* Sunny, warm Deep blue				**Crocus speciosus** *Height:* 10cm (4in) *Spread:* 8cm (3¼in) *Soil:* Ordinary *Site:* Open or light shade Violet	
Delphinium elatum (Larkspur) *Height:* 90-180cm (3-6ft) *Spread:* 45cm (18in) *Soil:* Ordinary *Site:* Open 'Blue Bees', light blue 'Blue Heaven', various shades of blue 'Blue Jay', mid-blue	**Echinops** (Globe thistle) *Height:* 90-120cm (3-4ft) *Spread:* 45cm (18in) *Soil:* Ordinary *Site:* Open 'Taplow Blue', deep lavender blue	**Eryngium** (Sea holly) *Height:* 90cm (3ft) *Spread:* 30cm (1ft) *Soil:* Ordinary, well drained *Site:* Open *E. alpinum*, steel blue *E. tripartitum*, deep blue	**Iris** *Height:* 90-120cm (3-4ft) *Spread:* 30cm (1ft) *Soil:* Ordinary, alkaline *Site:* Open *I.germanica* varieties, various shades of blue with other colours *I.sibirica*, light to deep violet blue	**Aconitum** (Monkshood) *Height:* 120cm (4ft) *Spread:* 30cm (1ft) *Soil:* Ordinary *Site:* Sun or light shade 'Audrey', lavender blue 'Marie Ballard', light blue 'Mistress Quickly', violet blue	**Ceratostigma plumbaginoides** (Leadwort) *Height:* 30cm (1ft) *Spread:* 25cm (10in) *Soil:* Ordinary, well drained *Site:* Sunny, sheltered Gentian blue
Hydrangea macrophylla *Height:* 1-2m (3½-6½ft) *Spread:* 1.2-2m (4-6½ft) *Soil:* Acid for blue flowers *Site:* Sun or semi-shade 'Blue Wave', light heliotrope 'Generale Viscomtesse de Vibraye', forget-me-not blue	**Lavandula** (Lavender) *Height:* 45-60cm (18-24in) *Spread:* 30cm (12in) *Soil:* Ordinary, alkaline *Site:* Open 'Grappenhall', lavender blue 'Hidcote', deep lavender blue			**Caryopteris clandonensis** (Blue spiraea) *Height:* 90cm (3ft) *Spread:* 60cm (2ft) *Soil:* Ordinary, well drained *Site:* Open 'Kew Blue', deep blue	**Perovskia atriplicifolia** *Height:* 1-1.5m (3½-5ft) *Spread:* 90cm (3ft) *Soil:* Ordinary, well drained *Site:* Sunny Lavender blue

White flowers

White is the great harmonizer. It is all the rainbow colours combined, reflected to the eye unaltered and in balance and, since it contains all the colours, it does not clash with any of them. It is also the great enlivener, the one that can be used to bring light into dark places and to cheer up colour combinations that are becoming too sombre.

Some people say that they do not like white flowers because they remind them of funerals. It would be just as apposite and far more cheerful to think of white as the wedding colour.

White gardens or white borders have been fashionable for a long time, but the most satisfactory of them are rarely devoted exclusively to white flowers. Silver and grey foliage is brought into them and also cream,

light lemon and pale shades of pink, blue and mauve. In this way white is made to seem even whiter and the whole composition is given greater moulding and variety.

The opposite approach to this is to use white for the boldest of contrasts with scarlet

or crimson or the deepest blues and purples. Many plants produce varieties with both white and strongly coloured flowers. In border phloxes, for example, there are bright red and deep purple varieties as well as white, and roses offer almost every imaginable shade of red and crimson as well as the purest of whites in varieties such as 'Iceberg' and 'Ice White'. Dahlias are equally versatile in this respect and petunias offer a wide selection of strong colours to go with snowy whites.

Colour schemes of all kinds are influenced by the size and texture of the flowers that produce them. There is a fundamental difference in the effect produced by the filmy clouds of white *Gypsophila* 'Bristol Fairy' or *Clematis flammula* and the more substantial blocks of white produced by white hydrangeas or

Arabis caucasica

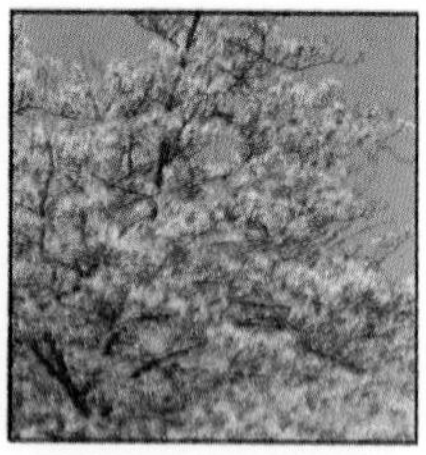

Amelanchier lamarckii

Crocus

Choisya ternata

Saxifrage

Narcissus 'Actaea'

	SPRING					SUMMER
ANNUALS/BEDDING	**Bellis perennis 'Monstrosa'** (Double daisy) *Height:* 15cm (6in) *Spread:* 15cm (6in) *Soil:* Ordinary *Site:* Open 'Fairy Carpet', white and rose	**Matthiola incana** (East Lothian stocks) *Height:* 45cm (18in) *Spread:* 25cm (10in) *Soil:* Ordinary, well drained *Site:* Sunny, sheltered 'Kelvedon White'	**Polyanthus** *Height:* 25cm (10in) *Spread:* 15cm (6in) *Soil:* Ordinary *Site:* Sun or moderate shade 'Triumph White'			**Alyssum maritimum** *Height:* 10cm (4in) *Spread:* 15cm (6in) *Soil:* Ordinary *Site:* Open 'Little Dorrit' 'Snow Carpet'
BULBS	**Anemone blanda** (Windflower) *Height:* 10-15cm (4-6in) *Spread:* 10cm (4in) *Soil:* Ordinary *Site:* Sun or partial shade 'Alba' 'White Splendour'	**Crocus** *Height:* 10m (4in) *Spread:* 8cm (3¼in) *Soil:* Ordinary *Site:* Open or light shade *C. chrysanthus* 'Snow Bunting' 'Jeanne d'Arc'	**Erythronium** (Dogs tooth violet) *Height:* 15-20cm (6-8in) *Spread:* 20cm (8in) *Soil:* Plenty of humus *Site:* Dappled shade 'White Beauty'	**Narcissus** (Daffodil) *Height:* 30-50cm (12-20in) *Spread:* 15cm (6in) *Soil:* Ordinary *Site:* Sun or light shade 'Actaea', small yellow and red cup 'Ice Follies', crown is cream at first 'Mount Hood' 'Silver Chimes', cup is cream 'Tresamble', touch of cream	**Tulip** *Height:* 30-60cm (12-24in) *Spread:* 10m (4in) *Soil:* Ordinary *Site:* Open 'Diana' 'Purissima' 'Schoonoord' 'White Triumphator'	**Galtonia candicans** (Summer hyacinth) *Height:* 90cm (3ft) *Spread:* 23cm (9in) *Soil:* Ordinary *Site:* Open
PERENNIALS	**Arabis caucasica** (Rock cress) *Height:* 15cm (6in) *Spread:* 30cm (12in) *Soil:* Ordinary, alkaline *Site:* Open 'Alba', single flowers 'Alba Plena', double flowers	**Iberis** (Candytuft) *Height:* 10-45cm (4-18in) *Spread:* 20cm (8in) *Soil:* Ordinary *Site:* Open *I. semperflorens* *I. sempervirens*	**Primula** (Primrose) *Height:* 10-30cm (4-12in) *Spread:* 15cm (6in) *Soil:* Ordinary *Site:* Shade *P. denticulata* 'Alba' *P. vulgaris* 'Snow Queen'	**Saxifraga** (Mossy saxifrage) *Height:* 8-20cm (3¼-8in) *Spread:* 20cm (8in) *Soil:* Ordinary *Site:* Partial shade 'Harstwood White' 'Pearly King' 'Wallacei'	**Viola cornuta 'Alba'** (Horned violet) *Height:* 15-20cm (6-8in) *Spread:* 15cm (6in) *Soil:* Ordinary *Site:* Partial shade	**Astilbe** *Height:* 45-60cm (18-24in) *Spread:* 30cm (12in) *Soil:* Ordinary, moist *Site:* Sun or light shade 'Irrlicht' 'White Gloria'
SHRUBS/TREES	**Amelanchier** (Snowy mespilus) *Height:* 4-5m (13-16½ft) *Spread:* 3-4m (10-13ft) *Soil:* Ordinary *Site:* Open *A. laevis* *A. lamarckii*	**Choisya ternata** (Mexican orange blossom) *Height:* 120-150cm (4-5ft) *Spread:* 120cm (4ft) *Soil:* Ordinary *Site:* Sunny, sheltered	**Clematis montana** *Height:* 6m (20ft) *Spread:* 2m (6½ft) *Soil:* Ordinary *Site:* Open There are also pink varieties	**Magnolia** *Height:* 2-5m (6½-16½ft) *Spread:* 2-4m (6½-13ft) *Soil:* Moderately acid *Site:* Open *M. stellata* *M. soulangeana* 'Alba Superba' *M. soulangeana* 'Lennei Alba'	**Prunus** (Cherry, almond) *Height:* 1-6m (3½-20ft) *Spread:* 60cm-4m (2-13ft) *Soil:* Ordinary *Site:* Open 'Avium Plena', double flower *P. glandulosa* 'Alba Plena', double flowers *P. yedoensis*, bluish white 'Shirotae', semi-double flowers 'Tai-Haku', single flowers	**Deutzia** *Height:* 2-2.5m (6½-8ft) *Spread:* 1-1.5m (3½-5ft) *Soil:* Ordinary *Site:* Open *D. magnifica* *D. scabre candidissima*

White varieties of *Matthiola incana* (**left**) provide freshness to the border in mid-summer. In full sun and on poor soils the papery blooms of *Cistus X cyprius* (**right**) are borne in profusion during the summer months. These Mediterranean shrubs are ideal for planting on dry sunny banks. The almond-scented flowers of *Prunus yedoensis* (**far right**) grace this elegant tree in early spring. Several named forms are available.

Chrysanthemum maximum. There is even a difference between the effect of single and double flowers of the same species — a more solid white from the double white arabis than from the single white wild form, for instance — which is why such differences are noted when describing these flowers below.

There are also many white-flowered climbers, most of all among the roses which range all the way in vigour from the 3m (10ft) 'Swan Lake' to the 10m (33ft) 'Kiftsgate', all of which can be used as backgrounds or allowed to mingle with other plants or spill out of trees. Clematis varieties of moderate vigour and sweet peas are particularly eligible minglers that are unlikely to smother the host plants used as support, and can make charming colour associations with them.

Galtonia candicans

Magnolia stellata

Chrysanthemum maximum

Ornithogalum umbellatum

Spiraea prunifolia 'Plena'

Viburnum tomentosum 'Mariesii'

				AUTUMN	
Iberis amara (Candytuft) *Height:* 30cm (12in) *Spread:* 15cm (6in) *Soil:* Ordinary *Site:* Open 'White Spiral'	**Gypsophila** (Baby's breath) *Height:* 45cm (18in) *Spread:* 23cm (9in) *Soil:* Ordinary *Site:* Open 'Covent Garden White'	**Lavatera rosea** *Height:* 60cm (2ft) *Spread:* 45cm (18in) *Soil:* Ordinary *Site:* Open 'Mont Blanc'	**Petunia** *Height:* 23-30cm (9-12in) *Spread:* 23cm (9in) *Soil:* Ordinary *Site:* Sunny 'Resisto White' 'Snow Cloud' 'White Joy'	**Aster** *Height:* 25cm (10in) *Spread:* 20cm (8in) *Soil:* Ordinary *Site:* Sun or shade 'Milady White'	
Gladiolus *Height:* 60-90cm (2-3ft) *Spread:* 20cm (8in) *Soil:* Ordinary *Site:* Open 'Alba Nova' 'Purity' 'Sancerre' 'Summer Snow'	**Lilium** (Lily) *Height:* 90-120cm (3-4ft) *Spread:* 25cm (10in) *Soil:* Ordinary *Site:* Sun or dappled shade *L. candidum* *L. martagon* 'Album' *L. regale*, flushed light yellow and purple	**Ornithogalum umbellatum** (Star of Bethlehem) *Height:* 15cm (6in) *Spread:* 15cm (6in) *Soil:* Ordinary *Site:* Sun or partial shade		**Acidanthera murielae** *Height:* 75cm (30in) *Spread:* 15cm (6in) *Soil:* Ordinary, well drained *Site:* Sunny, warm Purple blotch	**Dahlia** *Height:* 30-90cm (1-3ft) *Spread:* 45-90cm (18-36) *Soil:* Ordinary *Site:* Open 'Easter Sunday', creamy white 'Mistill Delight' 'White Klankstad' 'Wooton Wedding'
Chrysanthemum maximum (Shasta daisy) *Height:* 60-90cm (2-3ft) *Spread:* 30cm (12in) *Soil:* Ordinary *Site:* Open 'Beauté Nivelloise', single flowers 'Wirral Supreme', double flowers	**Dianthus plumarius** (Pinks) *Height:* 15-30cm (6-12in) *Spread:* 25cm (10in) *Soil:* Ordinary, alkaline *Site:* Open 'Mrs Sinkins' 'White Ladies'	**Gypsophila paniculata** *Height:* 90cm (3ft) *Spread:* 60cm (2ft) *Soil:* Ordinary, alkaline *Site:* Open 'Bristol Fairy', double flowers	**Paeonia lactiflora** (Chinese peony) *Height:* 90cm (3ft) *Spread:* 45cm (18in) *Soil:* Ordinary *Site:* Sun or partial shade 'Duchesse de Nemours'	**Aster novi-belgii** (Michaelmas daisy) *Height:* 30-90cm (1-3ft) *Spread:* 25-30cm (10-12in) *Soil:* Ordinary *Site:* Sun or shade 'Snowsprite' 'White Ladies'	**Cimicifuga** *Height:* 120-150cm (4-5ft) *Spread:* 45cm (18in) *Soil:* Ordinary *Site:* Half or dappled shade *C. racemosa*, ivory *C. simplex* 'White Pearl'
Escallonia iveyi *Height:* 3m (10ft) *Spread:* 1.5m (5ft) *Soil:* Ordinary *Site:* Sunny, sheltered	**Philadelphus** (Mock orange) *Height:* 1.2-3m (4-10ft) *Spread:* 1.2-1.5m (4-5ft) *Soil:* Ordinary *Site:* Open 'Beauclerk' 'Belle Etoile', flushed purple 'Sybille', flushed purple 'Virginal', double flower	**Spiraea** *Height:* 1.2-2.5m (4-8ft) *Spread:* 1.2-2m (4-6½ft) *Soil:* Ordinary *Site:* Open *S. prunifolia*, double flowers *S. vanhouttei* *S. veitchii*	**Viburnum** *Height:* 2.5-3m (8-10ft) *Spread:* 1.2-2.4m (4-8ft) *Soil:* Ordinary *Site:* Open *V. opulus sterile*, ball shaped flower clusters *V. plicatum*, ball shaped flower clusters *V. plicatum tomentosum*, flat flower clusters	**Erica** (Heath, heather) *Height:* 15-60cm (6-24in) *Spread:* 25cm (10in) *Soil:* Acid, no lime *Site:* Open *E. ciliaris* 'Stoborough' *E. cinerea* 'Alba Major' *E. cinerea* 'Alba Minor'	**Potentilla fruticosa** (Shrubby cinquefoil) *Height:* 1-1.2m (3½-4ft) *Spread:* 60cm (2ft) *Soil:* Ordinary *Site:* Sunny 'Abbotswood', starts in summer

Silver and grey foliage

Plants with silver or grey leaves have become so important to garden designers that whole books have been written about their selection and use, and some nurseries specialize in them. They can be used in gardens in two quite different ways: either as a relieving contrast to flower colours or, alternatively, in areas devoted almost exclusively to the silver or grey foliage, with flowers playing a definitely subordinate role, if admitted at all. Silver and grey gardens of the latter kind have become fashionable and, because many of the plants that have such leaves come from naturally dry climates, they can usually be grown with particular success in the gravel gardens which have also gained greatly in popularity in recent years.

Like white, silver and grey do not clash with anything and so can be used with any other foliage or with any flowers. Yet some combinations seem more satisfactory than others. Both silver and grey make delightfully restful combinations with blue and purple. Lavender and nepeta can actually supply both the grey leaves and the blue flowers, but many other combinations can be devised in which foliage and flowers come from different sources; silver *Cineraria maritima*, for example, with purple heliotrope or blue *Salvia patens*.

Pink flowers with grey foliage is another association almost certain to please, and again one may note that it occurs automatically when garden pinks, varieties of *Dianthus plumarius*, are planted. But by far the commonest natural alliance is between silver and grey leaves and yellow flowers, as in some gazanias, many senecios, *Santolina*, euryops and numerous verbascums.

Silver and grey also occur in much larger plants, including some big shrubs and trees. The willow-leaved pear, *Pyrus salicifolia* 'Pendula', is a particularly beautiful small tree that can be used as a centrepiece in a silver-grey scheme, and there are also many silvery or blue-grey conifers, some of which remain small either permanently or for a good many years. These small conifers combine particularly well with heathers, many of which have pink or reddish purple flowers and some have the added attraction of grey, yellow or copper-coloured leaves.

Many silver- and grey-leaved plants retain their leaves in winter, although rather few look their best at that time. Often the silver or grey

Anaphalis triplinervis 'Summer Snow'

Helichrysum splendidum

Pyrus salicifolia 'Pendula'

Senecio 'Sunshine'

Artemisia ludoviciana 'Silver Queen'

Stachys lanata

Leaves retained all the year

Artemisia tridentata
Shrub
Height: 1.2m (4ft)
Spread: 60cm (2ft)
Soil: Ordinary
Site: Sunny
Grey leaves

Centaurea cineraria
Sub-shrub
Height: 45cm (18in)
Spread: 30cm (12in)
Soil: Ordinary
Site: Sunny
Long, indented, white woolly leaves

Convolvulus cneorum
Sub-shrub
Height: 45cm (18in)
Spread: 30cm (12in)
Soil: Ordinary
Site: Sunny, sheltered
Narrow slivery leave

Eucalpytus gunnil
Tree
Height if pollarded: 2-3m (6½-10ft)
Spread if pollarded: 1.2m (4ft)
Soil: Ordinary
Site: Sunny, sheltered
Rounded silvery blue leaves

Helichrysum splendidum
Shrub
Height: 60cm (2ft)
Spread: 45cm (18in)
Soil: Ordinary, well-drained
Site: Sunny
Small silvery leaves

Senecio cineraria
Sub-shrub
Height: 60cm (2ft)
Spread: 30cm (1ft)
Soil: Ordinary
Site: Sunny
Deeply lobed white woolly leaves
'White Diamond' and 'Ramparts' are good varieties

Leaves from spring to autumn only

Achillea argentea
Herbaceous perennial
Height: 15cm (6in)
Spread: 25cm (10in)
Soil: Ordinary, well-drained
Site: Sunny
Small silvery leaves, small white flowers in late spring

Achillea taygetea
Herbaceous perennial
Height: 30cm (12in)
Spread: 38cm (15in)
Soil: Ordinary, well-drained
Site: Sunny
Finely divided grey leaves, pale yellow flowers in summer

Anaphalis nubigena
Herbaceous perennial
Height: 30cm (12in)
Spread: 30cm (12in)
Soil: Ordinary, well-drained
Site: Sunny
Small silvery leaves, pearly white flowers in autumn

Anaphalis triplinervis
Herbaceous perennial
Height: 38cm (15in)
Spread: 38cm (15in)
Soil: Ordinary, well-drained
Site: Sunny
Silvery grey leaves, pearly white flowers in autumn

Anthemis cupaniana
Herbaceous perennial
Height: 30cm (12in)
Spread: 45cm (18in)
Soil: Ordinary
Site: Sunny
Finely divided grey leaves, large white daisies in summer

Antennaria dioica
Herbaceous perennial
Height: 10cm (4in)
Spread: 15cm (6in)
Soil: Light, well-drained
Site: Sunny
Small grey leaves becoming green in winter, pink flowers in late spring

Euryops acreus
Shrub
Height: 30cm (1ft)
Spread: 30cm (1ft)
Soil: Ordinary
Site: Sunny
Small grey-blue leaves, small yellow daisies in late spring

Festuca ovina glauca
(Fescue grass)
Perennial
Height: 25cm (10in)
Spread: 20cm (8in)
Soil: Light, well-drained
Site: Sunny
Narrow blue-grey leaves

Helichrysum petiolatum
Herbaceous perennial
Height: 20cm (8in)
Spread: 60cm (2ft)
Soil: Ordinary, well-drained
Site: Sunny
Heart-shaped grey leaves

Leucanthemum hosmarense
Sub-shrub
Height: 23cm (9in)
Spread: 30cm (1ft)
Soil: Gritty, well-drained
Site: Sunny
Finely divided silver-grey leaves, large daisies in spring and summer

Onopordon arabicum
Biennial
Height: 2.5m (8ft)
Spread: 45cm (18in)
Soil: Ordinary
Site: Sun or partial shade
Broad, almost white leaves, purple thistle flowers in summer

Pyrus salicifolia 'Pendula'
(Willow-leaved pear)
Tree
Height: 4-5m (13-16½ft)
Spread: 3cm (10ft)
Soil: Ordinary
Site: Sunny
Narrow silvery leaves

appearance is produced by a dense covering of silky hairs or down developed by the plant to cut down water loss by evaporation from the leaf surface and so enable it to survive periods of drought. In damp climates, this covering collects moisture and may become sodden, possibly even causing the leaves to decay. Even without this final disaster, rain-soaked plants can look very bedraggled.

All silver- and grey-leaved plants succeed best in well-drained soil and open, sunny places. Many like soil that contains lime, either as chalk or limestone.

Stachys lanata (**left**) is a favourite plant, prized for its silver-grey foliage.

Gardens featuring silver and white plants (**right**) have a clean crisp appearance that generates a restful atmosphere. Many types of plants have silvery foliage, from low-growing perennials to stately trees. All can be used to good effect in the garden, especially with bold contrasting colours of seasonal bedding plants.

Verbascum bombyciferum

Artemisia schmidtiana

Ballota pseudodictamnus

Senecio 'Sunshine' (S. greyii)
Shrub
Height: 90cm (3ft)
Spread: 90cm (3ft)
Soil: Ordinary
Site: Sunny
Rounded grey leaves

Lavandula angustifolia
(Lavender)
Shrub
Height: 45-60cm (18-24in)
Spread: 30cm (12in)
Soil: Ordinary, well-drained
Site: Sunny
Narrow grey leaves

Stachys lanata
(Lambs ears)
Herbaceous perennial
Height: 25cm (10in)
Spread: 25cm (10in)
Soil: Ordinary, well-drained
Site: Sun or partial shade
Lance-shaped white woolly leaves and purplish-rose flowers. 'Silver Carpet is a low-growing variety without flowers

Teucrium fruticans
(Shrubby germander)
Height: 90cm (3ft)
Spread: 60cm (2ft)
Soil: Light, well-drained
Site: Sunny
Narrow silvery leaves, lavender flowers in summer

Artemisia absinthium
Sub-shrub
Height: 75cm (30in)
Spread: 45cm (18in)
Soil: Ordinary
Site: Sunny
Finely divided silvery leaves. 'Lambrook Silver' is a specially good variety

Artemisia arborescens
Sub-shrub
Height: 90cm· (3ft)
Spread: 60cm (2ft)
Soil: Ordinary
Site: Sunny
Finely divided silvery leaves

Artemisia ludoviciana
Herbaceous perennial
Height: 60cm (2ft)
Spread: 23cm (9in)
Soil: Light, well-drained
Site: Sunny
Silvery grey leaves

Artemisia schmidtiana
Herbaceous perennial
Height: 23cm (9in)
Spread: 20cm (8in)
Soil: Light, well-drained
Site: Sunny
Finely divided silvery leaves

Ballota pseudodictamnus
Herbaceous perennial
Height: 60cm (2ft)
Spread: 45cm (18in)
Soil: Poor or ordinary
Site: Sunny
Pale green leaves becoming white woolly

Cynara cardunculua
(Cardoon)
Herbaceous perennial
Height: 1.5m (5ft)
Spread: 60cm (2ft)
Soil: Light, deep
Site: Sunny
Large, deeply divided sliver-grey leaves

Romneya coulteri
(Californian tree poppy)
Sub-shrub
Height: 1.5m (5ft)
Spread: 60cm (2ft)
Soil: Light, well-drained
Site: Sunny, sheltered
Silver-grey leaves, large white poppies in late summer

Santolina chamaecyparissus
(Lavender cotton)
Sub-shrub
Height: 60cm (2ft)
Spread: 45cm (18in)
Soil: Ordinary
Site: Sunny
Small silver-grey leaves

Verbascum bombyciferum
(Mullein)
Biennial
Height: 1.5cm (5ft)
Spread: 30cm (1ft)
Soil: Ordinary
Site: Sunny
Large white woolly leaves, pale yellow flowers in summer

Veronica incana
Herbaceous perennial
Height: 10cm (4in)
Spread: 30cm (12in)
Soil: Ordinary, fertile
Site: Sun or partial shade
Narrow silvery-grey leaves, darkblue flowers in late summer

p.163

(Regent)

Red/yellow foliage

Flowers come and go but leaves are there for months on end, even throughout the year if the plant is an evergreen. So it is very important to consider foliage when colour-planning the garden. Although most leaves are green, there is an enormous variation even in this colour alone. There are the blue-greens of rue, some hostas and aquilegias, the narrow-leaved grass *Festuca ovina* 'Glauca', and many other plants; deep laurel greens; much livelier lime greens; muted sage greens; real grey-greens; and many more.

In addition to all this there is a diversity of other foliage colours, some of which would not have survived in the wild but were seized on by gardeners appreciative of their decorative merit and propagated by vegetative means because most would not reproduce the

unusual leaf colour from seed. There are yellow leaves, purple leaves, and some that are various shades of red, bronze or copper. All these colours can be just as effective as those of flowers, and can be used in precisely the same way to create harmonies and contrasts, to be eye-catchers (and for this, some of the all-yellow leaves such as those of *Catalpa bignonioides* 'Aurea', *Robinia* 'Frisia' and *Gleditsia* 'Sunburst' are particularly effective), or to tone down other colours which, on their own, may prove too strident.

Red, purple, bronze and copper make little or no difference to the vigour of plants. But when leaves are yellow, overall growth is usually slower, and the plant — be it tree, shrub or herbaceous perennial — may not grow as large as its normal green counterpart.

Yellow is also in general most fully produced when the light intensity is good; the colour may tend to become dull and greenish in the shade. Most yellow-leaved trees and shrubs can be planted in full sun. A few, however — notably the golden elders *(Sambucus)* — may suffer leaf scorch if the sunshine is too intense, and for these a position in good light but shaded from the sun around midday is best.

To all these leaf colours may be added the various colours of bark: the coral red of *Acer palmatum* 'Senkaki', the much deeper reds of the dogwoods *Cornus alba* and *C. sanguinea*; the yellow or orange of various willows such as the golden weeping willow *(Salix chrysocoma)* and two forms of the white willow *(S. alba)* named 'Chermesina' ('Britzensis' in some catalogues) and 'Vitellina'; the cinnamon of

Acer japonicum 'Aureum'

Humulus lupulus 'Aureus'

Juniperus media 'Old Gold'

Robinia pseudoacacia 'Frisia'

Taxus baccata 'Semperaurea'

Acer palmatum 'Atropurpureum'

YELLOW LEAVES

PERENNIALS

Hosta fortunei 'Aurea'
(Plantain lily)
Height: 45-75cm (18-30in)
Spread: 45cm (18in)
Soil: Ordinary
Site: Sun or partial shade
Young leaves soft yellow

Humulus lupulus 'Aureus'
(Hop)
Height: 6m (20ft)
Spread: 2m (6½ft)
Soil: Ordinary
Site: Open
Young leaves bright yellow

Milium effusum 'Aureum'
(Millet grass)
Height: 60cm (2ft)
Spread: 30cm (1ft)
Soil: Ordinary
Site: Open
Yellow

Valeriana phu 'Aurea'
(Valerian)
Height: 90cm (3ft)
Spread: 30cm (1ft)
Soil: Ordinary
Site: Open or light shade
Young leaves bright yellow

SHRUBS

Acer japonicum 'Aureum'
(Japanese maple)
Height: 3-4m (10-13ft)
Spread: 2m (6½ft)
Soil: Ordinary
Site: Open
Soft yellow

Calluna vulgaris
(Heather, ling)
Height: 20cm (8in)
Spread: 25cm (10in)
Soil: Acid, no lime
Site: Open
'Gold Haze', light yellow
'Robert Chapman', bronze and yellow

Cornus alba 'Aurea'
(Red-barked dogwood)
Height: 2-3m (6½-10ft)
Spread: 1.2m (4ft)
Soil: Ordinary, moist
Site: Open
Soft yellow

Ligustrum ovalifolium 'Aureum'
(Golden privet)
Height: 2-3m (6½-10ft)
Spread: 90-120cm (3-4ft)
Soil: Ordinary
Site: Open
Yellow

Lonicera nitida 'Baggesen's Gold'
Height: 90cm (3ft)
Spread: 90cm (3ft)
Soil: Ordinary
Site: Open
Yellow, becoming greenish yellow

Ribes sanguineum 'Brocklebankii'
(Flowering currant)
Height: 2-2.5m (6½-8ft)
Spread: 1.2m (4ft)
Soil: Ordinary
Site: Sun or light shade
Yellow

TREES/CONIFERS

Acer negundo 'Auratum'
(Box elder)
Height: 4.5-6m (15-20ft)
Spread: 3-4m (10-13ft)
Soil: Ordinary
Site: Open
Pale yellow

Catalpa bignonioides 'Aurea'
(Indian bean tree)
Height: 4.5-6m (15-20ft)
Spread: 5m (16½ft)
Soil: Ordinary
Site: Sunny
Soft yellow

Cupressus, Chamaecyaris and Cupressocyparis
(Cypress)
Height: 6-12m (20-39ft)
Spread: 3-5m (10-16½ft)
Soil: Ordinary
Site: Sunny
'Castlewellan Gold', greenish yellow
'Ellwood's Gold', yellow tipped
'Filifera Aurea', yellow
'Goldcrest', soft yellow
'Lanei', golden yellow

Gleditsia triancanthos 'Sunburst'
(Honey locust)
Height: 4.5-6m (15-20ft)
Spread: 3-4m (10-13ft)
Soil: Ordinary
Site: Sunny
Changing from deep to light yellow

Juniperus media
(Juniper)
Height: 60-120cm (2-4ft)
Spread: 2-4m (6½-13ft)
Soil: Ordinary
Site: Open
'Aurea', young leaves sulphur yellow
'Old Gold', bronzy-yellow

Robinia pseuodoacacia 'Frisia'
(False acacia)
Height: 5-9m (16½-30ft)
Spread: 3-4m (10-13ft)
Soil: Ordinary
Site: Sunny
Light yellow

Acer griseum; the shining mahogany of *Prunus serrula*; and the white of good forms of the common birch as well as exotic birches such as *Betula ermanii* and *B. papyrifera*.

In a few plants it is only the young growth that has coloured leaves. This is true of the herbaceous valerian named *Valeriana phu* 'Aurea', which has yellow leaves at first, and also two fine shrubs, *Pieris formosa* and *Photinia fraseri*, both of which have red leaves when young. They are very handsome for a few weeks in spring but relapse into greenness in summer.

Several varieties of *Cotinus coggygria* have striking purple foliage. These and the green-leaved forms are often suffused with superb shades of reds, yellows and oranges during autumn (**right**).

Cotinus coggygria

Pieris formosa

RED AND PURPLE LEAVES

		Ligularia dentata 'Desdemona'	**Phormium tenax 'Purpureum'**	**Rheum palmatum 'Atrosanguineum'**	
		Height: 90cm (3ft)	(New Zealand flax)	(Ornamental rhubarb)	
		Spread: 60cm (2ft)	*Height:* 2m (6½ft)	*Height:* 2m (6½ft)	
		Soil: Ordinary	*Spread:* 60cm (2ft)	*Spread:* 90cm (3ft)	
		Site: Open or light shade	*Soil:* Ordinary	*Soil:* Ordinary or moist	
			Site: Sunny, sheltered	*Site:* Open	
				Leaves red-purple beneath	

Sambucus	**Spiraea japonica 'Goldflame'**	**Corylus maximus 'Atro Purpurea'**	**Cotinus coggygria**	**Photinia fraseri**	**Pieris**
(Elder)	*Height:* 1.2m (4ft)	(Filbert)	(Smoke tree, Venetian sumach)	*Height:* 3-6m (10-20ft)	(Lily-of-the-valley-bush)
Height: 2.5-3m (8-10ft)	*Spread:* 1.5m (5ft)	*Height:* 2.5m (8ft)	*Height:* 2-3m (6½-10ft)	*Spread:* 1.8m (6ft)	*Height:* 2.4-8m (8-26ft)
Spread: 1.2-1.5m (4-5ft)	*Soil:* Ordinary	*Spread:* 2m (6½ft)	*Spread:* 2-2.5m (6½-8ft)	*Soil:* Ordinary	*Spread:* 2-2.4m (6-8ft)
Soil: Ordinary	*Site:* Open	*Soil:* Ordinary	*Soil:* Ordinary	*Site:* Sunny, sheltered	*Soil:* Acid, no lime
Site: Open or light shade	Leaves copper-yellow when	*Site:* Open or partial shade	*Site:* Sunny	'Red Robin', young leaves	*Site:* Open or dappled shade
S. nigra 'Aurea', yellow	young	Bark purple	'Foliis Purpureus', plum purple	bronze-red	*P.* 'Forest Flame', young leaves
S. racemosa 'Plumosa Aurea',			'Royal Purple', deep red-purple		red becoming cream
yellow, leaves much					*P. formosa* 'Wakehurst', young
divided					leaves bright red

Taxus baccata		**Acer palmatum 'Atropurpureum'**	**Acer platanoides 'Crimson King'**	**Fagus sylvatica 'Fastigiata'**	**Prunus cerasifera 'Nigra'**
(Yew)		(Japanese maple)	(Norway maple)	(Dawyck beech)	(Cherry plum)
Height: 2.5-5m (8-16½ft)		*Height:* 2-3m (6½-10ft)	*Height:* 9-18m (30-60ft)	*Height:* 9-18m (30-60ft)	*Height:* 6-7m (20-23ft)
Spread: 0.6-3m (2-10ft)		*Spread:* 2m (6½ft)	*Spread:* 8m (26ft)	*Spread:* 3m (10ft)	*Spread:* 4-5m (13-16½ft)
Soil: Ordinary		*Soil:* Ordinary	*Soil:* Ordinary	*Soil:* Ordinary, alkaline	*Soil:* Ordinary
Site: Sun or shade		*Site:* Open or dappled shade	*Site:* Open	*Site:* Open	*Site:* Open
'Davastonii Aurea', wide		Red-purple	Beetroot purple	'Dawyck Purple', leaves purple	Very dark purple
spreading, leaves edged					
yellow					
'Fastigiata Aurea', narrowly					
erect, leaves edged yellow					
'Semperaurea', bright yellow					
'Standishii', columnar, yellow					

Variegated foliage

Some leaves combine several colours — usually white, cream or yellow with green — but there are also pink, red and purple variegations in some plants. Such colours are not natural to the plant — although variegations do appear among wild plants — but correspond to reactions to various events: sometimes to virus infection, sometimes to mutations affecting only certain layers of tissue which may in turn determine whether the variegation appears in stripes, or as an edging to the leaf, or as a central blotch in it. All may be regarded as freaks, useful if the variegation is attractive, merely curious if it is ugly. In the wild, such freaks soon disappear because they are almost invariably less vigorous than the normal green-leaved type. Gardeners may, however, find them useful for various decorative pur-

poses, and keep them going mainly by vegetative means. Very occasionally, a variegation can be inherited by seed, a notable example being a white blotched variety of honesty *(Lunaria biennis)* which, because it is a biennial, can be kept going only by seed. Not only is this variegation unusual in being seed-borne but also in that it does not appear until the second year.

Variegations can be very decorative, especially when several colours combine, as shades of pink and cream do in the young leaves of the sycamore *Acer pseudoplatanus* 'Brilliantissimum' or in the leaves of some varieties of New Zealand flax *(Phormium)*.

Because of the way in which variegations originate there is often a risk that some growths may revert to the original green-

leaved form. Because these green-leaved stems are almost certain to be more vigorous and faster-growing than the variegated ones, any that appear must be removed as soon as possible or they may take over completely. Some variegated trees are grafted high up on main stems of the green-leaved type; with these there is an ever-present danger that stems may appear lower down on this main stem and quickly starve out the variegated head. Pruning to get rid of such green-leaved stems can be carried out at any time, even in summer. The offending stem must be removed cleanly right down to the trunk or to the variegated branch from which it has grown, with no stump left to give rise to a new crop of green stems.

The degree of variegation sometimes dif-

Hosta fortunei
'Albopicta'

Hedera helix 'Glacier'

Ilex aquifolium

Pachysandra terminalis
'Variegata'

Cornus alba 'Spaethii'

Elaeagnus pungens
'Maculata'

PERENNIALS

Brunnera macrophylla 'Variegata'
Height: 45cm (18in)
Spread: 45cm (18in)
Soil: Ordinary
Site: Sun or shade
White blotched

Hosta
(Plantain lily)
Height: 45-75cm (18-30in)
Spread: 45cm (18in)
Soil: Ordinary
Site: Sun or partial shade
H. albomarginata, leaves edged cream
H. fortunei 'Albo Marginata', leaves edged white
H. 'Frances Williams'
H. 'Thomas Hogg'
H. undulata, leaves white variegated

Iris
Height: 60cm (2ft)
Spread: 30cm (1ft)
Soil: Ordinary, alkaline
Site: Open
I. foetidissima 'Variegata', white striped
I. pallida 'Aureo Variegata', yellow striped
I. pallida 'Variegata', cream striped

SHRUBS/TREES

Acer negundo 'Variegatum'
(Box elder)
Height: 4.5-6cm (15-20ft)
Spread: 3.4m (10-13ft)
Soil: Ordinary
Site: Open

Acer pseudoplatanus 'Brilliantissimum'
(Sycamore)
Height: 3-6m (10-20ft)
Spread: 3-5m (10-16½ft)
Soil: Ordinary
Site: Open
Young leaves pink and cream

Aralia elata 'Variegata'
(Angelica tree)
Height: 2-4m (6½-13ft)
Spread: 1.5cm (5ft)
Soil: Ordinary
Site: Sunny, sheltered
Large, compound, creamy-white and green

Phormium tenax 'Variegatum'
(New Zealand flax)
Height: 2cm (6½ft)
Spread: 60cm (2ft)
Soil: Ordinary
Site: Sunny, sheltered
Cream striped leaves

Scrophularia aquatica 'Variegata'
(Water betony)
Height: 90cm (3ft)
Spread: 45cm (18in)
Soil: Ordinary, moist
Site: Open
Cream variegated

Sisyrinchium striatum 'Variegatum'
Height: 60cm (2ft)
Spread: 30cm (1ft)
Soil: Ordinary
Site: Open
Leaves grey-green striped white

Fuchsia magellanica
Height: 1.2-2m (4-6½ft)
Spread: 90cm (3ft)
Soil: Ordinary
Site: Sun or light shade
'Variegata', cream border to leaf
'Versicolor', leaves grey-green, pink and cream

Hebe andersonii 'Variegata'
(Shrubby veronica)
Height: 90cm (3ft)
Spread: 60cm (2ft)
Soil: Ordinary
Site: Sunny, sheltered
Cream variegated

Hedera (Ivy)
Height: to 6m (20ft)
Spread: 1.2-2m (4-6½ft)
Soil: Ordinary
Site: Sunny for variegation
H. colchica dentata 'Variegata', pale yellow
H. helix 'Glacier', grey-green and white
'Goldheart', dark green and yellow
'Goldheart' 'Marginata Elegantissima', grey-green, white and pink

Borders featuring mixed foliage plants (**right**) can be just as effective and attractive a part of the garden as those overflowing with bright flowering plants. Many people prefer the sculptural and subtle qualities such borders offer. Plants with variegated leaves are high on the list of favoured foliage subjects. These are available in all types, from ground-cover perennials to shrubs and climbers.

fers considerably from branch to branch. This is particularly noticeable with golden-variegated hollies which may produce some stems with wholly yellow leaves. It might seem clever to make cuttings of these stems and so produce a wholly golden holly, but plants that have no chlorophyll with which to manufacture food quickly die. The apparently all yellow-leaved trees and shrubs actually do have some chlorophyll, but it is masked by the yellow colour (whereas the yellow-variegated parts of the holly leaf have no chlorophyll at all). The same applies to white variegation — the more there is of it, the weaker is the plant. Another peculiarity of some variegations is that it is not carried in the root: take root cuttings from a white- or yellow-variegated Japanese angelica *(Aralia elata)*, for example, and all the resultant plants are green-leaved.

Euonymus fortunei 'Emerald and Gold'

Weigela florida 'Variegata'

Weigela (young shoots)

Cornus alba 'Elegantissima'
Height: 2-3m (6½-10ft)
Spread: 1.2m (4ft)
Soil: Ordinary, moist
Site: Open

Cornus alternifolia 'Variegata'
(Dogwood)
Height: 2-2.5m (6½-8ft)
Spread: 1.8m (6ft)
Soil: Ordinary
Site: Open
Leaves edged with white

Cornus controversa 'Variegata'
(Dogwood)
Height: 4-5m (13-16½ft)
Spread: 3-4cm (10-13ft)
Soil: Ordinary
Site: Sunny, sheltered
Cream variegated

Cotoneaster horizontalis 'Variegatus'
Height: 15cm-6m (6in-20ft)
Spread: 1-3cm (3-10ft)
Soil: Ordinary
Site: Open or light shade

Elaeagnus pungens
(Oleaster)
Height: 2-3cm (6½-10ft)
Spread: 1.5m (5ft)
Soil: Ordinary
Site: Sun or shade
'Aurea', yellow edge
'Maculata', yellow centre

Euonymus fortunei
Height: 15-60cm (6-24in)
Spread: 60cm (2ft)
Soil: Ordinary
Site: Sun or shade
'Emerald and Gold', yellow variegated
'Emerald Gaiety', white variegated
'Variegatus', grey-green edged white

Ilex (Holly)
Height: 3-15m (10-50ft)
Spread: 3m (10ft)
Soil: Ordinary
Site: Sun or shade
'Argentea Marginata', edged white
'Golden King', broadly edged yellow
'Golden Queen', edged yellow
'Madame Briot', yellow variegated
'Silver Queen', broadly edged white

Kerria japonica 'Variegata'
(Jew's mallow)
Height: 1.2-1.8m (4-6ft)
Spread: 90cm (3ft)
Soil: Ordinary
Site: Sun or shade
White variegated

Pachysandra terminalis 'Variegata'
Height: 15-20cm (6-8in)
Spread: Indeterminate, plant 15cm (6in) apart
Soil: Ordinary, moist
Site: Shady
White variegated

Rhamnus alaterna 'Argenteo-variegata'
(Buckthorn)
Height: 1.5-3m (5-10ft)
Spread: 1.5cm (5ft)
Soil: Ordinary
Site: Open
White variegated

Vinca
(Periwinkle)
Height: trailing
Spread: Indefinite, plant 30-45cm (12-18in) apart
Soil: Ordinary
Site: Sun or shade
V. major 'Variegata', yellow variegated
V. minor 'Aureovariegata', yellow variegated
V. minor Variegata', ivory white variegated

Weigela florida 'Variegata'
Height: 2-2.4m (6½-8ft)
Spread: 1.5m (5ft)
Soil: Ordinary
Site: Open
Creamy white border to leaf

TREES
&
SHRUBS

Introduction

The elegant *Sorbus* 'Lutescens' (**top**) is prized for the flush of silvery young leaves it bears in spring. It is not fussy over soil and position. Quite different in shape and leaf form is the wide-spreading *Juniperus x media* 'Pfitzerana Aurea' (**above**). Such conifers are ideal as ground cover and specimen plants. The full splendour of *Nyssa sylvatica* (**right**) is realised during the autumn, when its foliage turns to glorious shades of red, yellow and orange.

Perhaps we should start by defining our terms. A tree is a woody plant with a central stem, usually referred to as a trunk, from which branches may radiate. In contrast to a tree with its central trunk, a shrub produces a number of woody outgrowths from its roots. If we think of the oak as a typical tree, then the rose is a typical shrub.

When considering trees we tend to think of large plants, and of shrubs as smaller, but dimensions do not always fit such definitions. Some of the Himalayan climbing roses grow into and over very large trees, whereas many trees may be happier amid an alpine garden than elsewhere. It is convenient, although unscientific, to refer to the smaller trees — say, those under 1.5m (5 ft) — as bushes, as long as we also bear in mind that what may eventually become a large tree may perfectly well begin in the garden as a bush.

Most trees grow upwards, but there are a few trees (notably some junipers) which hug the ground and eventually cover a large area. When thinking of planting a tree, it is rare for anybody to consider such a plant as *Juniperus pfitzerana* — but a tree it is. Sometimes the distinction between a shrub and a tree is tenuous.

Most rhododendrons are technically trees, but in their youth so many of their branches seem to come from soil level that they have a shrub-like appearance. It is only when they become very old that their genuinely arboreal nature is apparent. Consequently, most of us think of rhododendrons as shrubs, and it does no harm to go on doing so. Both shrubs and trees are woody, after all, and it is this feature that tends to set them apart from other denizens of the garden.

One of the great gardening writers of the last century wrote in 1871: '. . . a few trees and shrubs, a plot of grass and comfortable walks (are) the three first essentials of a garden'. To this he added a herbaceous border, and claimed that anything else was mere embellishment. Nowadays, gardens are ordinarily smaller than was usual in the 1870s, but the essential truth of his statement remains valid. With large gardens there can be no question that he was absolutely right.

Siting trees in the garden
Trees are one of the most permanent features of the garden, so their siting is a matter of the utmost importance. Herbaceous plants, bulbs, or even small shrubs, can be transplanted if placed where they subsequently do not appeal. Trees once established, on the other hand, must be regarded as fixtures. It is in fact not impossible to move large trees, at considerable expense in both money and time, but it is certainly not practical for an amateur. Far better before planting your tree to give thought to all the possible advantages and disadvantages.

There are a number of uses for trees, apart from that of pure ornament. In a small garden, for example, a tree can be the focal point for the whole design. There can be more than one focal point. Alternatively, trees can be planted round the perimeter, to mark the limits of the garden and provide an attractive background for other plants; they can be used to provide shade, to provide spectacle in blossom, flower or attractive foliage; to provide colour in spring, autumn, or even in winter; and it would seem that there are few requirements of a gardener that a tree cannot be found to supply.

The main disadvantage of trees is that they grow slowly, so that it may be many years before they achieve the desired effect. Another drawback is that the larger trees have an equally large root system under the ground which must take nourishment from the soil, to the impoverishment of other plants. This need not, of course, be catastrophic, for the nutrients can be replaced either by chemicals or by garden composts and animal waste.

Some trees are poisonous. If there are young children in the vicinity, do not plant laburnum, for instance: the seeds are toxic, and small children may mistake them for peas and eat them with dire, possibly fatal, consequences. Even worse, the only part of the yew that is *not* poisonous is the red, fleshy cup that encloses the seed: it is this that children might well be tempted to taste, and by itself it would do them no harm — but if they bit into the internal seed that the cup surrounds, they would quickly become very ill.

Of course there are plenty of suitable trees besides laburnum or yew, but with young children you can never be too careful. Thorny trees could also cause distress. Hawthorns, if they have a decent trunk, are probably out of the reach of the young, but gleditsias may have thorns on their trunks. There is, however, a thornless form of the most common gleditsia —*G. triacanthos,* known as 'Inermis' — so if you wish to see at close quarters the delicate, fern-like leaves of the honey locust, it can be done without the risk of laceration.

Another disadvantage of trees is that the ground round about them becomes extremely dry, because the canopy of leaves above may be so thick that nothing can grow underneath. This is not such a disadvantage with deciduous trees (which shed their leaves in autumn) for spring bulbs and such early-flowering subjects as primroses grow happily underneath them, just as they do in the wild, and in the dry area just beyond the effects of the canopy Mediterranean plants such as cistus and the shrubby euphorbias may find conditions to their liking.

Many of the disadvantages of trees can thus be overcome with a little forethought — the ever-present watchword of the tree planter. Before planting, you should have some idea of the final dimensions of your chosen tree. If you decide to plant a cedar, let's say, what you will probably start with is a rather small stick, maybe 90cm (3ft) high and 30cm (12in) across . . . which gets taller and wider every single year, as year follows year — and 200 years is not an excessive age for a cedar — so you

The autumn tints are just beginning to show on this *Acer palmatum* 'Osakazuki' (**far left top**). Gradually the whole tree will turn a brilliant fiery red. The range of colours and leaf shapes among conifers is very wide. This blue spruce, *Picea pungens glauca* (**far left bottom**), forms a medium-sized tree with young foliage a striking shade of blue. Aptly named the golden rain tree *Koelreuteria paniculata* (**left**) bears abundant yellow flowers in mid-summer. Grow this medium-sized tree in good loam in a sunny position.

should bear the enormous eventual tree in mind when planting the tiny sapling. Patience may be required to wait to see it at all from indoors at first — but later, if you have planted it too close to the house it will eventually take all the light away and your electricity bill will soar.

It is a sound rule of thumb that no potentially large tree should be planted nearer the house than 10m (33ft); 15m (50ft) is preferable. Tree roots can also damage a house's foundations, so the further away from the house that forest trees are planted the better. Smaller trees may have additional dangers. Poplars, willows and alders in the wild tend to grow in wet places; their roots are particularly suited for seeking out water. Should there be the smallest fissure in nearby underground drainpipes, the roots of these subjects seek them out, enter, and crack them or block them with their roots. With these plants it is necessary to find out beforehand where your drainage system runs, and to be careful not to plant any of these subjects in its vicinity. Elsewhere in the garden they do no harm, and indeed, placing a weeping willow near a small pond is a favourite ploy of garden designers.

Types of trees
Trees may be divided into angiosperms and gymnosperms or, more colloquially, into broadleaved trees and conifers. The broadleaved trees include some plants with needle-like foliage, such as the tree heather, and

at the same time the seed heads of alders are shaped much like pine cones, but in spite of these unusual forms the distinction is generally quite clear. All trees are either deciduous — losing their leaves in the autumn, overwintering with bare branches, and producing fresh leaves in the spring — or evergreen, which keep their leaves throughout the winter. In fact, with some evergreens the leaves remain on the tree for several seasons; with others, the old leaves tend to fall away as the new leaves emerge.

The reason that some plants are evergreen whereas others are deciduous is not always clear-cut. Most oaks are deciduous, for example — but some, such as the cork and holm oaks, are evergreen. Usually it would seem that where winters are ordinarily excessively cold, dark, and with frequent strong winds, the tendency is for trees to be deciduous. They are less likely to be damaged by storms and, in that their leaves need daylight in which to function, the disadvantage of the loss of daylight in winter is minimized. Although this sounds

logical, there are plants such as holly which remain evergreen even in regions where short days occur annually, and in the same contrary fashion, the inhabitants of the coldest and stormiest regions in extreme latitudes are commonly evergreen pines and firs.

The ornamental value of trees
Fortunately the gardener need not be concerned about why a plant should be evergreen or deciduous, just with the results. Evergreen trees certainly enliven the garden during the winter months, but many of them tend to look a little heavy during the summer. Moreover, the delicate tracery of boughs and branchlets of deciduous trees during the winter often has its own fascination — so, if space allows, a judicious mixture of deciduous and evergreen trees probably gives the happiest result.

Deciduous trees can have other attractions during the winter. Many of them have attractive wood. The glistening white, cream, or pale pink trunks of various birches, for instance, contrast happily with the almost thread-like twigs of the past year's growth. The green and white striations of the snake-bark maples, of which there are a number, are particularly striking at this season, as is the flaking cinnamon bark of *Acer griseum* and the polished mahogany-like appearance of the trunks of the Tibetan cherry, *Prunus serrula.*

In other deciduous plants it is the young wood that is coloured. The coral-bark maple, *Acer palmatum* 'Senkaki', is coral-pink; the young growths of some varieties of *Salix alba* are especially vivid — 'Vitellina' is orange-yellow and 'Chermesina' has red bark. Another willow, *Salix irrorata,* has young wood that is purple overlaid with a silvery bloom. It is certainly possible to have colour in the garden in winter without evergreens.

Nevertheless, evergreens are naturally also colourful at this period. *Elaeagnus pungens* 'Maculata', which has gold splashes in the centre of its dark green leaves, gives an impression of sunshine even during the dullest days. There are a number of silver and yellow variegated hollies which look attractive throughout the year but are at their best during the winter. Some columnar conifers, mainly the thujas and false cypresses, have either golden or steel-blue foliage, as do some of the larger conifers such as the blue cedar, *Cedrus atlantica* 'Glauca', and the blue spruce *Picea pungens glauca,* of which a number of named forms exist. These large blue conifers are not altogether suitable for small gardens, where a single blue tree can be simply overwhelming; when surrounded by trees of more ordinary coloration, the effect is less intense.

Coloured foliage is not confined to winter. There are a number of deciduous trees which have golden or variegated foliage, producing a longer display than either flowers or coloured fruits do. The effect is enhanced if the variegated trees are used with restraint among green-leaved trees. Such restrained use should also apply to trees with purple leaves, such as the popular *Prunus cerasifera* 'Pissardii' and the purple beech. These look splendid in the spring as the leaves are unfurling, when the sun makes them glow like rubies, but they begin to look a bit heavy as the summer advances . . . and the purple beech does nothing at all in the autumn, when the green-leaved ones are turning golden.

Some leaves, indeed, achieve colour only at one season. *Pieris formosa forrestii* has flowers like the lily-of-the-valley in spring, followed by young growth that is a vivid red, contrasting with the green leaves of the previous season. In fact, the young growths are more showy than the flowers. Another evergreen, *Photinia X fraseri,* also has young growths in various shades of red, from the coppery red of 'Robusta' to the bright red of 'Red Robin'. Many trees have silvery young leaves, including several rhododendrons and the whitebeam, *Sorbus aria.* In others, such as the Indian horse chestnut, *Aesculus indica,* and the Golden Rain tree, *Koelreutera paniculata,* the

young leaves are bronzy. The young leaves of *Maackia chinensis* are a curious mixture of slate-blue and silver; the tree looks spectacular for a fortnight, but is rather dull thereafter.

Even more trees turn brilliant colours in the autumn. One of the most useful, although small, has the unwieldy name of *Malus tchonoskii;* it has an upright habit. Its leaves are silver, and turn a succession of flame-like tints before they fall in the autumn. Some of the maples previously mentioned for their handsome bark also colour red and gold before the leaves fall; those of the coral-bark maple, *Acer palmatum* 'Senkaki', on the other hand, turn butter yellow. *Acer palmatum* 'Osakasuki' turns a really fiery scarlet. The tupelo, *Nyssa sylvatica,* which is inconspicuous for most of the year — you may have to search to find the small greenish flowers at all — suddenly transforms itself into a pillar of fire. The Golden Rain tree, which has almost all the advantages — handsome young leaves, attractive mature foliage, late yellow flowers, followed by bronzy bladder-like capsules — closes its repertoire with golden, or occasionally scarlet, tints.

Tree shapes
The shapes of trees are significant. Basically, trees grow as pyramids: the older, lower branches extend for some distance, while the younger, upper ones progressively do so less and less. In a garden without competition from others, trees maintain this shape for a long time. In forests, as the trees enlarge, the light

is cut off from the lower branches, which die and fall off to expose the trunk. In a situation without competition, if a bare trunk is required, you may have actually to saw away the lower branches. Many nurserymen provide what are termed 'standards', in which the trunk (not infrequently of another species) is already formed. Standard amelanchiers, for example, are frequently amelanchiers budded on to the trunk of a whitebeam; and standard cherries are almost always budded on to a trunk of the wild cherry. In such cases it is essential to keep the trunk clear, or the stock may overtake the plant you require.

Shapes can alter, however. Many trees that are normally pyramidal have both fastigiate and weeping forms. Fastigiate trees are like spires in outline; the side branches rise perpendicularly rather than horizontally. The Lombardy poplar is a good example. Such forms are usually called 'fastigiata' in catalogues. Weeping trees have branches that tend to droop, with the branchlets hanging down. These are usually called 'pendula' in the catalogues, and the weeping willow is among the best known. A third type comprises the 'tabular' trees — those in which both branches and branchlets are horizontal, so that the trees look like a series of layers. The Cedar of Lebanon is a good example. In general, trees seem to be tabular by nature: no unusual tabular shapes have been recorded. As they age, some trees become round-topped and others flat, but not before the trees have acquired their full dimensions.

Weeping
Hybridization and selective breeding have produced a number of beautiful weeping trees, notably weeping willows and birches.

Conical
Many trees, especially conifers, assume a conical shape when mature. In a forest the lower branches may not develop fully.

Fastigiate
These trees have a narrow columnar shape. Prime examples are the Lombardy poplar and many garden forms of conifers.

Spreading
Most broadleaved trees assume an open spreading shape with a rounded top. The oak tree is a classic example of this type of growth.

Planting trees in the garden

The actual operation of planting trees requires care and forethought. It makes comparatively little difference whether the trees arrive from the nursery lifted from the ground or whether they have been kept in containers. It is claimed that container-grown trees can be planted at any time of the year, even when they are in flower, but this is only true to a limited extent. It is generally not the state of the tree when purchased that is important, as much as the ease with which it can become established. And to become established means making abundant root growth during its first season. A plant removed from a container in mid-summer normally survives, it is true, but makes little growth for the rest of the year — and so is more vulnerable to a bad winter, and is certainly slower again to get away in the following season.

In theory, the container-grown plant should get away more rapidly if planted at the correct season. This does not always happen, however, often because the roots have become so convoluted in their containers that unless they are teased out when planted, they take a long time to penetrate the soil in the garden. This has been found actually to be the case in some nurseries where plants that have unexpectedly made no significant growth have been lifted, and it has been seen that the roots have found it impossible to escape from the original soil ball, and have thus remained pot-bound. Unlikely though it sounds, therefore, it is best, if the container seems excessively full of roots, to shake the soil off the roots and try to rearrange them in a normal spread.

In nature most trees send down one long root to anchor the plant, and then send out roots in all directions to gather nourishment from the soil. In a container all the roots are forced into the shape of the container. In fact, they become distorted. So although one of the advantages of the potted plant is that it can be planted without disturbing the roots, there is also the fact that, to a limited extent, the roots become damaged just by being grown in a restricted space.

Sometimes the grower has no choice. Brooms have a long taproot, breaking which kills the plant. Brooms must on that account be grown in pots before planting out; it is very doubtful whether brooms lifted from the open ground would transplant successfully. It has also been found that clematis are very difficult to move unless grown in pots. Apart from these few exceptions, the majority of trees move quite happily from the open ground.

Acer pseudoplatanus 'Prinz Handjery' (**right**), a small tree for garden planting.

How to plant trees

| First dig a hole large enough to take the roots of the tree and loosen the soil at the bottom to a depth of at least 30cm (12in). | Insert a tree stake securely into the ground on the side facing the direction of the prevailing wind (i.e. into the wind). | Set the tree in the hole, carefully spreading out the roots. To prevent infection trim off any damaged or broken roots. | Add well-rotted manure or peat before returning the soil. Firm down and attach the tree to the stake with adjustable ties. | Prune the branches of newly planted bare-rooted trees by about one third to compensate for any damage sustained by the roots. | Having watered the tree thoroughly, apply a mulch around the base of the tree to a depth of 5cm (2in) to conserve moisture in the soil. |

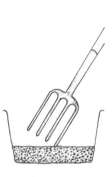 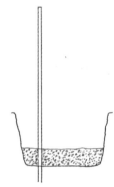  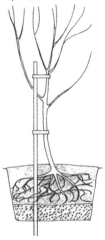 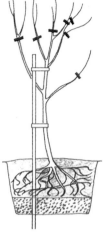 

When to plant trees

The period for planting trees varies somewhat according to the habit. Deciduous trees have an obvious dormant period when leaves are off them, and so are best moved at any suitable time between late autumn and early spring. Evergreens seem to be best moved either in mid-autumn or in mid-spring, although they are never fully dormant. If they are moved in mid-autumn, the soil is still warm enough to encourage some root growth before the cold weather discourages the roots from elongating. Similarly, by mid-spring the soil is warming up again and the roots should start to grow at once.

Whether you prefer the autumn to the spring may depend to a certain extent on where you live. Where spring is usually rather dry, autumn would seem to be a better time to plant evergreens, whereas where spring is wetter, spring may be preferred. It is not critical which of these seasons you choose, however, rather a matter of convenience. Deciduous trees have a longer period during which they can be planted, but since mid- to late winter may be very frosty in temperature climates, late autumn and early winter are slightly preferable.

Obviously, the main purpose behind all the methodology in planting trees is to get them established and growing as soon as possible. One way of actively encouraging this is to keep the tree out of the soil for as short a time as possible — which may entail preparing the site before the plant arrives. Of course some adjustment may be necessary, depending on the size of plant you then obtain, but some general spade-work can be carried out in advance. Excavate a circular hole about 1.2m (4ft) in diameter and 45cm (18in) deep. With a fork, loosen the soil for a further 30cm (12in) at the

bottom of the hole.

When planting a tree in the lawn, remove the turf around the hole so as to make a bed at least 2m (6½ft) — or preferably 3m (10ft) — in diameter (with the planting hole in the centre). Grass might otherwise take a lot of nutrients from the soil at the expense of the tree; indeed, one way of restricting the growth of trees is to allow a lawn to come up close to the trunk. (You may wish to do this much later, but not with a new tree.)

When the tree arrives, examine the roots and take off with secateurs any parts that may be cracked or split. Set the tree in the hole and ensure that the soil level is the same as that in which the tree was originally growing. Because there will inevitably be some subsidence as the soil firms down, heap up the soil a few centimetres above the old soil level, but not more. For many trees it is bad to be planted too deeply and, in the case of rhododendrons, it may prove fatal. It is at this time that you may have to make adjustments either upwards or downwards to your original excavation. Sprinkle some peat or well-rotted manure around the roots and cover them with soil. Then add a scattering of bonemeal or hoof and horn, or some slow-release chemical fertilizer.

The next thing is to stake the tree. Unless it is given time to establish itself in your garden, it will be very susceptible to the effects of wind. Rocking can harm the tree in two ways: it can break the roots, and it can cause an abraded hole through the outer layers to appear round the bottom of the trunk, into which rain can seep and rot the wood. So a good stake, although expensive, is essential, and is most easily inserted before you fill in the hole. It should be about 15cm (6in) from the trunk and carefully situated on the side of the prevailing wind, i.e. into the wind. Now fill in

the hole simultaneously treading the earth firmly around the roots. Once this is done, attach the tree to the stake. It is possible to buy adjustable ties which have a buckle, enabling you to loosen the tie as the trunk expands over the years. Wire or rope might chafe the trunk and cause damage, so a tie must be fairly wide and flexible.

However much care has been taken at the nursery, the roots of your new tree will have sustained some damage, so it is sound policy to lighten their burden and shorten the aerial parts of the tree by about one-third. In this way the roots are able to supply what is left. Conditions during the first year are critical for the tree, so be sure that the soil does not dry out. Moisture is best retained with a mulch; put this on in spring when the soil has become moist. Peat, farmyard manure or shredded bark are all suitable mulches, and should be put on to a depth of 5cm (2in). Garden compost, leaf mould or bracken are also suitable. A mulch is essential for the first year; repeated in succeeding years, growth is that much more rapid.

On no account should trees be planted when the ground is waterlogged or frozen. If such conditions do obtain when the plants arrive, they will be quite happy for some time in a cool shed; the roots should be covered in sacking, especially if frost is likely, but they do not need to be warm. If water lies for any length of time in the hole you have dug, you have probably chosen an unsuitable site and must think again. Many trees are unsuitable for soils with a high water table — but a local nurseryman should be able to advise you on this. It makes little difference with shallow-rooted plants such as rhododendrons, but some of the larger trees die if their roots descend to permanent water.

Small deciduous trees

The choice of trees, although for many reasons far less than it was some ten years ago, is still large, and we should perhaps start by considering small deciduous trees. By 'small', a final height of around 10m (33ft) is implied. Alphabetically, we should no doubt commence with *Abutilon vitifolium* and its hybrid *A. X suntense*. Rapid in growth, these are bushes rather than trees, with greyish leaves and lavender or deep mauve flowers in early summer; the flowers look like small hollyhocks. Usually the plant is not very long-lived, but it comes very rapidly from seed.

Many of the maples are rather too large for this category, but most of the snake-barks grow at moderate latitudes, as do the Japanese maples, which are forms of *Acer palmatum* cultivated for many centuries in Japan. Although they eventually make small trees, they are very slow-growing and take many years even to exceed bush dimensions. They resent excessive wind, but otherwise presen few problems, although chalky soil migh prove unsuitable. There are forms with green, variegated and purple leaves; many of them colour brilliantly in the autumn; and the young wood of 'Senkaki' has been mentioned already. The snake-barks include *A. capillipes, A. davidii, A. grosseri, A. pennsylvanicum* and *A. rufinerve:* all make small trees with striated trunks, and most also have good autumn colour. Giving the trunks a good scrub with a brush in the autumn shows them to the best advantage. *Acer griseum* has peeling bark, revealing cinnamon-coloured wood below and the most gorgeous autumn tints. It has apparently been known to make quite a large tree — but it grows almost infinitely slowly. Another species of *Acer*, the sycamore, is far too large for this section but has two dwarf forms with showily coloured young leaves: *A. pseudoplatanus* 'Brilliantissimum' and 'Prinz

Handjery'. The young leaves, often described as shrimp pink fade to greenish yellow.

The amelanchier is a marvellous small tree, with purplish young leaves, white flowers in late spring, and good autumn colours. Its botanical name is *Amelanchier X lamarckii,* but it is just as liable to turn up in catalogues as *A. canadensis, A. laevis* or *A. grandiflora.* Whatever alias it goes under, it is a first-rate small tree. Its Chinese relative, *A. asiatica,* has a more graceful habit and flowers even more freely. It does not turn colour in autumn but may then produce a second crop of flowers.

Berberis are usually regarded as smallish shrubs, but in suitable conditions some can attain quite a size; most of them are evergreen, however. But plants of the Carminea group, such as 'Barbarossa', can quickly reach 2m (6½ft). The yellow flowers open in early summer, but it is autumn when fruits and leaves turn crimson that the plant is at its best. *Berberis temolaica* can reach 3m (10ft), and has glaucous blue leaves on arching stems which make an impressive foliage feature. The plant is sometimes rather slow to re-establish itself after being moved.

Most of the buddleias tend to be shrubby in appearance, although they do have a short trunk. In the case of *Buddleia alternifolia,* though, it is worth shaping the tree to have a visible trunk at least 1m (3¼ft) tall so that its weeping character becomes evident. It has narrow, silvery leaves, and in mid-summer the branches are covered with small, fragrant lavender flowers. It is one of the most delightful small trees of any description. The common butterfly bush, *B. davidii,* seems to produce its best effects if annually pruned hard in early spring, making a rather awkward-looking plant for part of the year. This treatment does, however, result in longer panicles of flowers in late summer. There are a number of colour forms varying from white through various shades of mauve and violet to red and crimson-purple; 'Harlequin' has the

leaves variegated with ivory. In sheltered districts it is worth growing the large *B. colvilei,* which bears large crimson flowers in early summer. Young plants are frost tender, but older plants seem hardy. The showiest of all buddleias, it may reach 8m (26ft).

The Judas tree, *Cercis siliquastrum,* rarely exceeds 6m (20ft) in height, although it may spread sideways to a greater extent. Before the kidney-shaped leaves emerge, rosy purple pea-shaped flowers wreathe the branches and

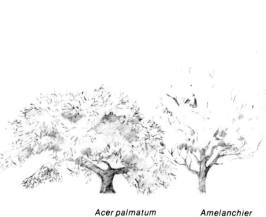

Acer palmatum   *Amelanchier X lamarckii*

Cercis siliquastrum

Cornus alba   *Buddleia davidii*

Cornus kousa chinensis (**left**) develops into an elegant small tree with large white flower bracts in mid summer. *Cornus florida rubra* (**below left**) produces its floral display in late spring and early summer. Rose-pink bracts surround the tiny flowers. *Amelanchier X lamarkii* (**right**) bears a mass of white spring blooms. For a deep pink spring show choose *Cratagus oxyacantha* 'Rosea Flore Pleno' (**below**).

may even sprout from the trunk. A few years' waiting achieves the full effect. Spring frosts may affect the flowers, which open in late spring; the tree is actually native to the Mediterranean and so unsuitable for very cold districts.

Clerodendrum trichotomum is more a large shrub than a tree, but it can reach 4.5m (15ft) or more. There are few late-flowering shrubs, but this one is at its best in early autumn, when it produces panicles of white, fragrant flowers about 2.5cm (1in) across and backed by dark crimson sepals. If the autumn is warm enough these may be followed by bright blue fruits which make an extraordinary addition to the repertoire of coloured fruits. Another large, late-flowering shrub is the Chilean *Colletia armata,* which covers itself in mid-autumn with small, fragrant white flowers. It is ferociously spiny, making gorse seem quite innocuous — but it does give a fine display at a time when there is little else, growing up to 2.4m (8ft) in height.

The dogwoods form an important group of garden plants, although their flowers are not outstanding. Three species — *Cornus florida, C. nuttallii* and *C. kousa chinensis* — have small flowers surrounded by large white bracts (pink in *C. florida rubra*) so that they give the effect of being covered with flowers. *C. florida* seems only to flower well in milder regions — colouring vividly in autumn — but the other two are more hardy, *C. kousa chinensis* being the best. The latter can in time make a tree up to 7m (23ft) tall, but such large plants are rare; the others are smaller. In addition, *C. kousa* can produce large red fruits like strawberries in autumn, although these are rarely seen if there is only one plant present. Cross-fertilization seems to improve the chances of this fruiting. *C. kousa* flowers in mid-summer; the others about three weeks earlier. In the same genus, *Cornus alba* is a suckering shrub that grows up to 3m (10ft) high with brilliant red bark, at its best in 'Sibirica'. 'Spaethii' has less brilliant wood, but the leaves are variegated with gold so that it is ornamental in summer as well as in winter. *Cornus controversa* makes a sizeable tree with tabular branches on which heads of cream flowers open in late spring. It is rather too large for this section, but its variegated form ('Variegata') remains a small tree rarely exceeding 6m (20ft). It has the same tabular habit, and the leaves have attractive silver variegation, making this one of the most appealing of small trees.

The *Corylopsis* group of shrubs bear racemes of flowers that look like large catkins. The earliest to flower is *C. pauciflora,* which needs an acid soil. It has primrose flowers in early spring. The others also have yellow flowers; one of the best is *C. willmottiae* 'Spring Purple', which can reach 2m (6½ft) or more, and in which the young leaves are plum-coloured. Mid-spring is the season for *Corylopsis,* for the flowers can be ruined by spring frosts.

The 'smoke' or 'wig' tree, *Cotinus coggygria,* is noteworthy for its circular leaves and the curious threads that surround the small flowers and give a smoky impression. The plants can reach 4m (13ft) high, but are usually smaller. Most forms colour well in the autumn and have threads that are fawn in hue; in 'Purpureus', however, the threads are pinkish. There are a number of purple-leaved forms with different names: 'Royal Purple', for example, has dark purple leaves. They all tend to turn crimson before falling.

The hawthorns, species of *Crataegus,* are splendid small trees with white flowers,

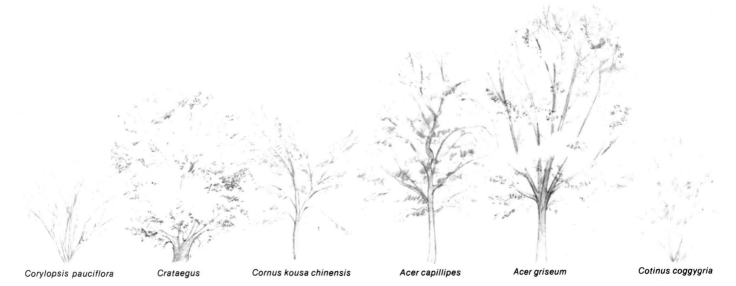

Corylopsis pauciflora   *Crataegus*   *Cornus kousa chinensis*   *Acer capillipes*   *Acer griseum*   *Cotinus coggygria*

coloured fruits, and often good autumn colour. Forms of May, *C. oxycantha,* have been found with double white flowers, and single and double red and pink flowers. These are showy when in bloom but have little to offer at other times. One of the best of the remaining species is the Washington thorn, *C. phaenopyrum,* which does not open its flowers until mid-summer, when flowering trees are scarce. Later it bears haws that look as if they had been dipped in scarlet sealing-wax; there are also splendid autumn tints in the foliage. The cockspur thorn, *C. crus-galli,* has very long thorns, up to 7.5cm (3in) long, but makes up for that with large, handsome flowers, large red fruits and a superb autumn display. Closely allied, but with even longer thorns, is *C. macracantha.* There are few species in this genus which are not good small trees.

Deutzias are delightful shrubs closely allied to the syringas but with smaller flowers in racemes. They rarely exceed 2m (6½ft) in height, although *D. scabra* can reach 3.6m (12ft). The flowers are mainly white, but there are some pale purple flowers such as 'Mont Rose' and 'Perle Rose'. They are shrubs rather than trees, and are delightful garden plants. Most flower in early summer, but *D. gracilis* comes out in late spring; *D. scabra* may well wait until mid-summer.

The oleasters contain both evergreen and deciduous species. Of the latter the Silver Berry, *Elaeagnus commutata,* is a suckering shrub with young leaves which really do look as though they were made from silver. *Elaeagnus angustifolius* can eventually make a moderate-sized tree with silvery willow-like leaves, small but extremely fragrant flowers, and eventually a polished trunk. It grows rapidly but seems to take its time to make a sizeable base; it is rather thorny.

In an acid soil, the various species of *Enkianthus* are well worth growing. They all make small shrubs — usually less than 2m (6½ft) high — and have remarkably sym-

In an acid soil *Ucryphia glutinosa* (**right**) will bear large white flowers in late summer and put on a splendid display of red and orange foliage in autumn. The snowdrop trees, *Halesia* (**below** and **below right**), are well named for the rows of droopy white flowers that adorn the branches in late spring. *Laburnum* 'Vossii' (**far right**) is prized for its early summer show of yellow, slightly fragrant flowers in pendulous racemes.

metrical growths, with the leaves in whorls. The bell-shaped flowers emerge at the same time as the leaves, and in the most frequently grown, *E. campanulatus,* they are pale yellow tipped with red. It can make a small tree up to 3.6m (12ft), and the leaves generally colour well in the autumn. If obtainable, *E. chinensis* makes a larger plant. The heather family really does require an acid soil, though.

Eucryphia glutinosa is a glorious small tree with pinnate leaves which usually colour well before falling, and in late summer white flowers up to 6cm (2¼in) across, looking like single roses. It prefers an acid soil and is the only deciduous species in cultivation.

Good autumn colour is not always easy to obtain on chalky soils, but the spindle tree, *Euonymus europaeus,* is a small tree that in autumn is bright with pink, orange-seeded fruits and flaming leaves. 'Red Cascade' is a particularly good fruiting clone. *E. latifolius* is rather more of a shrub, but has larger leaves and fruits which mature in early autumn.

Exochordas are spreading bushes with long

Elaeagnus angustifolius   *Genista aetnensis*   *Laburnum 'Vossii'*   *Exochorda X macracantha*   *Ekianthus campanulatus*   *Hamamelis japonica*

racemes of white flowers in late spring. *E. racemosa* is the most usually seen, and needs an acid or neutral soil. The larger, flowered hybrid *E. X macracantha,* however, tolerates some alkalinity as do most of the other species.

Most of the ash trees are too large for this section — but if it can be obtained, *Fraxinus mariesii* is one of the most elegant of small trees, with purplish young leaves, heads of creamy flowers in early summer, followed by purple keys (seeds). It is difficult to obtain but very rewarding.

The Mount Etna broom, *Genista aetnensis,* makes a tree up to 3m (10ft) with mainly leafless twigs covered in yellow pea-like flowers in mid-summer. The snowdrop trees, *Halesia,* require an acid soil but make very handsome small trees, covered with white, snowdrop-like flowers in late spring.

The witch hazels, *Hamamelis,* are noted mainly for their spidery yellow flowers which open at any suitable time from early winter to early spring. They tend to spread outwards rather than grow upwards and are not rapid in growth, although they start to flower when quite small. The Chinese witch hazel, *H. mollis,* is perhaps slightly preferable to *H. japonica,* but both are excellent plants. There are also hybrids between them, some — such as 'Diane' — that have reddish flowers; 'Jelena' is coppery. The leaves of witch hazels colour well before falling.

From New Zealand come two valuable late-flowering small trees, *Hoheria glabrata* and *lyalii,* which produce clusters of flowers like large cherry blossom at mid-summer. Their vulnerability to severe winter frosts may account for their relative rarity in temperate gardens. They are rapid in growth, with quite handsome greyish leaves, and are well worth the risk.

The superb Golden Rain tree, *Koelreutera paniculata,* which we have already mentioned, has been known to exceed a height of 10m (33ft), but this is fairly unusual; it is a plant no garden should be without.

The beauty bush, *Kolkwitzia amabilis,* makes a large spreading bush which covers itself with pink, yellow-throated bell-shaped flowers in early summer. The foliage is also quite attractive, although not exciting. Laburnum has very poisonous seeds, but the falling racemes of yellow flowers in early summer are extremely attractive, particularly in the hybrid usually known as 'Vossii', which has extra-long racemes.

Magnolias must be among the most popular of all flowering trees. The most frequently seen is *M. X soulangeana,* which bears white flowers, some with a blotch of purple at the base of the petals. There are also purple flowers in 'Lennei', which also flowers later than most, and reddish flowers in 'Picture' and 'Rustica rubra'. 'Alba Superba' is pure white. Although they eventually make trees to 10m (33ft), they are slow growers, but they flower from an early age. In districts where spring frosts are frequent, *M. sinensis* — which has hanging white flowers with a boss of crimson stamens — may be preferable. It does not flower until early summer. *M. wilsonii* is very similar. In sheltered districts, the huge-flowered *M. campbellii,* and *M. sargentii robusta,* which has pink, red, white or purple flowers, may be grown but they come into flower in early spring, are susceptible to wind damage, and do not flower until well-grown, so they are suitable only for sheltered gardens and patient gardeners. Smaller trees with smaller white flowers are provided by the hybrids *M. X loebneri* and *M. X proctoriana;* these start to flower quite soon. *M. X loebneri* 'Leonard Messel' has pale purple flowers.

The crab apples, species of *Malus,* make delightful small trees with attractive flowers; some species also have attractive fruits. There are also a number of hybrids with purple leaves. So many good ones are available that it is best to see a collection. *M. baccata,* is one of the best for fruit; *M. spectabilis* 'Riversii' has delightful semi-double pink flowers; and *M. tchonoskii* has silver young leaves and a very spectacular autumn display.

In acid soil, the sorrel tree, *Oxydendrum arboreum,* makes an attractive tree with flowers like the lily-of-the-valley in late summer and very brilliant autumn colours. It seems slightly temperamental, but where it grows well it is an unusual feature in any garden.

The mock orange, *Philadelphus,* tends to make bushes rather than trees, and the genus contains some desirable plants. *P. purpurascens* has white flowers with purple calices and is one of the first to appear in early summer. *P. coronarius* is the best known and has forms with golden and with variegated leaves. Some of the hybrids, however, are even better plants: 'Etoile Rose' is a smallish bush with a purple blotch at the base of the petals; 'Virginal' has double flowers; and *P. incanus* makes a much larger shrub and does not flower before mid-summer.

Prunus, the almonds, plums and cherries, is a very large genus of small trees, all highly

Magnolia soulangiana   *Malus baccata*   *Malus tchonoskii*   *Euonymus europaeus*   *Oxydendrun arboreum*   *Prunus sargentii*

suitable for the garden. One of the best, if a largish tree is needed, is *P. sargentii,* which covers itself in pink cherry blossom in early spring and turns crimson before the leaves fall in the autumn. Two species, *P. maackii* and *P. serrula,* are grown for their bark rather than their flowers. There are so many gems that again it is best to view a collection.

The willow-leaved pear, *Pyrus salicifolia,* makes a very attractive small tree with pendulous branches, silvery leaves, and the usual pear blossom.

Most rhododendrons are evergreen, but the azaleas contain some attractive deciduous species. Apart from the hybrids, particularly appealing are *R. albrechtii,* which has plum-purple flowers, and *R. schlippenbachii,* with large pink flowers; they do, however, flower in early spring, and so may be damaged by frosts. The North American *R. vaseyi,* which has smaller pink flowers, flowers later and might be more reliable in severe climates.

Robinias make attractive small trees with ferny leaves and racemes of purplish flowers — but they are very brittle, and must be sheltered from strong winds. The best known, *R. pseudoacacia,* is a large tree. The golden-leaved 'Frisia', on the other hand, seems of more moderate dimensions. *R. hispida* and *R. viscosa* are agreeable small trees.

The elders, *Sambucus* species, make small trees, and some of the golden-leaved forms of

S. nigra and *S. racemosa* are among the best golden trees for the garden. *S. racemosa* also has attractive red fruits. *S. canadensis* 'Maxima' has cream flower-heads up to 30cm (12in) across, followed by almost black fruits.

The genus *Sorbus* includes both the rowans and the whitebeams. For red fruit none is better than *S. aucuparia,* of which 'Edulis' has the largest fruits. *S. cashmiriana* has pink flowers and large pendulous white fruits; 'Joseph Rock' has yellow fruits and good autumn colour. *S. esserteauana* 'Flava' also has yellow fruits. *S. hupehensis* has glaucous blue leaves and pale pink fruits, as has the small graceful *S. vilmorinii.* Silver leaves are the main attraction of the whitebeam *S. aria.*

Stewartias are again attractive small trees for acid soils. They have white flowers in mid- and late summer, and usually good autumn

The large blooms of *Prunus* 'Shirotae' (**far left**) smother the branches of this compact Japanese cherry tree in spring. The blooms are pure white and fragrant, carried in long drooping clusters. An excellent garden tree growing up to 6m (20ft) in height. For delicate sprays of yellow-green foliage choose *Robinia pseudoacacia* 'Frisia' (**left**). This attractive tree, up to 6m (20ft) tall, will grow in any garden soil and tolerate polluted air. For an acid soil plant *Styrax japonica* (**above**). The white flowers are borne profusely in midsummer.

colour. *S. koreana* and *S. sinensis* eventually have handsome trunks with flaking bark. They resent being moved.

Styrax, with hanging white flowers at midsummer, are attractive small trees but slightly tender; they too require an acid soil. *S. japonica* is the easiest to obtain, and one of the best.

Syringas include all the lilacs and a number of pink-flowered hybrids called *S. X josiflexa,* of which 'Belicent' is probably the best. *S. velutina palibiniana* is a dwarf lilac which usually flowers in spring and again in autumn.

The viburnums include winter flowerers such as *V. X bodnantense,* berrying shrubs such as the Guelder rose *V. opulus* and *V. betulifolium,* fragrant flowers as in *V. carlesii* and its hybrids, and showy flowers as in the tabular *V. plicatum.* These tend to be bushy in habit, but can be trained with a trunk.

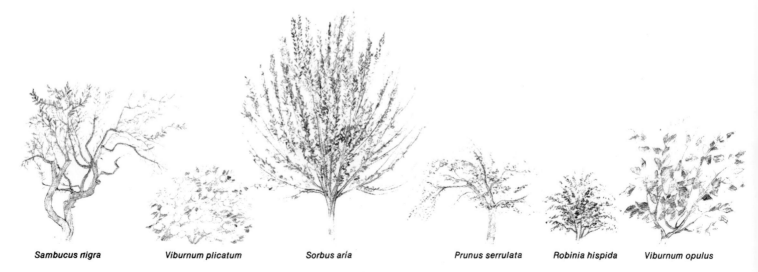

Sambucus nigra   **Viburnum plicatum**   **Sorbus aria**   **Prunus serrulata**   **Robinia hispida**   **Viburnum opulus**

Small evergreen trees and shrubs

Among the smaller evergreen shrubs the genus *Arbutus* is known from its fruits as the strawberry tree. Unlike most ericaceous plants, both the strawberry tree and its hybrid with the eastern Mediterranean *A. andrachne* known as *A. X andrachnoides,* are lime-tolerant. Both also flower and fruit at the same time, in late autumn. The rather more tender *A. arachne* flowers in spring. Apart from attractive fruits and flowers, strawberry trees also have ornamental cinnamon-coloured bark. The Californian madrona, *A. menziensii,* can make a larger tree and has panicles of white flowers in late spring followed by small orange fruits, also in panicles. This requires specifically acid soil and is on the tender side.

Azaras are smallish trees from Chile, with leaves of differing sizes opposite each other, and heads of fragrant but small yellow flowers in late winter and early spring. The plants do not tolerate too prolonged frosts.

In suitable districts, *Berberis darwinii* can make a small tree, although in cooler situations it is rarely more than a large bush. Its orange flowers are conspicuous in spring, but less colourful than the orange-red flowers of *B. linearifolia,* which always remains a smaller plant. The dark blue berries are covered with a plum-like bloom in the autumn.

The bottle brushes, species of *Callistemon,* do not like severe frosts. *C. citrinus* 'Splendens', however, which has crimson bottle brushes and rigid, needle-like leaves, is reasonably easy to cultivate; the yellow *C. salignus* seems even hardier. They grow readily and rapidly from the dust-like seeds, at least in the early stages. Acid soil seems preferable. The flowers girdle the twigs, which continue to elongate briefly after the buds have formed. The colour comes not from petals but from filaments of the stamens.

Acid soil is also necessary for the camellias, but in spite of their exotic appearance the majority are hardy even in very cold districts. They flower in early spring, so it is as well to locate them where they do not catch the early morning sun — where, in fact, the flowers if frosted overnight can thaw out slowly, so possibly escaping damage. Most popular are the various cultivars of *C. japonica,* occurring in single, semi-double, and fully double forms, in colours ranging from deep red through pinks to white; some even have striped petals; one or two have fringed petals. They also vary in habit: some spread and others are erect — but all flower in early and mid-spring. They start flowering when quite small but can eventually make fairly sizeable trees, although they are rather slow-growing.

Callistemon salignus **(left)** produces its creamy bottlebrush flowers in early summer above the evergreen foliage.

Camellias **(below)** bring colour to the garden in spring. Many varieties are available in reds, pinks and white.

In 1924 George Forrest introduced *Camellia saluenensis* from China, which bears pale pink flowers in late winter. A delightful shrub in itself, albeit more tender than *C. japonica,* it has been much used as a parent in hybrids, which are often better garden plants than *C. japonica.* One of these hybrids is *C. X williamsii,* from which a number of cultivars have been developed, flowering from late winter to late spring. 'Donation' is probably the best known of these. Most of the plants are various shades of pink; 'Francis Hanger', however, has white flowers. A good example of hybrid vigour is 'Salutation', which is perfectly hardy but which has *C. saluenensis* and *C. reticulata* — both somewhat tender species — as its parents. *C. reticulata* has the larger flowers, but both need a fairly mild climate to survive. *C. saluenensis* has alternatively been crossed with the small-flowered *C. cuspidata* to produce 'Cornish Snow', which has small white flowers in very early spring and attractive copper-coloured young growth. Although the flowers are small, they are produced with great freedom. In very mild districts it may be possible to grow *C. grantha-*

Pyrus salicifolia

Sorbus aucuparia

Sambucus racemosa

Syringa velutina palibiniana

Arbutus unedo

Berberis darwinii

miana, a plant from Hong Kong, with large white flowers in early winter followed again by coppery young growth. *C. sasanqua* has small flowers in winter, but seems to experience difficulty in flowering in too temperate climes, apparently requiring a consistently hot summer to initiate flowers.

Ceanothus tend to succumb to severe winters, but they come up rapidly from cuttings. No other tree has such fine blue flowers. With the exception of the hybrids 'Burkwoodii' and 'Autumnal Blue', they all flower in late spring or early summer. The earliest to flower is also one of the largest, *C. arboreus,* of which 'Trewithen Blue' has the best colour. Most of the species come from the western USA, mainly California, which indicates its ideal conditions. The genus can hybridize in the wild, and in fact the reasonably hardy *C. X veitchianus* is one of such natural hybrids; 'Cascade' makes a weeping tree. *C. thyrsiflorus* is one of the hardiest of the species. 'Autumnal Blue' and 'Burkwoodii' flower from mid-summer to early autumn but do not make so massive a display at any one time as do the spring flowerers.

Cistus are mainly rather small bushes, although *C. ladanifer* can attain 3m (10ft) in height. They come up rapidly from seed or from cuttings, but they can succumb to prolonged winter frosts — in any case, they are not very long-lived plants. The flat, rose-like flowers open over a long period in late spring and early summer, but each flower lasts only a day to be replaced by another flower the next day. *C. albidus* has silvery leaves and rather muddy purple flowers. During winter, the leaves of *C. laurifolius* — one of the hardiest species — turn glaucous grey. The bud-scales of the white-flowered *C. populifolius* are bright red. *C. ladanifer* has large white flowers with a crimson blotch in the centre; it seems to do best on acid soil, whereas the other species grow in any soil. All need a sunny situation.

The larger cotoneasters are mainly

The bright blue blooms of *Ceanothus x veitchianus* (**above**) are borne in profusion during late spring and early summer. A sunny spot and light soil will suit it best. White flowers smother the arching stems of *Cotoneaster conspicuous* (**right**) in early summer. Bright red berries follow in the autumn.

Erica lusitanica (**above**) may reach 3m (10ft) high. The pink flower buds formed in winter open in early spring into fragrant white flowers. The superb deep pink blooms of *Kalmia latifolia* 'Clementine Churchill' (**right**) grace this 1.5m (5ft) bush in mid-summer. Grow kalmias in a lime-free soil.

evergreen. Most are grown for their numerous coloured fruits. The exception is *C. conspicuus,* some forms of which are prostrate and are commonly trained to fall over walls or down banks. They have quite large white flowers in early summer, produced singly along the branches, followed by large crimson berries in the autumn. Most of the others are moderate trees belonging to the 'Watereri' group of hybrids between *C. salicifolius* and the deciduous *C. frigidus.* These have heads of rather dull cream flowers in mid-summer, followed by great heads of red or yellow fruits in autumn. The fruits of 'Salmon Spray' are (not surprisingly) salmon pink; those of 'Rothschildianus' are creamy yellow. *C. lacteus* and *C. glaucophyllus serotinus* flower in late summer and retain their fruits until late winter.

Crinodendron hookeranum, the Japanese

lantern tree, is a gem albeit on the tender side. Its crimson, drooping, lantern-like flowers open in late spring or early summer. Like so many Chilean shrubs, it needs shade around the roots and an acid or neutral soil. Once established, it usually regenerates, although it can be damaged during severe winters: the flower buds are formed in autumn and a bad winter may therefore disrupt the next season's flowers.

There are at least two evergreen species of *Elaeagnus* which deserve mention. *E. macrophyllus* has almost circular leaves, silver on both sides when young but later only on the underside, and small but very fragrant white flowers in mid or late autumn. *E. pungens* 'Maculata', with a bright gold splash in the centre of each leaf, is one of the glories of the winter garden; it spreads more widely than it

Cotoneaster frigidus

Embothrium coccineum lanceolatum

Elaeagnus pungens

Erica arborea

Ceanothus arboreus

ascends, and grows rapidly. The variegation is not apparent in the leaves before they are fairly well developed — so patience and considerable caution is required before removing shoots that look as though they are reverting.

The Chilean fire bush *Embothrium coccineum lanceolatum* is yet another spectacular Chilean requiring acid soil and shade for its roots. It dislikes root disturbance, so must be brought into the garden as a young plant, preferably container-grown; it also likes a fairly moist root run. The rather spire-like small tree's branches, when mature, are covered with spidery orange-scarlet flowers in late spring and early summer, and justify all the trouble required to grow this shrub successfully.

There are three tree heathers suitable for temperate gardens: the rosy purple *Erica australis,* which is also the tenderest; *E. arborea,* which can form a true tree in sheltered districts, and which has fragrant white flowers in mid- to late spring; and the smaller but earlier-flowering *E. lusitanica,* which has pink buds that open to white flowers in early spring. All need acid soil. In milder districts, some of the South African species, like *E. canaliculata* — which can reach 5m (16ft) — might be tried.

Escallonias are fairly low-growing for the most part, with arching stems and heads of pink or red flowers from early summer to early autumn. *E. X iveyi,* however, is a much larger tree, up to 5m (16ft) tall, with white flowers in late summer and early autumn. Many of the hybrids grow excellently near the sea, seemingly impervious to salt spray.

The evergreen eucryphias are generally somewhat tender, but there are two hybrids with the hardier Chilean deciduous *E. glutinosa* that grow in most places with acid soil. *E. X intermedia* 'Rostrevor' is a hybrid between *E. glutinosa* and *E. lucida* from Tasmania: it makes a fairly upright small tree which does not flower before maturing, but then covers itself in small white flowers in late summer and early autumn. *E. X nymansensis* 'Nymansay' makes a columnar small tree with large white flowers in late summer and early autumn. Both hybrids have white flowers much like single roses in appearance.

Fatsia japonica — more popular in the last century — makes a handsome foliaged evergreen, with large palmate leaves and heads of greenish flowers in late autumn. There is an attractive variegated-leaved form.

Garrya elliptica is grown for its ornamental catkins, which on male plants may be up to 7.5cm (3in) long; those on female plants are much shorter. The trees are at their best in mid- and late winter, and greyish-green in colour. Female plants produce quite showy purple fruits in autumn. The plant rarely exceeds 2.5m (8ft) in height, and can be damaged in severe winters (as might be expected of a Californian plant).

Halimium atriplicifolium, a close relative of the cistus, has silvery leaves and bright yellow flowers up to 3.5cm (1½in) across in early summer. It makes a moderate bush and is very desirable, but it is tender and suitable only where moderate winters are to be expected.

Some of the hoherias are evergreen. One of the best is *H. sexstylosa,* which has shiny green poplar-shaped leaves and clusters of white flowers in early autumn. It makes a small tree, up to around 5m (16½ft), and is the hardiest of the evergreen species, but can be damaged in very severe winters.

Most of the kalmias are small shrubs for the alpine garden, but *K. latifolia,* the calico bush, can make a bush up to 1.5m (5ft) tall, with rhododendron-like leaves and panicles of pink flowers at mid-summer. The flowers are saucer-shaped and up to 2.5cm (1in) across: pale pink when open, but deep pink in bud. The bush needs an acid soil and a fairly well-lit situation. 'Clementine Churchill' is so deep a pink as to be described as red in catalogues.

The bay, *Laurus nobilis,* can exceed the 10m (33ft) limit, but for most purposes should be considered here. It is grown mainly for its glossy, aromatic leaves, much used in cuisine. It can be damaged in bad winters, but usually regenerates.

There are a number of *Leptospermum* species in cultivation, all requiring an acid soil and all unable to tolerate too cold a winter. The manukas of New Zealand are most often seen making small trees up to 4.5m (15ft) tall, with small leaves and somewhat starry flowers in early summer, varying in colour from white through pink to deep red; some cultivars have double flowers, such as 'Red Damask'. *L. lanigerum (pubescens),* with silvery leaves, and the not dissimilar *L. cunninghamii,* are less tender and have white flowers. *L. cunninghamii* flowers later than other species, in mid-summer.

The privets contain a few ornamental small

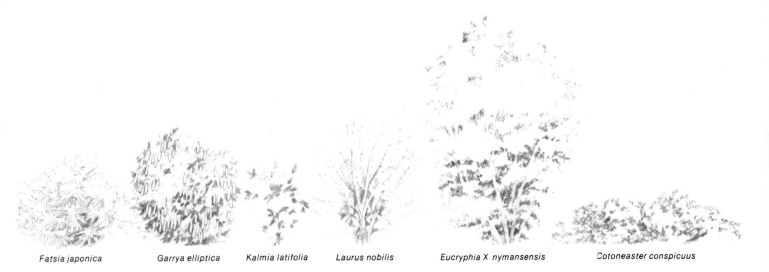

Fatsia japonica   *Garrya elliptica*   *Kalmia latifolia*   *Laurus nobilis*   *Eucryphia X nymansensis*   *Cotoneaster conspicuus*

trees with handsome leaves and panicles of creamy flowers in late summer and early autumn. *Ligustrum japonicum* and *L. lucidum* can make sizeable trees, up to 7m (23ft) or more. *L. lucidum* has two attractive variegated forms. It is common to think of privets as evergreens, but in fact most species are deciduous. The golden-leaved common privet, *L. ovalifolium* 'Aureum' can make a noble specimen if planted on its own.

Of the evergreen magnolias, *M. grandiflora* has large, fragrant cream flowers throughout the summer and early autumn. It needs wall protection in cold areas; elsewhere, it can make a large, round-headed tree. Although it also requires a good depth of soil, the acidity or alkilinity seems inconsequential. Of the various named clones, the underside of the leaves of 'Exmouth' is covered with reddish brown 'fur' (tomentum), and 'Goliath' starts to flower much sooner than other cultivars. The other evergreen magnolias — *M. delavayi*, which has very large leaves and short-lived flowers in late summer, and *M. nitida*, with shining leaves and moderate flowers in late spring — are tender plants and do not tolerate very severe winters.

Mahonias are useful bushes that usually flower in late autumn and through the winter. They have large, spiny, pinnate leaves up to 30cm (12in) long which are generally tinged purple when emerging. The best seem to be the hybrids between *M. japonica* and *M. lomariifolia*, known as *M. X media*, with cultivars such as 'Charity', 'Buckland' and 'Winter Sun', all with heads of racemes of yellow flowers which open at any time from late autumn to late winter or early spring. *M. japonica*, which has a bushy habit and pale yellow flowers smelling of lily-of-the-valley is more likely to open in late winter or early spring; *M. lomariifolia*, with its gawky habit and deep yellow flowers, usually obliges in early winter. The plants all grow vigorously but must be left to bush out at their own rhythm:

removing the growing point only causes it to produce a replacement. *M. pinnata*, of garden origin, makes a small bush with deep yellow flowers in mid- and late spring. All the plants have quite handsome bluish fruits.

The myrtles are useful evergreens for their late flowering and, in suitable districts, attractive and edible fruits. One of the best is *M. apiculata (luma)*, which can make an attractive small tree with light brown bark peeling to reveal the cream-coloured wood beneath. The flowers open in late summer and early autumn. *M. cheken* is a smaller tree with a slightly later flowering season. The European *M. communis* also flowers in mid and late summer; it makes a bush up to 4m (13ft) high. All the myrtles like full sun and a sheltered situation.

There are a large number of evergreen olearias, often known as daisy bushes which have the advantage of flowering quite late in the season. The most frequently seen is *O. X haastii*, with rather small, rounded leaves and heads of fragrant white daisies in late summer. *O. avicenniifolia*, often offered (incorrectly) as *O. albida*, has pointed leaves and wider corymbs of flowers in early autumn. *O. phlogopappa (gunniana)* flowers in late spring. *O. macrodonta* has holly-like leaves and flowers in early summer; and *O. stellatula* 'Splendens' (also known as *O. gunniana* 'Splendens') has flowers in late spring of lavender blue or pale pink.

Osmanthus armatus has holly-like leaves and fragrant white flowers in mid-autumn; the leaves of *O. heterophyllus*, alternatively, are even more holly-like but the flowers open in early spring.

The evergreen photinias contain some interesting trees, of which the hybrids between *P. glabra* and *P. serrulata* — known as *P. X fraseri* — are remarkable for their brilliantly-coloured young growths. 'Red Robin' has almost cerise growths, and usually flushes two or three times in the season. In any case, once the plants are large enough they can be clipped

Rhododendron yunnanense (**above**) produces masses of pale pink flowers in late spring. It is evergreen in mild sites but may lose some leaves during hard winters. It will thrive in lime-free soil and dappled shade.

The abundant white flowers of *Pyracantha rogersiana* (**right**) give way to a generous crop of autumn berries. An excellent hardy shrub for sun or shade. Many viburnums are suitable for garden planting. One of the best is *Vibrunum tinus* (**far right**). The flat heads of white flowers are borne through winter until early spring.

in early summer to encourage a second flush of growth. 'Robusta' has rather more coppery-coloured new growth. It is said to be hardier than other clones — but none seems particularly tender.

With equally brilliant new growth is *Pieris formosa forrestii*, which bears flowers like the lily-of-the-valley. This has been crossed with *P. japonica* to derive 'Forest Flame', which has slightly narrower and shorter leaves that soon turn pink and then cream before turning green. *P. japonica* 'Bert Chandler' seems identical, except that it has the narrow leaves and smaller dimensions of *P. japonica*. *P. japonica* itself is a smaller bush with coppery young growth and flowers in early spring, before *P. formosa*. There are forms with pink flowers —

Ligustrum lucidum

Olearia haastii

Photinia X fraseri

Pieris formosa forrestii

Rhododendron

Ligustrum ovalifolium

Mahonia japonica

'Christmas Cheer' and 'Daisen' — and an attractive slow-growing cultivar with variegated leaves.

Pyracanthas tend to make tall bushes, much like hawthorns but evergreen, with heads of white flowers in early summer and brilliant red, orange or yellow fruits in autumn and early winter. *P. coccinea* 'Lalandei', which has scarlet fruits, is most often seen, but *P. atlantioides* 'Aurea' and *P. rogersiana* 'Flava' have good yellow fruits. *P. angustifolia* has orange fruits.

The most popular of flowering evergreen trees and bushes are the rhododendrons, for which an acid soil is essential. They have a long flowering period from winter to late summer and grow in most situations, although

dappled shade suits the majority. The so-called hardy hybrids grow in full sun. All tend to flower profusely, although not always annually, and with smaller plants great benefit is derived by removing the flower heads as soon as they have faded to prevent them from forming seed. They vary in height from prostrate bushes to sizeable trees, and there seems to be some correlation between the size of the leaves and the amount of light they enjoy: apparently, the more light is available, the smaller the leaf. Many, like the hardy hybrids, have the flowers in large trusses; others, such as the attractive *R. yunnanense,* have azalea-like flowers in groups of three. A number, such as *R. bureavii, R. mallotum* and *R. fulvum,* have the young leaves covered in orange tomentum which persists on the underside; yet others, such as *R. thomsonii, R. cinnabarinum roylei* and *R. campanulatum aeruginosum,* have glaucous blue-green leaves so that the foliage is often as ornamental as the flowers. This is particularly so with the large-leaved plants of the *falconeri* and *grande* groups. These big-leaved trees are not effective in very windy districts, for the leaves can be easily damaged. *R. sinogrande* can produce leaves 80cm (32in) long and 30cm (12in) wide. The young leaves of all these big-leaved species are delightfully silvery.

Apart from very many rhododendron species, there are also numerous hybrids. The

season starts in late winter with *R. dauricum* and *R. mucronulatum,* small bushes with magenta flowers, and ends in late summer with the large tree *R. auriculatum,* which has large fragrant white flowers not produced on young specimens.

There are a few useful evergreen viburnums, of which the laurustinus (*Viburnum tinus*), with heads of white flowers which open from early winter to late spring, is deservedly popular. A Mediterranean plant, it can suffer in bad winters but is nevertheless not as tender as its more attractive form from the Canary Islands, *V. rigidum. Viburnum X burkwoodii* has the fragrant *V. carlesii* in its parentage, and correspondingly bears fragrant flowers in late spring and early summer. 'Anne Russell' and 'Park Farm Hybrid' are clones from this cross. *V. davidii* makes a mound-shaped bush and tends to be unisexual so two or more plants should be grown together. The dull white flowers, which open in early summer, are followed by turquoise-blue fruits that persist throughout the winter and are then very striking.

'Pink Pearl' (**below**) is a popular hybrid for garden planting. The rose-pink flowers, fading in colour as they mature, are borne on vigorous shoots in early summer. In moist sheltered conditions the shrub will grow over 4.5m (15ft) in height and spread. This evergreen hardy hybrid, in common with all other rhododendrons, needs an acid soil to flourish. In chalky soils prepare a peat bed in which to grow these beautiful shrubs and trees.

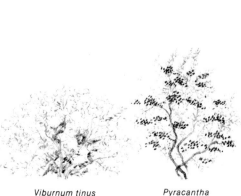

Viburnum tinus   *Pyracantha*

Large trees

The larger trees — of anything from 10m to 60m (33ft to 200ft) or more tall — not surprisingly take a long time to reach full dimensions, although most are fairly sizeable after ten years. They therefore require considerable patience on the part of the gardener before their full potential is achieved. Because they are such permanent garden features, the bigger trees need positioning and selecting with unusual care.

Among the *acers* are some sizeable examples. The box elder, *A. negundo,* has pinnate leaves and makes a moderate-sized tree. The white variegated 'Variegatum' is deservedly popular for its conspicuous leaves, but 'Auratum', with golden leaves, is also attractive. The Norway maple, *A. platanoides,* is a rapid grower and has heads of green flowers in mid-spring before the leaves unfurl; at that time it looks very attractive, although appearing rather heavy later. 'Crimson King' and 'Schedleri' have purple leaves and purplish flowers. *A. rubrum* has quite brilliant red flowers in mid-spring and may colour well in the autumn. 'Schlesingeri' is said to be of particularly good autumnal colour. Plants on acid soils, however, always seem to colour better than those on alkaline. *A. saccharinum,* the silver maple, has leaves that are silvery below and usually of good autumn colour; again it is a rapid grower. The sugar maple, *A. saccharum,* rarely seems to display splendid colours outside its native USA.

The horse chestnuts are splendid trees, with panicles of flowers in late spring. *Aesculus carnea* is comparatively small, although large enough for this section, and has reddish panicles in late spring and early summer. The horse chestnut itself, *A. hippocastanum,* on the other hand, has white

The splendid *Catalpa bignonioides* (**left**) bears showy flowers (**above**) in mid-summer, followed by slender seedpods.

Fraxinus excelsior 'Pendula' (**below**), a magnificent tree.

flowers with reddish stamens. 'Baumannii' has double flowers and so does not produce conkers. The Indian horse chestnut, *A. indica,* is the best of the lot: the emerging leaves are bronzy, and the panicles open a month later than other horse chestnuts, in early to mid-summer.

The Tree of Heaven, *Ailanthus altissima,* has very large leaves like an enormous ash, up to 1.2m (4ft) long; it does well in towns.

The alders, species of *Alnus,* have no objection to moist situations but are otherwise not very brilliant. Yet 'Aurea' and 'Ramulis Coccineis' — cultivars of *A. incana* — have yellow young shoots and leaves, and the catkins, which appear in early spring, are at that time red and showy.

The birches contain some of the most handsomely barked trees, but are very territorial, throwing out surface roots well beyond the spread of the canopy. The bark of *Betula albosinensis* tends to be pinkish; that of *B. lutea* is amber-coloured; shining white bark is alternatively provided by *B. ermanii, B. jacquemontii* and the European *B. pendula.* The cultivar 'Youngii' makes a very attractive weeping

form of this last species. The North American *B. papyrifera* also has attractive bark, and may additionally have quite handsome gold leaves in autumn. The birches are difficult to distinguish — but are most attractive.

The sweet chestnut, *Castanea sativa,* has long, rather foetid catkins in mid-summer, and has both white and yellow variegated forms.

Catalpas are useful trees for their late flowering — at mid-summer or just after — but

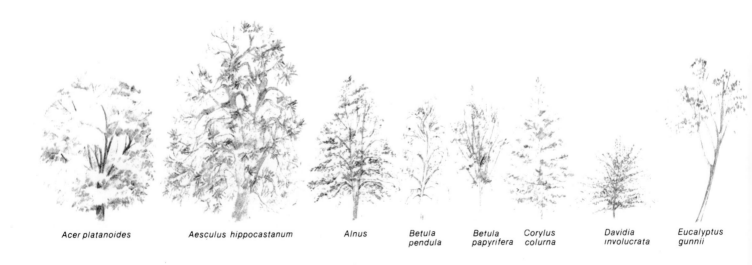

Acer platanoides   Aesculus hippocastanum   Alnus   Betula pendula   Betula papyrifera   Corylus colurna   Davidia involucrata   Eucalyptus gunnii

are comparatively short-lived; specimens are said to decline after fifty years. *C. bignonioides* is the commonest, and has panicles of flowers like small foxgloves, white with yellow or purple markings. 'Aurea' has golden yellow leaves. *C. fargesii*, from China, has pinkish flowers.

The Turkish hazel, *Corylus colurna*, unlike most of the hazels, makes a large tree with a fine spring display of catkins and curiously corrugated bark. Specimens over 18.5m (60ft) are not uncommon.

The dove tree, *Davidia involucrata*, has leaves much like those of a lime tree, but after a few years covers itself in late spring with heads of inconspicuous flowers, each surrounded by two large white bracts of papery consistency up to 30cm (12in) in length and about 10cm (4in) across. A flowering specimen is a magnificent sight. Although it looks so exotic it seems unmoved even in the worst winters.

Eucalyptus gunnii, from Tasmania, is the hardiest of these Australasian trees and soon attains a moderate size. The emerging leaves are attractively silvery. *E. niphophilia* has attractive green, grey and cream bark, but is rather slow in growth.

The beeches are handsome trees of large dimensions; the best are forms of the European *Fagus sylvatica*. Of the various forms, 'Purpurea' and 'Riversii' have purplish leaves; 'Heterophylla' is the cut-leaved beech, with lobed, rather narrow leaves; 'Rohanii' is a purple-leaved slow-growing form of this; 'Dawyck' is a fastigiate (steeply conical) form, and 'Pendula' is a weeping form. All seem to thrive in any type of soil, although 'Rohanii' seems to be slower in growth than the others.

The manna ash, *Fraxinus ornus*, has heads of small white flowers in late spring and early summer, and the usual pinnate ash leaves. *F. sieboldii* is similar, but is said to have good autumn colour; it may be difficult to obtain. The common ash, *F. excelsior*, has no beauty of flower, but 'Jaspidea' has yellowish wood that is bright in winter, and 'Pendula' makes a tent of green.

Gymnocladus dioicus is rather slow growing but has some of the largest leaves to be found in any garden. They are pinnate and pinkish when unfurling, turning a clear yellow before falling. The young wood is silver-grey and handsome during the winter. Apparently, the beans were used as a substitute for coffee by early settlers in North America.

The hollies include a number of medium-sized, rather slow-growing trees which can make perfect pyramids; alternatively, the lower branches can be removed to display the smooth trunk. To obtain berries, plants of both sexes should be planted. Most of the arboreal (tree-like) forms are either from the European *Ilex aquifolium*, the common holly, or from its hybrid with the Canary holly *I. perado* known as *I. X altaclarensis*, which has larger, less spiny leaves than the common holly. Of all these there are quite a few yellow and white variegated forms — usually with misleading names. Thus 'Golden King' is a female plant, and 'Golden Queen' is male. *I. latifolia*, from Japan, has extremely large leaves and requires a sheltered situation. Patience is needed with hollies; they resent moving, and must be brought into the garden as small plants.

The walnuts, species of *Juglans*, make attractive trees with perfumed leaves and edible fruits. The ordinary walnut comes from *J. regia*. All are slowish growers and usually take a long time before they start to fruit.

Liquidambar styraciflua has maple-like leaves and, once it is well established, good autumn colour. The tulip tree, *Liriodendron tulipifera*, has oddly-shaped leaves like a horse's saddle, which turn a good yellow before falling. Its flowers are greenish with an orange base, and not showy.

The southern beeches are rapid growers, although not very long-lived. *Nothofagus antarctica*, which has very small leaves and rather twisted growths, is among the most attractive.

Paulownias make handsome flowering trees, with their panicles of blue-purple in late spring. The best seems to be *P. fargesii*, which flowers sooner than the better known *P. tomentosa*, which may have its flowers damaged in winter whereas those of *P. fargesii* seem less liable to be affected. Trees can reach a height of 20m (65ft).

Poplars are rapid in growth but are not among the most attractive of large trees. The young leaves of the *canadensis* group, however, are attractively copper-coloured, and the white poplar, *Populus alba*, has silvery leaves. *P. X generosa* can increase at the rate of 2m (6½ft) per year. The necklace poplar, *P. lasiocarpa*, has very large, red-veined leaves but seems hard to preserve.

The various oaks, species of *Quercus*, make attractive slow-growing trees; a collection should be inspected to find one suitable for the specific conditions. The red oak, *Q. rubra*, seems to be the fastest grower.

Robinia pseudoacacia is the well-known false acacia, which has fragrant white flowers in early summer. *R. X ambigua* makes a smaller tree with pale pink flowers of which 'Bella Rosa' and 'Decaisneana' are the best cultivars.

The lime tree, *Tilia*, has fragrant flowers at mid-summer; the most attractive is the weeping silver lime, *T. petiolaris*, which has pendulous branches and silver undersides to the leaves. It is probably a form of *T. tomentosa*, also with silver undersides to the leaves.

Zelkovas make very attractive slow-growing trees, not unlike elms but with no propensity to disease. *Z. carpinifolia* and *Z. sinica* are both splendid — but *Z. serrata* has the added bonus of good autumn colour.

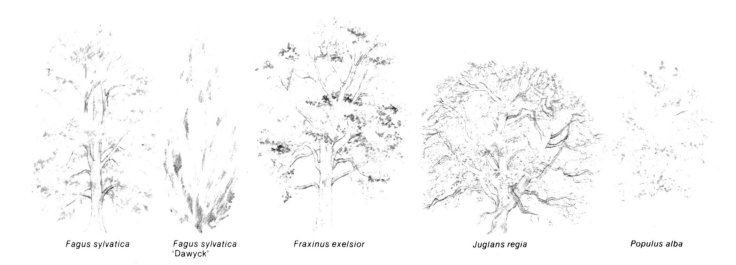

Fagus sylvatica

Fagus sylvatica 'Dawyck'

Fraxinus exelsior

Juglans regia

Populus alba

Conifers

Conifers differ from the other plants so far discussed in that they have no beauty of flower, although occasionally the fruits are ornamental. Most either have thin, needle-like leaves, or their twigs are covered with overlapping scale-like leaves. Conifers are among the oldest surviving plants and can be found in all climates, from the Arctic to the tropics. Usually they are very intolerant of atmospheric pollution — it seems always to be the conifers which are the first victims of acid rain, for example — and they are thus generally unsuitable for town gardens. Soil reaction (acid or alkaline) seems often of little importance, but it is known that young conifers, in particular, live in symbiosis with a fungus that 'infects' the roots; the roots actually make little growth if the fungus is not present. Spent hops appear to stimulate the growth of the fungus, and should be forked in (if obtainable) when the conifers are being planted. Fortunately the fungus appears to be naturally present in most soils. The great majority of conifers are evergreens, but there are some deciduous ones, including some of the most attractive.

I also include among the conifers — but only because otherwise it has no category of its own — the maidenhair tree, *Ginkgo biloba*, which seems to have survived unchanged for some 160 million years. Deciduous, it has stalked, fan-shaped leaves like a frond of maidenhair fern, which turn a clear yellow before falling. Plants are unisexual, and the fruits are plum-like, yellow in colour — and offensive to the nose when the flesh is crushed (although the seeds are eaten in the east). Normally it makes a pyramidal tree, but there are fastigiate forms, and also a pendulous variant that is less consistent.

The dawn redwood, *Metasequoia glyptostroboides*, was known only as a fossil until

1941 when a stand was discovered in China. It makes a tall, conical tree up to 35m (116ft) high in the wild, and develops a buttressed trunk. A rapid grower, in spring it covers itself with bright green needle-like leaves which turn russet in autumn before falling. It seems to do best in a fairly moist situation. Propagation from cuttings is easy; used occasionally as a hedging plant, it is best as a single specimen.

The swamp cypress, *Taxodium distichum*, is not dissimilar but grows, as its English name implies, in very wet situations. Mature trees may throw up 'knees' — woody outgrowths from the roots up to the surface and above, which convey oxygen to the roots in waterlogged soil. Vivid green young leaves turn russet before they fall. The tree requires either acid or neutral soil, but otherwise seems trouble-free.

The best-known deciduous conifers are the larches: almost all are large trees with very vivid young green leaves. Larches make excellent specimens; probably the best is a hybrid of unknown provenance known as *Larix X pendula*, which makes a large tree with long hanging branchlets up to 1m (3¼ft) in length, so that a well-grown tree is extremely handsome. It is thought to be a hybrid between the European *L. decidua* and the North American *L. laricina*; the plant has been known since 1739. The Japanese larch *L. kaempferi*, much like the European larch, has a clone 'Blue Haze' which has glaucous-blue leaves — seemingly an unnecessary refinement in a larch.

Abies, the silver fir, is a genus of large trees in which the cones are large and held pointing upwards; the broadish needles are silvery on the underside. The young growths are often damaged by late spring frosts. Most species seem to do best in regions of high rainfall, although the Mediterranean *A. cephalonica* and *A. pinsapo* are exceptions. Most of the species make very large trees, with branches emerging in whorls up the trunk. *A. delavayi*

Hardly recognisable as a conifer, the curious *Ginko biloba* (**above**) is botanically classified as one. *Juniperus communis* 'Compressa' (**right**) is ideal for planting in a rock garden. It grows slowly to form a dwarf column. For even smaller spaces *Picea abies* 'Little Gem' (**below**) forms compact mounds.

Ginkgo biloba   Metasequoia glyptostroboides   Taxodium distichum   Larix laricina   Abies pinsapo   Abies cephalonica   Cedrus atlantica   Cedrus deodara

and *A. speciosa* have bluish cones. *A. koreana* has violet cones, but is a much smaller tree and slow growing; its cones apparently form at quite an early age.

The cedars also all make large, handsome trees, pyramidal at first but later flat-topped with a tabular habit. Although given different specific names, the differences between *Cedrus atlantica, C. deodara* and *C. libani* are very slight. The deodar has pendulous branchlets and is slightly more ornamental when young; it also has a reputation for being more tender. There is an attractive glaucous form of *C. atlantica*. None of the cedars is a rapid grower.

The spruces, species of *Picea*, may be confused with the silver firs, but the cones always droop and there are small peg-like projections where old needles have fallen. The classic Christmas tree is the Norway spruce, *P. abies*, of which there are many variants, including a number of dwarf forms. The North American *P. breweriana* and the Himalayan *P. smithiana* are among the most beautiful of mature trees, with very long pendulous branchlets that turn the tree into a green fountain. But they are slow growers and do not produce these hanging growths until well matured. *P. pungens* 'Glauca' has glaucous-blue leaves; 'Koster' seems the best form of this, but 'Globosa' and 'Hoopsii' are naturally shorter and more suitable in restricted spaces.

The pines, species of *Pinus*, have needles in bundles generally longer than those of the other genera discussed. In some of the rather tender Mexican pines, such as *P. montezumae*, the needles may be up to 25cm (10in) long. Pines generally make attractive trees, pyramidal when young, with branches in whorls and more flat-topped when mature, and with very ornamental trunks. The Scots pine, *P. sylvestris*, is among the best, but most species are pleasant to look at, and all make largish trees eventually.

The hemlocks, species of *Tsuga*, have a rather more graceful habit and are distinguished by their small cones. The Douglas fir, *Pseudotsuga menziesii*, is a rapid grower. The Californian redwoods, the giant *Sequoiadendron giganteum* and the almost equally large *Sequoia sempervirens* — the tallest tree in cultivation, at 110m (366ft) — are all excellent subjects... where space allows.

The conifers with overlapping scale-like leaves are rather more tolerant of pollution than those with needles, but naturally do not enjoy it. Between the two groups come the junipers, some of which have needles whereas others have scales. They are mainly small plants, although the pencil cedar *J. virginiana* can make a sizeable tree which has an attractive columnar habit. The savin, *J. sabina*, is a large prostrate tree which can cover very large areas in the wild. The young leaves are needles, whereas the mature leaves are scales. Two of the best forms — 'Hicksii' with glaucous leaves, and 'Tamariscifolia' with green leaves — have needles and no scales. *J. X media* 'Pfitzerana' makes a spreading horizontal tree with scale-like leaves. 'Blue Cloud' has glaucous scales.

The false cypress, chamaecyparis, usually makes a columnar tree with scale-like leaves, but some of the forms of *C. obtusa* and *C. pisifera* retain their juvenile needles. Forms of Lawson's cypress, *C. lawsoniana*, are widely available, ranging from the blue-grey 'Allumii' to the rather dwarf 'Aurea Densa' with golden foliage, and there are innumerable variations in between. The Nootka cypress, *C. nootkatensis*, tolerates the coldest conditions. The true cypresses (of the genus *Cupressus*) are commonly somewhat frost-tender coming as they do from such areas as California and the Mediterranean. Most make very attractive columnar trees.

So do the species of *Thuja*, not easily distinguished from *Chamaecyparis* and again tending to make handsome columnar specimens. *T. occidentalis* 'Rheingold', a slow-

The dark foliage of *Chamaecyparis notkatensis* 'Glauca' (**above left**) is formed in flat sprays tightly clothed in scale-like leaves. *Taxus baccata* 'Fastigiata' (**above**) develops into a dense column of dark green foliage. *Abies koreana* (**left**) is prized for its neat shape and attractive purple cones.

growing conical bush with gold foliage, is among the most popular of smaller conifers. Forms of *T. plicata*, on the other hand, can make extremely large specimens. All the species have proved very variable, and it is only by viewing a collection that a suitable selection can be made.

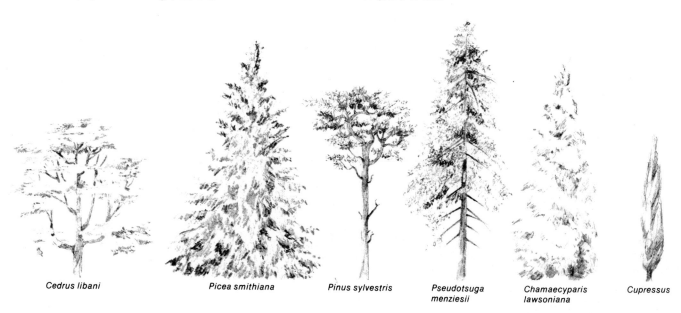

Cedrus libani　　*Picea smithiana*　　*Pinus sylvestris*　　*Pseudotsuga menziesii*　　*Chamaecyparis lawsoniana*　　*Cupressus*

BACKDROPS
&
BOUNDARIES

Introduction

Hedges can provide distinctive features as well as effective boundaries. Yew grows so densely that it can be trimmed into arches (**right**) to echo the formal style of this garden pool.

Most of us seek that sense of privacy, even if it is sometimes illusory, which a boundary fence or hedge gives us. It marks our plot out from the others, and forms a framework for the garden. You do not have to be a recluse to want privacy or to define your boundary.

Walls, fences and hedges do more than mark out our territory, however. To a large extent they are the setting, the backdrop, or the stage in which we set our plants. They are part of good garden design.

There are, of course, times when a visible barrier is *not* the right answer. If the view from your home is a stunning one, the last thing that you'll want to do is block it out. Even so, you'll probably want to keep animals either in or out of your garden, and to have some physical mark of your territory. If you are ambitious, and the site is suitable, you could even make a modest ha-ha; but there are other boundary markers, such as a post-and-chain, which can be small and unobtrusive. Even plastic-coated wire mesh with low-growing shrubs in front can be effective. Whatever the size and shape of your garden, there are good ways and there are bad ways of marking what is, after all, its external skeleton.

Since hedges and screens are a backcloth for many of your plants, and an integral part of any well-designed garden, it would be a mistake to think of them only as boundary markers. *Internal* hedges, or walls, play an important role that should not be overlooked.

A screen, whether it is a hedge, a wall, or a fence, also benefits the plants. It can provide shelter and possibly even a microclimate within the garden — but some provide shelter more efficiently than others.

Deciding what you want

You will need to take into account both the *function* of the 'fence' and the *appearance*. Ignore either consideration and you may well regret the decision.

If you are disabled or infirm, or simply do not like the aspect of hard physical work in gardening, then the required amount of initial effort and of later maintenance may also affect your decision.

The pros and cons of the major alternatives are set out below, but do not overlook the less obvious benefits: a hedge requires a lot more maintenance than a wall, but it is better at filtering the wind without causing turbulence, and it is more likely to encourage wildlife. There are also drawbacks to hedges that may not be obvious at first; if you want to use a hedge or living screen as an attractive background for your borders, you will also have to cope with the fact that it will impoverish the soil for the other plants near by.

Walls

Few gardeners would doubt their competence to plant a hedge; yet for those with neither the muscle-power nor the confidence that comes with DIY jobs well done, the prospect of building a wall can seem daunting. It is not difficult if you take it in logical steps and easy stages and if you have not done a job like this before, it can give you a tremendous sense of satisfaction when it is finished.

The advantages of a wall are its robustness and lack of maintenance. If it is high enough it may also make a satisfactory background for many wall-trained plants, from fan-trained fruit to decorative wall shrubs. A brick or solid block wall is also more peep-proof than most wooden fences of the same height. A brick or concrete wall does not have to be unimaginative; there are many permutations of materials and patterns that you can try.

The disadvantages are mainly two-fold: cost and effort. This applies mainly to brick, and to a lesser extent to concrete blocks. All materials, even in natural dry stone walling, have to be laid on a firm base, which generally means proper concrete foundations.

In addition to the cost of the bricks or blocks there will be the expense of concrete (and possibly hardcore) and mortar. This can add quite substantially to the total outlay — especially if you decide to hire a concrete-mixer too.

Laying a wall can be hard physical work, and should not be rushed.

A solid wall can cause a lot of wind turbulence; this is much less of a problem with pierced blocks (often called screen blocks, although they do not offer a screen of privacy).

Fences

Fences are generally cheaper than brick or concrete, and much more 'instant' than a hedge. New, they can also look quite attractive; but difficulties come with age. Then they begin to look jaded, and gaps and cracks all too frequently precede different types of rot and the structure's eventual collapse. Quality can be as variable as the design — and there is a bewildering range to choose from.

Advantages include instant cover or privacy at less cost (and probably time) than a brick or concrete wall.

Disadvantages include the fact that if you want your fence to last, you will have to apply a preservative every second year, and even then a fence is likely to succumb long before a wall. Many are not peep-proof (although this may not matter).

Hedges

Hedges are hard to beat for sheer variety of shape, colour and form. Some are evergreen, some deciduous, some have flowers, a few have the bonus of berries, many with much more interesting shape and form than the useful but overworked privet. A hedge can range in height from 30cm (1ft) or so (such as the dwarf box *Buxus suffruticosa*, and dwarf lavenders) to screens more than 4.5m (15ft) high (such as *X Cupressocyparis leylandii*).

Advantages: sheer variety, and the ability to provide the *changing* interest associated with living plants, are always attractions. Low cost is another. (If you can take cuttings, and have the patience, a hedge may cost you nothing.) Even if you have to buy plants, it still almost certainly works out cheaper than a fence or a wall.

Disadvantages: revolve around the additional problems of growing other plants close to the hedge, and the effort of keeping a hedge trimmed.

Do not be afraid to mix

The danger of looking at the options in turn in isolation is that you may miss the possibility of good combinations that might give you the best of all worlds.

On these and the following pages there are examples in pictures of fences on walls, hedges with fences, and hedges with walls. The results can be aesthetically pleasing; alternatively, in such a combination the attractions of one may offset the shortcomings of the other. Or you could perhaps improve things by 'grafting on' a different type of background to one that is already there.

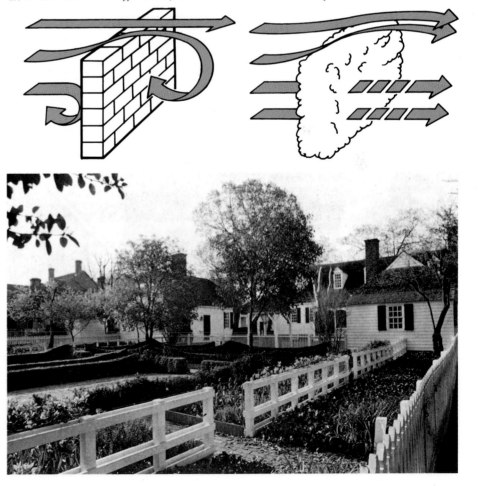

Garden walls create turbulence on their leeward side (**above right**); hedges 'filter' the wind to shelter plants effectively.

Picket fencing, ranch style fencing and elegantly trimmed hedges harmonize in this American garden (**right**).

Fences

A fence is by far the quickest way to screen your garden or mark your boundary. It is obviously more 'instant' than a hedge — which may take several years to grow to the height that you require — and quicker than a brick or block wall to erect.

Wooden fences

Although most fences are close-board or something similar (because these offer privacy), there are many other options well worth considering.

Most fences provide more than merely a screen for people: they offer protection to plants in exposed places and even a framework for suitable climbers (if you provide the necessary additional support).

For complete privacy, a close-boarded fence is the answer. Interwoven fencing is a good screen from a distance, but not peep-proof at close quarters.

Posts

A fence is only as strong as its supports. A solid fence offers a lot of wind resistance and requires stronger posts than an open fence. Sizes generally vary between 50mm x 75mm (2in x 2½in) and 100mm x 150mm (4in x 6in). You should also allow sufficient depth in the ground; as a guide, a low fence intended to rise 60cm (2ft) above ground needs at least 30cm

(1ft) below ground. For a fence 1.8m (6ft) high, there should be at least 75cm (2ft 6in) of post below ground.

The fence manufacturer should advise on the size of posts required — if in doubt, though, err on the large side even if it means paying a bit more.

All timber posts should be treated with a preservative, preferably pressure or vacuum impregnated by the fencing supplier. If you cut the timber for any reason, this is likely to expose untreated timber in the centre; overcome this by soaking the cut end in a preservative.

Concrete posts solve the problem of rot, but not everyone likes the appearance. In the right setting, however, they can be perfectly acceptable. Most are cast with grooves to take a fencing panel, and this does make erection a little easier.

A less common option is a metal post — again with grooves in to take a fence panel.

You must be careful to order the right type and number of concrete or metal posts — for, as opposed to working with wooden posts, you need to specify what is required in the way of corners, and ends, together with the number of intermediate posts (because of the position of slots for the panels).

Chain-link and other wire fences

The posts at each end of a wire, chain link or chestnut paling fence need struts to take the strain when the wire is pulled tight.

Metal post supports

If you do not like the idea of digging or boring holes, and perhaps mixing concrete to pack back into them, you could use a metal fixing post instead. There are several kinds, varying in sophistication, but the principle in all is the same.

The metal stake is driven into the ground using a sledge-hammer or club hammer (there is a fitment available to protect the top of the post support while you drive it in).

The advantages of metal supports are that they demand less effort than digging and filling holes, and you do not have to buy, carry, and mix concrete. The posts can be smaller (although the saving on the post does not in itself pay for the cost of the post holder), and do not rot in the ground.

The disadvantages are that you must make sure the post fits, and it is not always easy to drive them in absolutely straight (which is vital). In some circumstances you may find they look obtrusive, even though only a small section is visible at the base of the post.

Concrete panels

The panels are slotted into the grooves in the concrete posts. Do not do this until the concrete anchoring the posts has set firmly.

The panels sometimes seen around commercial premises are undisguised concrete and hardly attractive. There are finishes available, however, that you might find acceptable as a surround to a patio. Although one

---

Erecting a wooden fence

1 Start by marking the line of the intended fence with string stretched between two stakes, and lay the posts in approximately the right positions. Remember that the distance between the center of one post and the next is not the length of the fencing panel, but the panel plus post.

2 Make the first hole. You can dig this out with a spade, but a post-hole borer should make easier work of it.

3 Pack bricks or rubble around the base to hold the post upright, and check for plumb in both directions, using a long spirit-level. Once you are confident that it is true, pack more rubble around the base to firm it, and check verticals again.

4 Lay the first panel on the ground butted up to the post as a guide to the correct positioning of the next post. Make the next hole.

5 Insert the second post as the first, but also check that the two are the same height by using a string stretched taut at the final

height, or by using a spirit-level on a board spanning the two.

If the fence has rails that have to be jointed to the post, fit the rails into the first post before you position the second (an extra pair of hands really is essential).

6 Fix the panel into position with galvanized nails or screws. You may find it easier to use brackets to fix the panels. It is in fact more convenient to fix these to the posts before you erect them.

7 Always use a line stretched between the ends at the height of the top of the fence, to ensure that the height is even.

8 Try to ensure that the main part of a timber fence does not come into contact with soil. Either use a gravel board (which you can replace more easily if it rots), or rest the fence on a layer of bricks or blocks.

9 Finally, firm the posts again, double-checking that they are vertical. Small posts can be firmed with rammed earth and rubble, but it is generally better to concrete in posts with more than about 90cm (3ft)

above ground. If you are setting the posts in concrete, nail temporary struts to keep the post in position until it sets (wait for a few days before removing them).

WARNING: **do not attempt to erect tall or solid fences on a windy day, or if strong winds are forecast.**

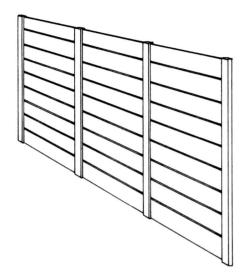

Fences made with concrete panels (**above**) can provide a durable boundary but may have a rather 'industrial' appearance. Choose panels with a more attractive finish than just plain concrete, a simulated brick or a 'shiplap' pattern for example. Make sure that the posts are correctly aligned before sliding the panels one by one into the preformed grooves.

side has the traditional finish and the usual concrete strip appearance, the other (ideally 'inside') side has an imitation brick finish. The effect is one of a white brick wall, but you can paint it with any good quality exterior grade emulsion paint to make a potentially exciting backdrop for your plants.

Concrete comes in other disguises too — as simulated stone walls, or in an overlapping 'shiplap' pattern, for instance. It is worth shopping around to see what is locally available.

A word of warning about erecting a concrete fence: the posts must align *exactly*, or you will find it difficult, if not impossible, to slide the inflexible panels into the grooves that should — but do not — correspond.

Wire mesh

Probably not taken seriously enough as a form of fence, the various wire mesh fences available are not serious contenders for a front garden boundary. Yet they have potential as useful dividers between back gardens where you want a fairly open outlook and are not bothered about privacy. They are also useful where the garden borders open countryside, many of them being inconspicuous, especially when shrubs are planted against them.

A wire fence, especially chain-link, can be both strong and cheap. It is also easy to erect (see below), but the job must be done properly if disappointment is not to follow. It is imperative that wire fences are properly strained and kept taut.

Galvanized wire should last for 10 years or more; plastic-coated wire should have an even longer life, and also looks better.

Erecting a chain-link fence

Chain-link is quick and easy to put up, but time and care must be taken to erect the posts properly. Posts bought directly from the fence manufacturer are likely to be made of angle iron, although some makes of fencing are also designed to be fixed to wooden or concrete posts. Some steel supports are plastic-coated. Screwed eye-bolts can be used to tension the line wires between concrete or timber posts; also needed are stretcher bars and winding brackets as well as strainer bars. If you are in doubt about the necessary bits and pieces, ask the supplier's advice.

1 Start by marking out the line of the fence with string, then inserting the posts into levelled ground. The holes for angle-iron supports should be about 45cm (18in) square and 60cm (2ft) deep for a fence of about 1.2m (4ft) height; increase the depth to about 75cm (2ft 6in) for taller fences. Straining stay holes can be smaller — about 45cm (18in) by 30cm (1ft), and 45cm (18in) deep. Intermediate posts should not be more than 3m (10ft) apart.

Ideally, the posts should be concreted into position. Make sure that the straining bars are positioned on the right side to take the strain.

2 Once the posts are fixed firmly, unroll the line wire and strain it between the posts. For a fence of 1.2m (4ft) or less, two wires will be sufficient, but for more than this height use a third wire. The wires are fixed to the winders bolted to the angle-iron at end and corner posts. It is threaded through suitable holes in the intermediate posts.

3 Unroll the fence against the first post, and pass a stretcher bar through the last row of meshes, bolting this to the post.

4 Unwind the roll, keeping it as taut as you can, and use wire or string to fix it temporarily to the line wires. Fasten the mesh to each intermediate and straining post in turn, maintaining tension. Wherever there is a change of direction, use a stretcher bar to bolt the chain link to the post.

Finally, fix the fence to the line wires with tying wire. Ideally, it should be fixed to the top wire every 15cm (6in), but intervals of 45cm (18in) should be adequate along the bottom and middle wires.

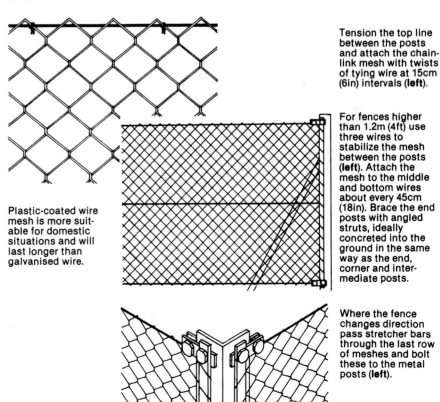

Plastic-coated wire mesh is more suitable for domestic situations and will last longer than galvanised wire.

Tension the top line between the posts and attach the chain-link mesh with twists of tying wire at 15cm (6in) intervals (**left**).

For fences higher than 1.2m (4ft) use three wires to stabilize the mesh between the posts (**left**). Attach the mesh to the middle and bottom wires about every 45cm (18in). Brace the end posts with angled struts, ideally concreted into the ground in the same way as the end, corner and intermediate posts.

Where the fence changes direction pass stretcher bars through the last row of meshes and bolt these to the metal posts (**left**).

Garden walls come 'alive' (**top** and **above**) when covered in climbing plants.

Planting near a wall

The ground near walls and fences is often much drier than the rest of the garden. This means the plants there have to be watered more often than the rest of the garden, and it also means careful planting.

Make the hole about 30cm (1ft) away from the wall. (If you want the plant to go up the fence or wall, you can train it towards it, using a sloping cane if necessary.)

Always incorporate plenty of moisture-holding material, such as peat, well-rotted compost, or manure.

After planting, water well and then mulch the moist ground with damp peat, pulverized bark or compost.

Making them more beautiful

No matter how tasteful or how well constructed boundary walls and fences are, their appearance can usually be improved by plants.

Low walls and fences of 1.2m (4ft) or less in height do not really call for intensive planting; in any case, climbers are clearly unsuitable for a wall or fence of that height. It is best to make a feature of such a wall or fence rather than try to hide it. (In fact, if you feel that you have to hide a low fence or wall, the chances are you have made the wrong choice in the first place.)

Of course, a previous owner may have committed the error of putting it up, leaving you with a decision either to pull it down and start again, or to make the best of what is there. If you feel that it has to be improved, try to use shrubs, particularly evergreens, to soften the overall effect. Alternatively, low walls can be extended in height with either closeboard or trellis panels, allowing you more privacy, and more scope for planting climbers and wall shrubs.

Climbers and wall shrubs (**right**) add elegance to any garden wall. Choose from the wide range of flowering plants and striking foliage shrubs available.

The sort of plants that you can use to liven up an unexciting fence or wall are:
- climbers;
- all shrubs;
- ordinary shrubs, particularly evergreens; or
- 'architectural' plants.

Climbers

Climbers are generally not the easy solution that they may seem at first thought. Most of them are far suitable more for climbing a house wall or up a specially prepared trellis or other support. Virginia creeper (*Parthenocissus quinquefolia*) and Boston ivy (*Parthenocissus tricuspidata*) can cover a building superbly but are not for garden walls and fences; sweet peas and morning glories (*Ipomoea rubro-caerulea*, syn *I. violacea*) are among the most attractive annual climbers, but neither makes a good screen, nor can they fend for themselves without a suitable support.

There are, however, a few plants that do climb and clothe without much help and with no need to erect netting or trellis for them to grow up. Some ivies are among the most useful, but there are other plants equally so,

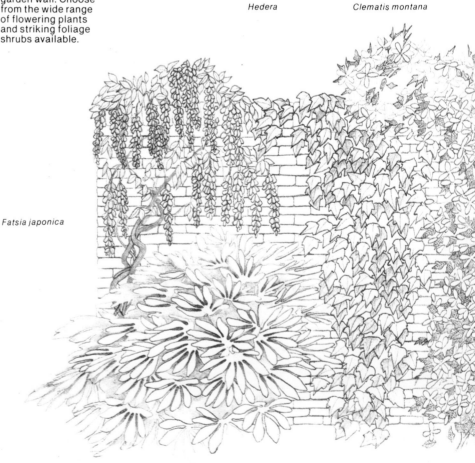

Wisteria

Hedera

Clematis montana

Fatsia japonica

such as *Polygonum baldschuanicum* and various loniceras (honeysuckles).

Ivies are particularly useful because they are evergreen, and there are many variations in leaf colour and shape. Two large-leaved varieties of outstanding merit are the Persian ivy *Hedera colchica* 'Dentata Variegata', and the Canary Island ivy *H. canariensis* 'Glorie de Marengo', also called 'Variegata'. Both these variegated ivies look interesting all the year round, although the Canary Island ivy may look the worse for wear in very cold areas.

The ordinary *H. helix* varieties are also suitable, although these tend to look better on walls than on fences. There are dozens of varieties from which to choose.

Another evergreen to consider is the Japanese honeysuckle *Lonicera japonica* 'Aureoreticulata', which has golden reticulation on bright green leaves. It tends to lose leaves in a severe winter.

Deciduous climbers are obviously less desirable, assuming the object is to cover the fence or wall, but there are also some useful plants in this category.

The mile-a-minute, or Russian, vine *(Polygonum baldschuanicum)* is a rampant plant that covers a large area quickly, and crowns the fence or wall with foaming masses of small creamy flowers in late summer and through autumn. Not a particularly pretty plant, it is fine though if you want quick cover.

For a really pretty flowering climber, it is difficult to beat clematis. Some initial support is required, such as netting or a trellis, but then species such as *C. montana* simply romp along the fence. The species is white, but the pink variety 'Rubens' is justifiably more popular.

If you are prepared to use a trellis of some kind, the various large-flowered hybrids can make a spectacular show. One of the most popular, 'Nelly Moser', actually does best on a shady fence (its colour is stronger out of sunlight): a useful bonus.

Wisterias must rank among the most desirable of all climbers and wall shrubs, but only a large, tall wall can do them justice. If your wall is suitable, and you have the patience to wait for a few years to see it at its full glory, a wisteria can be very rewarding.

For an annual climber that covers a fence quickly, try the Japanese hop, *Humulus japonicus.* The variety 'Variegatus' is particularly decorative.

There are many other climbers that you could try, including honeysuckle.

Pyracantha   Elaeagnus pungens 'Maculata'

The pink-and-white blooms of *Clematis* 'Nelly Moser' (**above left**) flourish on a garden wall. Climbing plants create a 'vertical' aspect to the garden (**right**).

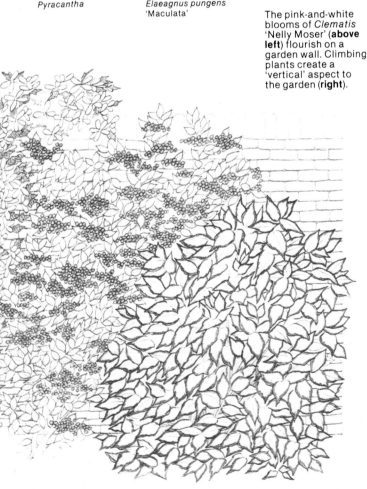

Wall shrubs

Although most wall shrubs grow equally well in the open, they usually have some feature or 'habit' that makes them specially suitable for growing against a structure such as a wall. Some, for example, have become known as wall shrubs because they are not particularly hardy and tend to grow better with the protection offered by a wall.

Pyracanthas come high on the list of desirable plants because, apart from summer foliage (and some small white flowers), there is the bonus of autumn and winter berries.

'Ordinary' shrubs

There are so many good shrubs that it is always difficult to single out a few. But the shortlist can be confined to plants that are:

- evergreen;
- able to grow well against a fence or wall;
- widely available; and that
- make a good screen/provide good cover.

High on the list must be the variegated hollies *Elaeagnus pungens* 'Maculata', and *Viburnum tinus*. Many conifers provide year-round cover and interest, of course, but their shape tends to be more upright and less bushy than those mentioned.

'Architectural' plants

You do not have to have a densely planted area to offset the boredom of a long wall or fence. Often, one or two really striking plants can enliven the scene and act as focal points.

A large clump of phormium, a single yucca, or a large castor oil plant (*Fatsia japonica*) may be all that is needed.

A large-leafed ivy, Dentata variegata / softens the outline and colour of its wall.

Living screens

For sheer impact, there is no substitute for the living boundary or screen formed by a hedge, even though it needs regular maintenance.

Apart from the regular trimming or pruning that is necessary with all hedges, there is one other big drawback: waiting for results.

Yet despite the extra work involved, a hedge is much preferred by many gardeners, for, besides marking the boundary, a hedge can, by illusion, extend it; it can blur the boundary even while defining it.

Often treated as a background against which to set other plants, a hedge can also be something beautiful in its own right. There are some spectacular flowering hedges to consider, and certainly many more pleasing evergreens than privet. Many of the most useful hedging plants are described on the following pages.

Big is not necessarily best

Because it is natural to want to see results quickly, there is the temptation to buy tall hedging plants. Resist it. They often take several seasons to become established and to start growing again, and frequently they lack the dense base that can be achieved by planting small and clipping early.

Small plants are cheaper, as well as better, in the long run.

To speed your hedge along, it is better to put money and effort into preparing the ground well.

Deciding what you want

It is worth being quite clear what you want from your hedge — a screen, something to keep animals in or out, a barrier to muffle sound from a busy road, or a decorative feature that contributes its own quota of beauty to the garden. The possible requirements are numerous.

The Table below includes all the plants described on the subsequent pages. It should enable you to find a hedge that suits your needs, whether you want a formal evergreen screen or an informal flowering hedge.

Planting distances differ according to whether you require a screen or a hedge. Distances between plants for a screen are

Name	Evergreen/deciduous	Recommended height	Formal/informal
Berberis darwinii	evergreen	1.2 – 1.8m (4 – 6ft)	formal/informal
Berberis x stenophylla	evergreen	1.8m (6ft)	informal
Berberis thunbergii	deciduous	0.4 – 1.8m[1] (1½ – 6ft)[1]	formal/informal
Buxus sempervirens	evergreen	0.3 – 1.2m[1] (1 – 4ft)[1]	formal
Carpinus betulus	deciduous[2]	1.5 – 2.4m (5 – 8ft)	formal
Chamaecyparis lawsoniana	evergreen (conifer)	1.5 – 2.4m (5 – 8ft)	formal
Cotoneaster lacteus	evergreen	1.8 – 2.4m (6 – 8ft)	informal
Crataegus monogyna	deciduous	1.5 – 2.4m (5 – 8ft)	formal
X Cupressocyparis leylandii	evergreen (conifer)	3 – 4.5m (10 – 15ft)	formal
Cupressus macrocarpa	evergreen (conifer)	2.4 – 5m (8 – 10ft)	formal
Elaeagnus x ebbingei	evergreen	1.2 – 1.8m (4 – 6ft)	formal
Euonymus japonicus	evergreen	1.5 – 1.8m (5 – 6ft)	formal
Fagus sylvatica	deciduous[2]	1.5 – 2.4m (5 – 8ft)	formal
'Flamboyant'	deciduous	2.4 – 3m (8 – 10ft)	formal
Forsythia	deciduous	1.2 – 1.8m (4 – 6ft)	informal
Griselinia littoralis	evergreen	1.5 – 2.1m (5 – 7ft)	formal
Ilex aquifolium	evergreen	1.5 – 1.8m (5 – 6ft)	formal
Lavandula spica	evergreen	0.3 – 1.2m[1] (1 – 4ft)[1]	informal
Ligustrum ovalifolium	semi-evergreen	1.2 – 1.8m (4 – 6ft)	formal
Lonicera nitida	evergreen	0.6 – 1.2m (2 – 4ft)	formal
Potentilla	deciduous	1 – 1.2m (3 – 4ft)	formal/informal
Prunus ceracifera 'Nigra'	deciduous	1.5 – 2.4m (5 – 8ft)	formal/informal
Prunus x cistena	deciduous	1.2 – 1.5m (4 – 5ft)	informal
Prunus laurocerasus	evergreen	1.5 – 1.8m (5 – 6ft)	formal
Rosa	deciduous	1 – 1.8m (3 – 6ft)	informal
Rosmarinus	evergreen	1.2 – 1.5m (4 – 5ft)	informal
Spiraea x arguta	deciduous	1.2 – 1.5m (4 – 5ft)	informal
Taxus baccata	evergreen	0.9 – 1.8m (3 – 6ft)	formal
Thuya plicata	evergreen (conifer)	1.5 – 2.4m (5 – 8ft)	formal

[1] Depends on variety
[2] Old leaves remain throughout winter

greater, for the plants themselves are to become bigger; close spacing keeps the plants more compact for a low hedge. Recommended spacings for each plant are given on the appropriate page. Also in the Table, the likely number of necessary cuts in a year will help you to decide whether a particular hedge is too labour-intensive for you.

What is a hedging plant?

Some of the plants grown as hedges could reach 9m (30ft) or more if grown as individual plants. Others could make specimen shrubs if grown in isolation. What makes them into a hedge is the close spacing (which restricts their growth and modifies their habit), coupled with clipping and pruning.

The dramatic difference between a beech tree and a beech hedge should be sufficient to demonstrate how even a seemingly unpromising plant can be tamed and trained into a first-class hedge. Do not rule a plant out simply because you do not normally associate it with your idea of a traditional hedge. On the other hand, be cautious with plants that you do not know will work; not every plant responds.

Living screens can be grown in almost any shape, size and colour (**below**). Many potentially very tall conifers can be kept in check to create dense attractive hedges. Colour and fragrance are provided by such plants as lavender and roses. For a long flowering season choose a potentilla or for a spring 'blaze' forsythia is hard to beat.

Main features	Cuts/year
foliage/flowers	one
flowers	one
foliage	one/two
foliage	one/two
foliage	one
foliage	one
foliage/berries	one
foliage	one/two
foliage	one
foliage	one
foliage	one
foliage	one
foliage	one
foliage	one
flowers	one
foliage	one
foliage	one
foliage/flowers	one
foliage	six
foliage	six
flowers	one
foliage	one
foliage	one
foliage	one
flowers	one
foliage/flowers	one
flowers	one
foliage	one
foliage	one

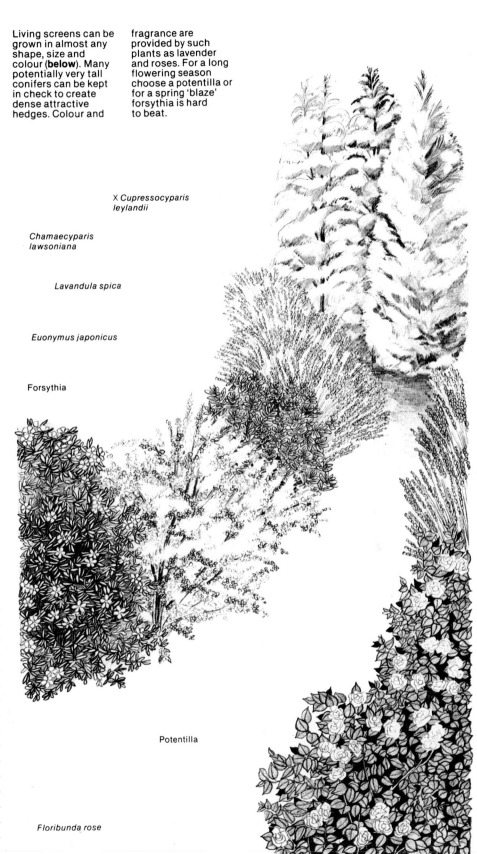

X *Cupressocyparis leylandii*

Chamaecyparis lawsoniana

Lavandula spica

Euonymus japonicus

Forsythia

Potentilla

Floribunda rose

Plants to grow by a hedge

Hedges make a fine backdrop for many plants, but unfortunately they also cause problems for plants close to them. There is a potential shade problem, the ground near the base is always very dry because the soil is largely protected from driving rain, and the soil is also likely to be impoverished.

Whatever is planted close to a hedge has to compete for light, moisture and food.

As a very rough guide, anything that you plant within a distance of half of the height of the hedge is likely to suffer unless you choose particularly tolerant plants. So a 1.8m (6ft) hedge could cause problems for a distance of about 90cm (3ft). If the hedge backs a large border, you probably need a path at the back anyway in order to be able to trim the hedge, and in these circumstances a 1.2m (4ft) hedge is likely to cause fewest problems.

The main difficulty arises with narrow beds between lawn and hedge. It is those borders narrow enough to be reached over to trim the hedge that are the most difficult in which to grow plants.

Nature has adapted plants to grow in even the most adverse spots, however, and some of the possible candidates are listed below. But because most of them are fairly tough does not mean that you can neglect them — they do need special care while they are becoming established.

Always water the plants regularly and thoroughly until they are established. Even if they tolerate dry soil normally, give them an extra chance to start with.

Be prepared to feed the plants, at least perennials for the first year. Foliar feeding has the advantage of feeding the plants without encouraging the hedge to compete.

Because the plants likely to succeed near hedge range from shrubs to annuals, they have here been grouped under type. But do not be afraid to mix them — there is nothing wrong mixing shrubs and herbaceous perennials, nor annuals with perennials. Often, however, it is best to keep to one or two plants in a small bed for real impact.

Bergenia cordifoia (**above**) is excellent for spring colour in the shade of a hedge.

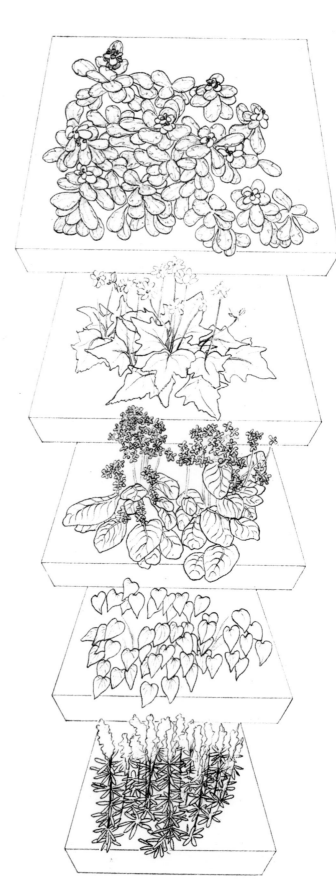

The plants: Herbaceous perennials

Ajuga reptans: Bugle Excellent as a ground cover plant. There are several good varieties, all of them suitable. Most of these ground-hugging plants have attractive coloured and variegated leaves. They have the considerable merit of being evergreen. Small spikes of blue flowers appear in late spring and early summer, but its main use is as a foliage ground cover.

Anemone X hybrida: Japanese anemone Useful if you want a late-flowering herbaceous plant. The usually white or pink flowers (it depends on variety) are carried on stems about 60-90cm (2-3ft) tall in late summer to mid-autumn.

Bergenia Another useful evergreen ground cover, but with striking flowers in spring. The large, round leaves often take on a reddish-purple hue in winter. Most varieties have pink flowers; the height seldom rises to more than 30cm (1ft).

Epimedium perralderianum Although almost evergreen, the leaves usually look the worse for wear by the end of winter. The bronze-yellow flowers in mid-to late spring are not particularly conspicuous, but it is a useful if slow-growing plant. The height is of about 30cm (1ft).

Euphorbia: Spurge There are many different spurges, but *E. robbiae* is one of the most suitable for this situation. Its habit is always interesting, with rosettes of dark green leaves, over which yellowish-green flowers are carried in early to mid-summer. Its height is of about 45cm (1½ft). *E. wulfenii* is also a possible candidate, but is a much bolder plant, reaching 1.2m (4ft).

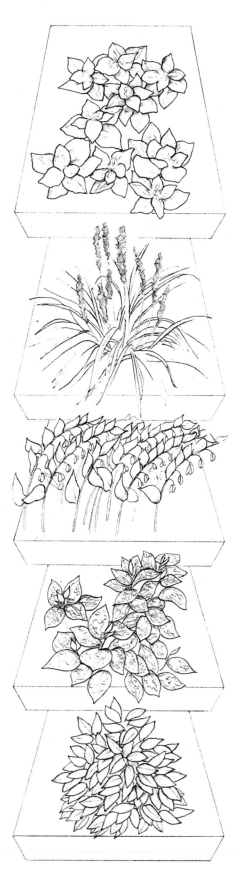

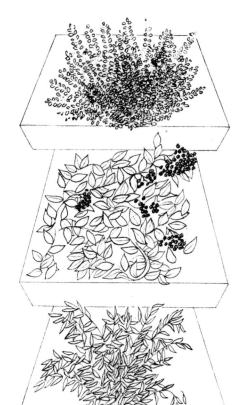

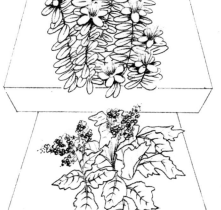

Lamium maculatum
Another low-growing
carpeting plant.
There are several
varieties, with either
pink or white flowers
in mid-spring to early
summer. It is grown
mainly as a foliage
plant, however; the
leaves are usually
marbled or splashed
with white.

Liriope muscari
An established
clump of this distinc-
tive plant is always
interesting when in
flower in late summer
to mid-autumn. Its
foliage is evergreen
and rush-like, with
blue spires of flowers
resembling a grape
hyacinth. Its height is
of about 30cm (1ft).

*Polygonatum X
hybridum:* Solomon's
seal
Frequently sold as *P.
multiflorum*, but
useful whatever its
name. The greenish-
white bell flowers
hang down from ar-
ching stems in late
spring and early sum-
mer. The height is of
about 75cm (2½ ft).

Pulmonaria
Can be used as a
ground cover, or as
isolated 'clumps' —
either way, a
desirable plant.
There are several
species and varieties
available, generally
with spotted or mottl-
ed leaves, and with
pink, violet, and blue
flowers in mid to late
spring.

Shrubs
Aucuba japonica
Only suitable near a
large hedge, other-
wise probably too
big.

Berberis
Dwarf kinds can be
used, or larger ones
if the hedge is
substantial in size.

Cotoneaster
A diverse family,
some species of
which make small
trees, others ground-
hugging carpeters.
For planting in a
small bed near a
hedge, a dwarf kind
such as *C. dammeri*
or *C. salicifolius*
'Repens' is probably
best. Both these are
evergreen.

Danae racemosa:
Alexandrian laurel
Not a spectacular
plant, but a useful
evergreen with
glossy green leaves
and orange berries,
appreciated most in
winter.

Hedera: Ivy
Ivies are very ver-
satile. In addition to
the uses described
elsewhere in this
book, they make a
fine ground cover for
difficult sites.

*Hypericum
calycinum:* Rose of
Sharon
A tough plant that
completely takes
over its bed in time.
The evergreen leaves
give year-round cover
(although they can
look tatty in winter
and may drop), but it
is worth growing just
for its vibrant display
of large yellow
flowers from early
summer to early
autumn. Height:
30-45cm (1-1½ ft).

Mahonia aquifolium:
Holly-leafed berberis
An evergreen shrub
growing 60-120cm
(2-4ft). Its leaves take
on red and purple
tints in winter.

Planting and training

Planting a hedge

Every hedge is intended on planting to remain in place for a long time, so there is only one chance to prepare the ground properly. It is easy to be tempted to short cuts, but thorough preparation helps the hedge to become established more rapidly.

Prepare the ground in advance by digging two spits deep (a spit is the depth of a spade blade), and incorporate as much well-rotted manure or compost as can be spared. Level the ground and rake in a general fertilizer at about 140g per sq m (4oz per sq yd) before planting.

Excavate holes at the spacing recommended for the hedge, large enough to take the root-ball, and for the roots to be spread out if the plants are bare-root.

Always firm the soil around the plants, and water thoroughly.

Container-grown trees can be planted at any time, provided the ground is not frozen or waterlogged, but bare-rooted and balled plants are generally best planted from mid-autumn to early spring. Mid- to late autumn is a good time for deciduous hedges, but evergreens are better planted in spring — mid- to late spring is satisfactory — so that they are not exposed to water loss from the leaves before the soil has warmed up enough for the roots to grow and take up more moisture.

There should be no need to stake your hedge, but if the site is very exposed it is a good idea to provide a temporary screen or fence. If this is too much for the horticultural budget, stretch strings or wires between stakes to support the intervening plants.

After planting

Water your hedge if the weather is dry, at least until it is established — especially if you want your hedge to grow quickly while it is young. Soak the ground thoroughly rather than sprinkling the surface, even if it means doing so less often.

Feed it with a foliar feed regularly for the first year. This may seem an extravagance for a hedge — it is certainly not essential — but even if you never feed it again, it is worth a little extra effort to get the hedge moving as quickly as possible.

Prune early. Shaping and forming your hedge can begin as soon as you have planted it. Cut back straggly stems, and even upward growth if you want a row of even plants. (The only exceptions are plants, such as tall conifers, that you want to grow up as a *high* screen.)

Tall windbreaks and screens

For a tall windbreak or screen, some of the plants listed on pages 30 and 31 are suitable, but you must plant them further apart. Bear in mind that such tall screens are really suitable only for a fairly large garden.

Shaping the hedge

The terms 'pruning' and 'trimming' can mean much the same thing, but pruning implies a more careful and individual selection of the shoots to be cut than trimming with hand shears or electric hedgetrimmers.

Always shape your hedge carefully, and use secateurs for large-leaved plants such as laurels. (If you use shears on these, the mutilated leaves are conspicuous and ugly, especially as they die.)

An *informal* hedge is not clipped or pruned to a neat, regular shape. A *formal* hedge is clipped to produce 'flat' surfaces.

Although most formal hedges are rectangular in cross-section, like a wall, it is better to taper the sides, narrowing them towards the top. The lower part then receives more light, and the wedge shape offers the best form of wind protection without causing too much turbulence.

After planting (or in spring if planted earlier), cut back all growths to half or two-thirds of their length. Remove any straggly shoots.

An informal hedge needs little more formative pruning, but at the end of the first summer a formal hedge should be pruned or trimmed again to form the outline shape of the hedge. It is a good idea to make two wooden frames to the desired shape and size of the hedge (obviously not its final size) and stretch strings between these, so that you have a clear idea of the shape to prune to.

Topiary, the art of pruning and shaping hedging plants into sculptural features to decorate the garden, has been a traditional pursuit for centuries. Early training may involve the use of wire to hold growing stems in the required shapes. With expert trimming and meticulous attention to detail, fantastic shapes can be achieved with plants such as privet and yew. These privet peacocks (**right**) perch atop crisply clipped blocks formed from the same plant.

Pachysandra terminalis Eventually forms good evergreen ground cover, about 30cm (1ft) high. The white-splashed 'Variegata' is much more attractive than the green form against a dark hedge.

Vinca: Periwinkle Both *V. minor* and the larger *V. major* are worth growing if there are no restrictions to their spreading habit. Neither grows much more than 30cm (1ft) high, and there are variegated forms that are more striking against a dark background.

Balsam *(Impatiens balsamina)* has colourful flower spikes and most varieties range between 30-45cm (1-1½ ft). Even more spectacular are the more popular kind of *impatiens*, the Busy Lizzies. There are many varieties, usually little more than 15cm (6in) in height, most of which provide a bold splash of colour for the summer.

Both these *impatiens* are half-hardy.

Shaping hedges for decorative effect is not a pursuit reserved solely for stately homes. These elegant shapes (**left**) herald the entrance to a modest house.

Yew hedging is ideal for precise trimming. These smooth shapes (**left**) create a striking feature in this Victorian garden.

DIFFICULT
SITES

Very dry sunny banks

Anyone who has explored the hillsides in Mediterranean countries must be aware that many plants flourish in hot, dry, arid conditions. A very dry sunny bank in the garden may, in the spring and summer, present very similar conditions. So why not try turning it into a little bit of Mediterranean hillside? It is easy if the right plants are chosen.

Sun and soils

A bank that receives sun for much of the day can become extremely hot in spring and summer. The sun rapidly dries out the soil, so that plants at times have minimal moisture. The rate at which the soil dries out depends also on the type. If it is a heavy clay, for instance, it will take longer to dry out than a sandy or gravelly soil and the sun bakes it hard on the surface. Sandy and gravelly soils cannot hold on to large amounts of moisture — rain rapidly drains through them to the lower levels, out of reach of plants' roots. So shortage of moisture can be very severe on a sunny bank with sandy or gravelly soils.

Dry sunny banks can be used to grow a wide variety of plants that thrive in arid conditions (**below**)

Spartium junceum in fragrant bloom (**above**)

For autumn colour try the bulb *Nerine bowdenii* (**top**) The unusual flowers of *Phlomis fruticosa* (**above**)

PLANTS FOR A DRY SUNNY BANK
Botanical Name
SHRUBS
Artemisia arborescens
Cistus
Colutea arborescens
Cytisus X beanii
Cytisus X kewensis
Genista hispanica
Genista lydia
Helichrysum angustifolium
Helianthemum
Lavandula officinalis
Perovskia atriplicifolia
Phlomis fruticosa
Phygelius capensis
Potentilla fruticosa
Rosmarinus officinalis
Salvia officinalis 'Purpurascens'
Santolina chamaecyparissus
Spartium junceum
Ulex europaeus 'Plenus'
Yucca filamentosa
PERENNIALS
Acaena microphylla
Acanthus spinosus
Anthemis cupaniana
Echinops ritro
Eryngium
Euphorbia myrsinites
Potentilia 'Gibson's Scarlet' and 'William Rollinson'
Sedum
Sempervivum
Thymus serpyllum cultivars
Verbascum hybrids
Zauschneria californica
BULBS
Allium
Crocus
Nerine bowdenii
Tulipa tarda

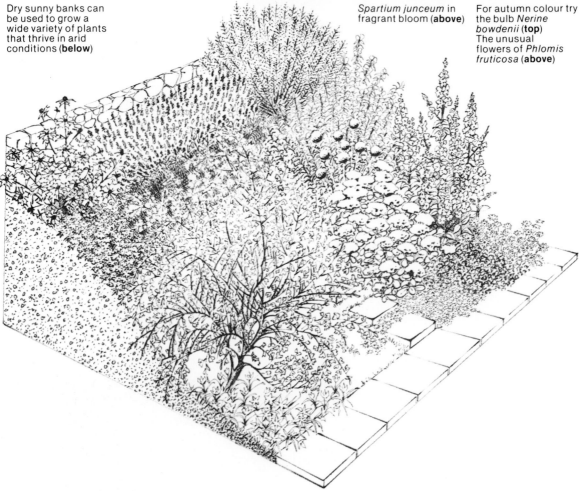

The paper-thin petals of *Cistus albidus* sparkle in the sunshine (**right**)

Common Name	Height	Spread	Colour	Season of interest	Notes
Wormwood	1m (3.3ft)	1m (3.3ft)	Yellow	Summer	Feathery silvery leaves
Rock rose	0.6–2m (2–6.5ft)	0.6–2m (2–6.5ft)	Red, pink, purple, white	Summer	Evergreen
Bladder senna	2.4m (8ft)	2.4m (8ft)	Yellow	Summer/Autumn	Balloon-like seed pods
Broom	45cm (18in)	90cm (3ft)	Yellow	Spring	–
Broom	45cm (18in)	1.2m (4ft)	Pale Yellow	Spring	–
Spanish gorse	60cm (2ft)	2m (6.5ft)	Yellow	Summer	Very spiny
Broom	60cm (2ft)	1.8m (6ft)	Yelow	Spring	–
Curry plant	60cm (2ft)	60cm (2ft)	Yellow	Summer	Grey leaves
Rock rose	15cm (6in)	60cm (2ft)	Wide range	Summer	–
Lavender	90cm (3ft)	90cm (3ft)	Grey-blue	Summer	Grey leaves
–	1.2m (4ft)	90cm (3ft)	Violet-blue	Summer	Grey leaves
Jerusalem sage	1m (3.3ft)	60cm (2ft)	Yellow	Summer	Grey woolly leaves
–	90cm (3ft)	60cm (2ft)	Scarlet	Summer	Evergreen
Shrubby cinquefoil	0.6–1.2m (2–4ft)	0.6–1.2m (2–4ft)	Yellow, orange, red, pink, white	Summer	–
Rosemary	2m (6.5ft)	2m (6.5ft)	Mauve	Spring/Summer	Evergreen
Purple-leaf sage	30cm (12in)	60cm (2ft)	Purple leaves	–	–
Cotton lavender	60cm (2ft)	60cm (2ft)	Yellow	Summer	Woolly silvery leaves
Spanish broom	2.4m (8ft)	2.4m (8ft)	Yellow	Summer	Green stems
Double gorse	2m (6.5ft)	2m (6.5ft)	Yellow	Spring	Very spiny
Adam's needle	60cm (2ft)	90cm (3ft)	Cream	Summer	Sword-like leaves
New Zealand burr	50cm (2in)	45cm (18in)	Crimson	Summer	Bronze leaves
Bear's breeches	1.2m (4ft)	60cm (2ft)	White and purple	Summer	Deeply cut spiny leaves
–	15cm (6in)	30cm (12in)	White	Summer	Grey scented leaves
Globe thistle	90cm (3ft)	60cm (2ft)	Steel blue	Summer	Grey-green leaves
–	0.6–1.2m (2–4ft)	45–60cm (18–24in)	Blue	Summer	Leaves often spiny
Spurge	15cm (6in)	30cm (12in)	Sulphur yellow	Spring	Blue-grey leaves
Cinquefoil	45cm (18in)	45cm (18in)	Red and orange respectively	Summer	–
Stonecrops	Prostrate to 45cm (18in)	15–45cm (6–18in)	IYellow, pink, red or white	Summer	Fleshy leaves
House-leeks	Prostrate	15–30cm (6–12in)	White, yellow, pink or red	Summer	Fleshy leaves in rosettes, often red, pink or purple
Thyme	Prostrate	60cm (24in)	Pink, red or white	Summer	Aromatic leaves
Mullein	1.2m (4ft)	60cm (2ft)	Mainly yellow or pink	Summer	Large woolly leaves
Californian fuchsia	45cm (18in)	45cm (18in)	Bright red	Summer	Greyish leaves
Ornamental onions	30cm (12in) to 1.2m (4ft)	30–45cm (12–18in)	Pink, red or yellow	Summer	Plant bulbs in groups
–	10–15cm (4–6in)	10–15cm (4–6in)	Mainly yellow, orange blue or purple	Spring	Plant bulbs in groups
–	60cm (24in)	About 15cm (6in)	Pink	Autumn	Plant bulbs in groups
Tulip	15cm (6in)	10cm (4in)	White and yellow	Spring	Plant bulbs in groups

How plants cope

There are many plants that actually revel in these seemingly arid conditions, and a fair selection may be found in the accompanying table. But how is it that some plants succeed in these hot dry conditions, whereas others simply shrivel up and die?

The answer is that many plants have to become specially adapted to arid conditions: in many parts of the world, plants thrive on hot, dry, rocky hillsides with virtually no soil, or they can be found in semi-deserts where very little rain falls.

Some of these plants have very deep roots which can tap supplies of moisture many feet below the surface. Others have fleshy or swollen roots and stems, also leaves, which store water towards periods of drought. Many plants from hot climates have woolly or waxy leaves. The wool, hair or waxy coating prevents the leaves from rapidly losing moisture during hot weather.

To help the plants along

In the garden there is never any need to give the plants a difficult time — it is possible to help them grow and really flourish by preparing the soil well for them before planting.

To ensure that the soil does not dry out too rapidly, plenty of organic matter can be dug in: well-rotted manure, garden compost, peat, spent hops, mushroom compost or shredded bark. This acts as a sponge and helps to retain moisture, so is particularly important if the soil is sandy or gravelly.

Dig a dry sunny bank to at least the depth of a spade before planting, and place a layer of organic matter in each trench. If the bottom of the trenches seems very hard and compacted, break it up with a fork, to the depth of the fork's own tines if possible, so that the roots of plants are able to grow deeply in search of moisture.

Also try to mix organic matter into the surface of the soil. Before planting it is a good idea to prick into the surface of the soil a general-purpose fertilizer.

To make a feature as interesting as possible, and to imitate a natural rocky hillside, consider using a few specimen rocks. A few pieces of well-shaped natural rock, their bases partly sunk in the soil, should do the trick and also provide a cool root run for some of the plants. Some of those recommended in the table can be effectively grown over a rock, such as *Cytisus*, helianthemums, *Acaena*, sempervivums and thymes.

Planting tips

Plants put out new roots and become established more quickly if the planting-hole is well prepared. Mix some moist peat into the bottom of the hole, and also into the soil removed, before returning it around the roots. Make sure the roots — or the ball of soil around the roots — are moist before planting.

Looking after the plants

Try not to leave plants to their own devices once they are planted — a little care and attention will encourage them to grow that much better.

Water them thoroughly if the soil is dry after planting. Then, during the first season after planting, apply water whenever the soil starts to dry out. It is best to water plants on a bank with a garden sprinkler attached to a hosepipe to give a gentle rain-like effect. The water is then less likely to run off, as would be the case with a watering can or hosepipe.

To prevent soil from being washed down a bank during periods of heavy rain, to help prevent rapid drying out of the soil in hot weather, and to create a pleasing natural appearance, consider covering the soil after planting with a layer of shingle or stone chippings, both of which are available from the larger garden centres. A layer 2.5-5cm (1-2in) deep is sufficient. This also helps to prevent weed growth.

An annual feed in the spring, with a fertilizer such as blood, fishmeal and bone, ensures that the plants do not have a starved appearance.

Wet and flooded areas

Gardeners with very wet soil that may become waterlogged or hold surface water in the winter, could be forgiven for giving up gardening in despair. Yet a most attractive garden could be created in such conditions by choosing moisture-loving plants.

It may not, of course, be the entire garden that is affected — maybe just an area at the foot of a slope, for example, where water drains down from a higher level.

Generally it is the heavier types of soil that commonly lie wet — like clay. If you live in a low-lying peaty area (fen country, for example), then you also may have very wet soil.

The royal fern (*Osmunda regalis*) develops into a fine specimen plant in moist conditions (**above**). Here the delicate pale green fronds take on the hues of autumn. The lovely blotched blooms of monkey flower (*Mimulus luteus*) dazzle the eye all summer long (**left**). The stunning white flower spathes of *Zantedeschia aethiopica* 'Crowborough' (**far left**). The spathes of *Lysichitum americanum*, a brilliant yellow (**left**). A wide variety of moisture-loving plants (**below**), including the plumes of *Aruncus* and *Astilbe*, the upright spikes of *Lobelia*, the broad leaves of *Hosta*.

PLANTS FOR WET AND FLOODED A...
Botanical Name
TREES AND SHRUBS
Acer negundo
Alnus cordata
Alnus glutinosa
Alnus incana
Betula pendula
Betula nigra
Cornus alba varieties
Cornus stolonifera 'Flaviramea'
Rhamnus frangula
Salix alba 'Chermesina'
Salix alba 'Vitellina'
Sambucus nigra 'Albovariegata'/'Aurea'/ 'Purpurea'
Sambucus racemosa 'Plumosa Aurea'
Taxodium distichum
PERENNIALS
Astilbe X arendsii cultivars
Filipendula ulmaria
Gunnera manicata
Ligularia
Lysichitum americanum
Mimulus guttatus/luteus
Osmunda regalis
Zantedeschia aethiopica

The right way to start

It pays to improve soil before attempting to plant anything. Drainage of surplus water needs to be effected, and the soil should be 'opened up' as much as possible to allow air to penetrate to the roots of the plants. In bad cases of waterlogging there is very little air in the soil, a situation that can result in the death of plants, even those which are moisture-lovers.

Soil preparation involves deep digging — to two depths of the spade (known as double digging). This ensures that the lower soil (the subsoil) — which may be hard and compacted, preventing surplus water from draining down to the lower levels of soil well away from plant roots — is well broken up.

During digging, work in plenty of grit or coarse sand, which has the effect of keeping the soil open and therefore well drained and aerated. Mix it well into the subsoil and into the top layer. There may be no need to prepare the entire garden in this way — only the beds and borders, and certainly any area in which it is intended to lay a lawn.

Take care with planting

Planting-holes on wet sites need to be prepared specially well so that plants have every chance to become established quickly. Make each planting-hole sufficiently large to take the roots of the plant without cramping them. Before inserting the plant, dig the bottom of the hole to the depth of a fork and make sure it is well broken up. Mix into the bottom a liberal quantity of peat, or one of the proprietary planting mixtures available from garden centres.

The soil removed should be replaced around the plant, but first thoroughly mix into it plenty of peat or planting mixture which makes it easier for the plants to quickly root into the surrounding soil.

Aftercare of plants

Lavish care and attention on your plants to ensure good growth. Feeding is important on wet soils because plant foods can be washed down into the lower levels of soil, out of reach of the roots. (This is known as leaching.) Carry out a regular feeding programme in the spring and summer, when plants are growing. Use a general-purpose fertilizer or blood, fishmeal and bone.

Wet gardens often have problems with slugs and snails: these creatures love damp conditions. Use slug pellets.

Common Name	Height	Spread	Colour	Season of interest	Notes
Box elder	6m (20ft)	4.5m (15ft)	–	Summer	'Variegatum' has white and green foliage
Italian alder	12m+ (39ft+)	–	–	Spring/Summer	Spring catkins
Common alder	9m+ (30ft+)	–	–	Spring/Summer	Spring catkins
Grey alder	12m+ (39ft+)	–	–	Spring/Summer	Spring catkins
Silver birch	10m+ (33ft+)	–	Yellow autumn foliage. White peeling bark	Summer/Autumn	–
River birch	10m+ (33ft+)	–	Pinkish-white bark	Summer	–
Shrubby dogwood	2.4m (8ft)	2.4m (8ft)	Red stems	Winter	'Sibirica' has red stems in winter. 'Elegantissima' and 'Spaethii' have variegated foliage
Shrubby dogwood	2.4m (8ft)	2.4m (8ft)	Yellow stems	Winter	–
Alder buckthorn	2.4m (8ft)	2m (6.5ft)	Yellow autumn foliage	Autumn	Red fruits
Scarlet willow	10m+ (33ft+)	–	Orange-scarlet shoots	Winter	Usually cut back for winter shoots
Golden weeping willow	15m+ (49ft+)	–	Yellow shoots	Winter	Usually cut back for winter shoots
Elder/Golden elder	2.4–3.6m (8–12ft)	2.4–3.6m (8–12ft)	Cream and white/yellow/ purple foliage	Summer	–
Golden cut-leaf elder	2.4–3.6m (8–12ft)	2.4–3.6m (8–12ft)	Golden foliage	Summer	–
Swamp cypress	10m (33ft)	4.5m (15ft)	Green/bronze	Spring/Autumn	Fresh green spring growth. Foliage turns bronze in autumn. Deciduous conifer. Red-brown bark
–	0.6–1m (2–3.3ft)	45–60cm (18–24in)	Shades of red and pink, plus white	Summer	
Meadow sweet	1m (3.3ft)	60cm (2ft)	Creamy white	Summer	Fragrant flowers. The cultivar 'Aurea' has golden foliage and is only 30–45cm (12–18in) high
–	3m+ (10ft)	3m+ (10ft)	Foliage	Summer	Massive rhubarb-like leaves. 'Bottlebrush' flowerheads
–	1.2m (4ft)	60cm (2ft)	Yellow, orange	Late summer	Daisy-like flowers. Large leaves, up to 30cm (12in) across
False American skunk cabbage	90cm (3ft)	1.8m (6ft)	Yellow	Spring	Arum-like flowers with green spadix
Monkey flower	45cm (18in)	45cm (18in)	Yellow with red spots and plain yellow	Summer	–
Royal fern	1.2m (4ft)	1.2m (4ft)	Pale green fronds	Summer	'Purpurascens' has purple-copper foliage
Arum lily	1m (3.3ft)	1m (3.3ft)	White	Spring/Summer	Cultivar 'Crowborough' is hardier than the type species

Small concrete backyards

A small concrete back yard, devoid of plant life, is certainly a depressing sight, yet it can be turned into a most delightful patio garden.

'Patio' is a Spanish word meaning the inner courtyard of a house, where the house is built in the form of a square, enclosing an open space. In hot climates the patio garden often has a pool and perhaps a fountain, and plants are grown either in soil beds or in ornamental containers. The idea is to create a cool shady place — a refuge from the heat of the day.

You can turn a small concrete back yard into a similar haven of tranquillity. And if it is surrounded by a brick wall or a fence, then so much the better, for it will then be a very private little world.

Many city or suburban houses have nothing more than a yard at the back, yet many have been turned into the most delightful patio gardens.

Varying the surface
A very simple and practical idea for making an area of nothing but concrete more interesting is to have some areas of gravel. This immediately provides a pleasing contrast in textures. The same advice applies if the back yard is covered with concrete paving slabs.

There are two ways of creating such gravel areas. The simplest is to lay the gravel direct on the concrete; a layer about 2.5-5cm (1-2in) deep is sufficient. The material to use is pea shingle, which is readily available from builders' merchants and some garden centres.

The gravel must be retained in some way or it will not stay in its allotted place. This is easily achieved with the aid of small concrete curbing or edging stones, or with a single layer of ornamental walling bricks. These ideally should be cemented in place.

If the gravel is placed directly on to concrete, you will have to find containers in which to grow plants on it. If, however, you wish to grow plants in soil beds topped with gravel, you will have to break up and lift some of the concrete, then dig out the soil to a depth of about 30cm (1ft), and replace it with good topsoil or with potting compost. Before refilling, though, break up the bottom of the hole to the depth of a fork, for the subsoil is bound to be compacted. This helps surplus water to drain away and ensures that plants can easily root into the lower soil.

Plants for gravel areas
Particularly suitable plants for these gravel areas, whether they are to be grown direct in soil or in ornamental containers and tubs, are those with bold or dramatic foliage that give an exotic atmosphere, imitating the patio gardens of hot countries.

Phormiums or New Zealand flax have the

most dramatic leaves of all: they are sword-shaped and held erect. And what is more, the foliage is evergreen. They need a sunny situation, although they do not mind partial shade. Some of the modern cultivars have very colourful foliage. Try the following: *Phormium cookianum* 'Tricolor', leaves striped green, white and red, height: 90cm (3ft); also *P. tenax* cultivars: 'Bronze Baby', deep bronze leaves, 60cm (2ft) high; 'Purpureum', purplish leaves, height: 2m (6½ft); 'Sundowner', cream-pink and greyish-purple, height: 90cm (3ft); 'Thumbelina', purple-bronze, 30cm (1ft) high; 'Yellow Wave', golden-yellow and green, height: 75cm (30in); 'Dazzler', deep red, similar height; and 'Variegatum', cream and green, 2m (6½ft) in height.

The *yuccas* have stiff sword-like evergreen leaves and also need a sunny situation. They are generally grown as single specimens rather than in groups. There are several to choose from, such as *Yucca filamentosa*, whose leaf edges have curly threads, height: about 60cm (2ft); *Y. filamentosa* 'Variegata', with green and cream striped leaves; *Y. flaccida* 'Ivory', noted for its creamy white flowers, height: about 60cm (2ft); and *Y. gloriosa*, popularly known as Adam's needle, which forms a trunk-like stem topped with spine-tipped leaves, and produces creamy white flowers, height: up to 2m (6½ft).

The *hostas* or plantain lilies are dwarf herb-

Flagstones, a narrow border, climbing wall plants and a wide variety of planted containers transform this small back yard (**above left**) into a haven of colour and interest. Ablaze with the bright blooms of pelargoniums and petunias, this back yard (**left**) also features the cooler contrasts of sempervivums and herbs. Lack of space should never cramp your gardening ambitions. Here a compact yard (**below left**), viewed from the house, features an ornamental pond, a luxuriant planting of choice foliage and flowering subjects and a classical statue as a focal point.

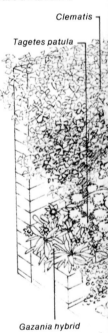

Clematis

Tagetes patula

Gazania hybrid

aceous plants with large, bold leaves, which come in various shades of green, also bluish grey and variegated cream, white and green. There are many cultivars; choose any which appeal. They have lily-like flowers in summer, generally lilac or white. The plantain lilies are particularly useful for shady parts of the garden, for they like moist soil. They look particularly fine growing at the edge of a pool.

Rodgersias are also grown mainly for their attractive foliage, which is bold and hand-shaped. They can be grown in sun or partial shade, and prefer reasonably moist conditions — so keep them well watered. A popular cultivar is *Rodgersia pinnata* 'Superba', with bronzy purple leaves. Height: about 90cm (3ft).

The ornamental grasses associate well with many plants, particularly plants with bold foliage like the *hostas* and *rodgersias*. There are many grasses to choose from. All of the following are perennial in habit and appreciate a sunny spot: *Helictotrichon sempervirens*, blue-grey foliage, 45cm (18in); *Cortaderia selloana* 'Gold

Crazy paving (**above**) enhances an informal planting. A sword-like phormium (**top right**) in a patio corner. *Rodgersia pinnata* 'Superba' (**above right**).

Band', leaves striped yellow and green, 75cm (30in); *C. selloana* 'Sunningdale Silver', variety of pampas grass, with creamy white plumes of flowers, 2m (6½ft); *Festuca glauca*, blue-grey foliage, 30cm (12in); *Holcus mollis* 'Variegatus', green and silver variegated, 30cm (12in); *Miscanthus sinensis* 'Zebrinus', the zebra grass, whose leaves are banded with gold, 2m (6½ft); and *Phalaris arundinacea* 'Picta', popularly called Gardener's garters, a vigorously spreading grass with green and white striped leaves, height: 60cm (2ft).

Prostrate or low-growing junipers are useful for contrasting with spiky or grassy leaves. There are many to choose from, such as *Juniperus horizontalis* 'Bar Harbor', completely prostrate with grey-green foliage; *J. X media* 'Old Gold', height and spread about 90cm (3ft); and *J. sabina tamariscifolia*, a flat-topped bush with deep green foliage, 30 cm (12in) high, and a spread of about 1.2m (4ft). They like sun or partial shade.

The evergreen shrub *Fatsia japonica* has large, bold, hand-shaped leaves and makes a specimen about 2.4m (8ft) in height and spread. White flowers are produced in autumn. It is a good shrub for shade, but takes full sun.

In areas where the climate is perhaps a little milder, you could try the Chusan palm *Trachycarpus fortunei*, which has large fan-shaped leaves on a thick trunk. It is slow growing but eventually makes a specimen well over 2m (6.5ft) in height, and the leaves have a similar spread. Sun is needed, plus a spot sheltered from wind.

There are all kinds of hardy ferns that can be planted in cool shady spots, including around the edge of a pool where the soil is moist.

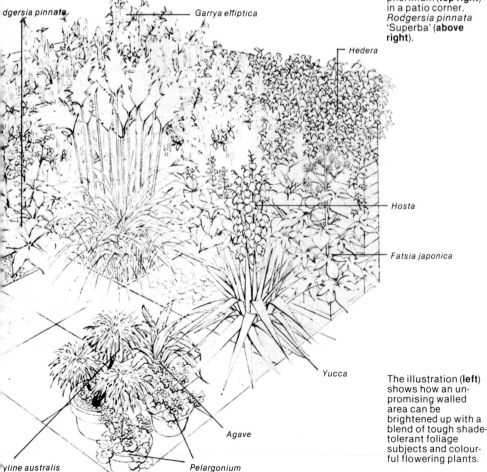

dgersia pinnata · Garrya elliptica · Hedera · Hosta · Fatsia japonica · Yucca · Agave · ·yline australis · Pelargonium

The illustration (**left**) shows how an unpromising walled area can be brightened up with a blend of tough shade-tolerant foliage subjects and colourful flowering plants.

A new dimension

To add another dimension, consider a pool. Such an attraction is very easy to put in these days, using one of the small prefabricated pools obtainable from garden centres or water-garden specialists, made from rigid fibreglass or plastic. A formal square or rectangular pool is generally more in keeping than an informal shape. Moreover, to avoid your having to dig a hole in the concrete, the pool could be raised — simply by placing it on the concrete and building up the sides with bricks or ornamental walling blocks. The variation in height adds life to an otherwise flat area.

Water also provides the patio garden with another texture, reflecting the sky and plants, and creating further interest. Miniature waterlilies are available for small pools, and around the edge, in the shallow water, marginal aquatics like marsh marigold and perhaps a water iris could be planted. Include some submerged oxygenating plants or 'water weeds', and introduce some fish. For best results, choose a sunny place for the pool.

Make best use of vertical space

If the yard is surrounded by a wall or fence, there are then ideal supports for climbing plants which can be trained to horizontal wires or to trellis panels fixed to the wall or fence.

There are many climbers and wall shrubs to choose from, even for shady aspects, such as winter jasmine, *Jasminum nudiflorum*, with yellow flowers; ornamental ivies with green or variegated foliage; Virginia creeper; and *Garrya elliptica*, which has greenish catkins in winter.

For sunny walls and fences choose from the wide range of clematis, climbing and rambling roses (these two subjects look well together and can be allowed to intertwine); honeysuckles; and summer jasmine, *Jasminum officinale*, with white scented blooms.

Bold splashes of colour in stylish containers (**above**) create a superb miniature garden. Here pelargoniums, *Impatiens*, begonias and fuchsias predominate. Screens and trellis work (**left and far left**) form a striking background to patio plants. A cramped town back yard may seem an unpromising site but here (**below left**) a small patio is engulfed by a 'jungle' of foliage and flowering plants.

Containers for plants

A look around a good garden centre reveals a wide range of ornamental containers, in all shapes, sizes and materials.

Very popular are terracotta pots and vases, as well as modern concrete tubs. Traditional wooden tubs are also attractive. Classical urns are very much in keeping with a patio garden. In order to fill every available inch of space, make use also of window boxes and hanging baskets.

For a large container for planting, consider constructing a floor box. This structure is essentially a raised bed and may be built directly on concrete or paving from timber, railway sleepers, bricks, walling blocks, or similar building materials.

All containers must have drainage holes in the base. Before adding compost, place a layer of drainage material in the bottom, such as pebbles, stones or broken clay flower pots. Top this layer with coarse peat, and then fill up to within a couple of centimetres (roughly an inch) of the top with a proprietary potting compost. A large raised bed should be filled with good quality topsoil, which will probably have to be bought in.

Colourful plants for containers

It is not only permanent plants, recommended earlier, that can be used in containers, but also temporary subjects to give colour in spring and summer — the spring and summer bedding plants.

For summer colour in shade, try *Begonia semperflorens* (wax begonia), fuchsias, *Impatiens* (busy lizzie), and the annual *Mimulus* (monkey flowers).

For summer colour in sunny parts of the garden there is a very wide choice indeed: pelargoniums (geraniums), petunias, French and African marigolds, *Nicotiana*, tuberous begonias, *Verbena, Lobelia*, Gazanias, Livingstone daisies, *Heliotrope* and ageratums.

Spring bedding plants suitable for shade include polyanthus, forget-me-nots and coloured primroses. For sun, plant bulbs such as tulips and hyacinths, and plants such as double daisies and wallflowers.

For a hot sunny spot, try some succulent plants in pots outdoors for the summer, such as the century plant *(Agave)* and *Cordyline australis*, (the cabbage palm), but remember these have to be taken indoors in early autumn in temperate climates.

Hard-wear areas

Some parts of the garden receive very hard wear. Consequently, they never really look attractive — more often than not they are an eyesore To improve this situation it is generally a case of re-thinking in terms of more resilient surfaces and tougher plants.

The main problem areas commonly centre on parts of a lawn — or even the whole lawn if it is small — especially the areas used for sitting on or as playing areas for children. The grass simply becomes worn away.

Play areas themselves often look very shabby, perhaps down to nothing more than bare earth where the grass has completely died out. In wet weather, such areas often become mud patches. Plants around a play area may look rather untidy; they do not readily make new growth after being damaged or trodden on.

Areas around the house doors are obviously used a great deal, and again may resemble a children's play area. Other vulnerable parts of a garden are borders or beds alongside drives and paths.

But there is really no need to put up with shabby areas. Choose the right kinds of plants, the appropriate surfacing materials — and hard-wear areas can be considerably improved and in time even look attractive, yet *still* be used just as much. After all, a garden is meant to be used as well as being decorative.

Hard-wear lawns

The lawn is without doubt the most vulnerable part of a garden, used more than any other for sitting and playing. Consequently, bare patches quickly appear as the surface becomes very compacted, and muddy patches develop in wet weather. Tiny lawns, the norm in modern pocket-handkerchief gardens, come off worse than larger grass areas because use is concentrated in one area. With a large lawn, the area actually in use can at least be moved around before damage occurs, to give the worn grass a chance to recover.

A lawn that is to be subject to hard wear should be made by sowing a grass seed mixture which produces a resilient turf. These mixtures contain a high proportion of

ryegrass; a typical composition is: three parts perennial ryegrass *(Lolium perenne)*, a broad-leaved grass which grows in tufts; four parts chewings fescue *(Festuca rubra commutata)*, which is a tufted drought-resistant grass with thin leaves that produces a fine appearance; two parts crested dog's-tail *(Cynosurus cristatus)*, which grows in broad-leaved tufts and is also drought-resistant; and one part rough-stalked meadow grass *(Poa trivialis)*, a broad-leaved grass that spreads by runners above the ground. Many mixes, such as Sprinter, contain dwarf ryegrass which produces a less tufty-looking lawn.

On no account use a grass seed mix formulated for a luxury lawn. These mixtures contain very fine grasses, such as browntop

The variegated leaves of *Euonymus fortunei* 'Silver Queen' (**left**) are usefully tough.

Resilient ground cover is provided by *Cotoneaster dammeri* (**above**).

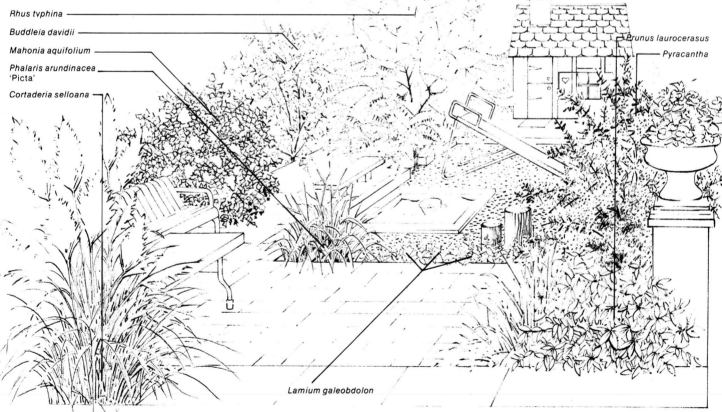

Rhus typhina

Buddleia davidii

Mahonia aquifolium

Phalaris arundinacea 'Picta'

Cortaderia selloana

Prunus laurocerasus

Pyracantha

Lamium galeobdolon

bent *(Agrostis tenuis)* and chewings fescue, which do not stand up to hard wear. Chewings fescue is used in utility mixes mainly to improve the appearance of a lawn — to give a 'thick pile'.

It is also possible to have special grass seed mixtures made up that contain clover. Most people would consider this to be a weed, but a lawn with a high proportion of clover is nevertheless very hard wearing and, as a bonus, stays green during drought conditions. It is also possible to have an entirely clover lawn. For clover mixtures or pure clover, contact a specialist lawn grass seedsman. Clover can be mown exactly like an ordinary lawn to give a fairly smooth surface. Alternatively, it can be allowed to grow fairly tall and flower before it is cut.

Gravel areas
A very tiny lawn is not a practical proposition if the area is to be used a great deal. One alternative is to consider laying gravel. Admittedly, the surface is not as soft as grass but it can look neat at all times, especially if perhaps some containers are grouped on it, filled with colourful plants.

A gravel area is easily constructed. First, make sure the area is as level as possible before setting garden curbing stones around the edges to contain the gravel, ideally bedded in cement. Next, sprinkle dry cement all over the soil — a layer about 12mm (½in) deep will be sufficient. Fork this into the top 5-7.5cm (2-3in) of soil, mixing it well in. Do this preferably when the soil is moist but not wet. Then firm the soil really well, ideally by using a heavy garden roller. Eventually the cement hardens and binds the soil together, giving a very hard surface. Subsequently, cover the area with gravel — pea shingle from a local builders' merchant — to a depth of about 5cm (2in).

If any weeds grow through the gravel, spray them with a proprietary path weedkiller. It is also a good idea to rake the gravel about once a week to keep it looking neat and level. Apart from that, no maintenance is needed.

Sitting-out areas
Within a larger lawn that is used for sitting, why not consider constructing a special sitting-out area — a hard surface for a table and chairs? It can certainly be more comfortable — no longer does your chair sink into the lawn, nor does your table rock crazily, endangering

Hypericum calycinum (**above**) is an outstanding ground cover plant for hard-wear areas. Once established, it forms a dense growth of evergreen leaves that are smothered in showy yellow flowers throughout the summer.

For an exceptionally robust and rewarding shrub it is hard to beat the low-growing *Prunus laurocerasus* 'Otto Luyken' (**below**). The attractive white flower spikes are borne above the glossy evergreen foliage in spring.

things upon it. You will also be able to sit out when the grass is very wet.

Mark out an area of suitable size — it could be formal (square or oblong) in a formal garden, or perhaps an irregular shape in a more informal garden. Some superb paving materials are available today, as a visit to a garden centre reveals. Paving slabs come in all shapes, sizes and colours; an alternative is natural-stone paving, particularly in a cottage garden. Paving should be laid on a foundation consisting of about 15cm (6in) of well-rammed hardcore, topped with a thin layer of sand. Lay paving slabs preferably on mortar, and leave a 6mm (¼in) gap between them. The gaps should later be grouted with cement and sand to prevent weeds from growing through.

Play areas
Small children need somewhere to play, and it is a good idea to allocate one specific part of the garden for this purpose, where they can dig

TOUGH PLANTS FOR HARD WEAR AREAS

Botanical name	Common name	Height
SHRUBS		
Berberis X stenophylla	Barberry	2.4m (8ft)
Buddleia davidii	Butterfly bush	2.4m (8ft)
Cornus alba	Shrubby dogwood	2.4m (8ft)
Cotoneaster horizontalis	–	60cm (2ft)
Cotoneaster species	–	60cm-3.6m (2-12ft)
Elaeagnus X ebbingei	–	3m (10ft)
Euonymus fortunei	–	Prostrate or low growing
Hedera colchica	Persian ivy	Prostrate
Hedera colchica 'Dentata Variegata'	Variegated Persian ivy	Prostrate
Hypericum calycinum	St John's wort	30cm (12in)
Kerria japonica 'Pleniflora'	Jew's mallow	2.4m (8ft)
Leycesteria formosa	–	2m (6.5ft)
Lonicera pileata	Shrubby honeysuckle	60cm (2ft)
Mahonia aquifolium	Oregon grape	1.5m (5ft)
Prunus laurocerasus 'Otto Luyken' and 'Schipkaensis'	Dwarf cherry laurels	60cm (2ft)
Pyracantha	Firethorn	3.6m (12ft)
Rhus typhina	Stag's horn sumach	3.6m (12ft)
Ribes sanguineum	Flowering currant	2.4m (8ft)
Symphoricarpos albus	Snowberry	1.8m (6ft)
PERENNIALS		
Cortaderia selloana	Pampas grass	2.4m (8ft)
Elymus arenarius	Lyme grass	60cm (2ft)
Lamiastrum galeobdolon 'Variegatum'	Yellow archangel	30cm (12in)
Phalaris arundinacea 'Picta'	Gardener's garters grass	60cm (2ft)

holes, make a 'camp', and have a swing, slide and climbing frame. This should also, to some extent, act as a protective measure for the rest of the garden, keeping it looking good, most of its plants safe from tiny feet and garden toys.

Furthermore, if ever you are talked into buying a tent, put it up in the play area and *not* on the lawn; if a tent is erected on the lawn even for only a few days, the grass beneath turns yellow, and takes some time to recover.

A play area needs a suitable surface, certainly not grass or soil, or it will end up as a mud patch. A fairly new idea is to surface it with pulverized or shredded bark, which gives a very soft, well-drained surface and can be laid directly on to well-firmed soil. A depth of about 5-7.5cm (2-3in) is sufficient. If children fall over on this they do not hurt themselves and, what is more, they keep clean.

Plant life need not be entirely absent from a play area — indeed, some groups of suitable shrubs not only make it look more attractive

but may possibly be appreciated by youngsters as they play amid them. The play area could also be surrounded (or partly surrounded) by shrubs, not only as a partial screen, but so that children know exactly which is their part of the garden.

Of course such shrubs must be really tough, and ought also to be quick-growing. Some of them could be flowering shrubs — but avoid prickly or thorny kinds. Particularly recommended are *Buddleia davidii* cultivars, shrubby dogwoods with coloured stems, and *Kerria japonica* 'Pleniflora'. Also avoid any shrubs which produce berries in case small children might be tempted to eat them (although the berries of most garden shrubs are not poisonous).

Smartening up access areas
Other hard-wear areas are those around the house doors, around gates, and borders or beds alongside drives and paths. For these

areas, which are liable to be trodden over occasionally, if not regularly, one suggestion is to clothe the soil with really tough ground-cover plants: there are some that can put up with the occasional heavy foot.

Plant ground-cover plants in bold groups or drifts, setting the plants fairly close together so that they quickly close up and provide dense cover. Most of the ground-cover plants recommended here can be planted approximately 30-45cm (12-18in) apart in every direction.

Before planting, however, it pays to prepare the soil well by digging in plenty of well-rotted manure or garden compost, and pricking in some sterilized bonemeal or a general fertilizer. Feed and water the plants well and they will grow vigorously.

Suitable tough ground-cover plants include *Cotoneaster horizontalis*, *Euonymus fortunei* cultivars, *Hedera colchica*, *Hypericum calycinum*, *Lonicera pileata* and *Lamiastrum galeobdolon* 'Variegatum'.

Spread	Colour	Season of interest	Shade tolerance	Notes
3.6m (12ft)	Golden yellow	Spring	√	Evergreen, prickly
2.4m (8ft)	Blue, purple, red, mauve, white	Summer		Deciduous, fragrant flowers
2.4m (8ft)	White	Summer	√	Red stems, deciduous. Several cultivars available
2-2.4m (6-8ft)	White	Summer	√	Red berries in Autumn. Deciduous. Ideal for ground cover
Variable	White	Summer	√	Many species and cultivars, all with colourful autumn berries
3m (10ft)	White	Autumn	√	Evergreen, silvery grey leaves
Variable	–	–	√	Ground cover. Evergreen. Many cultivars have variegated leaves
Variable	–	–	√	Dark green evergreen leaves, large and heart-shaped. Ground cover plant
Variable	–	–	√	Cream and green variegated leaves. Ground cover
Variable	Yellow	Summer	√	Evergreen ground cover, very vigorous
2m (6ft)	Yellow	Spring		Deciduous, forms thickets of growth
2m (6.5ft)	White and claret	Summer	√	Deciduous, produces purplish berries in autumn
1.2cm (4ft)	Greenish	Spring	√	Ground cover shrub, semi-evergreen, bright green foliage
2m (6.5ft)	Yellow	Spring	√	Glossy, deep green evergreen, spiny foliage. Blue-black berries
1m (3.3ft)	White	Summer	√	Evergreen leaves. Good ground cover
3.6m (12ft)	White	Summer	√	Grown for red, orange or yellow autumn berries, evergreen, spiny
3.6m (12ft)	Pale red	Summer		Good autumn leaf colour. Crimson berries
2.4m (8ft)	Red, crimson or pink	Spring		Deciduous, black autumn berries
1.8m (6ft)	Pink	Summer	√	Grown for its large white berries. Choose one of the cultivars
2m (6.5ft)	Silvery plumes	Summer/Autumn		Arching, grassy evergreen leaves. 'Sunningdale Silver' is a good cultivar
Indefinite	Grey-blue	Summer		A vigorous grass with grey-blue foliage. Needs plenty of space to spread
Indefinite	Yellow	Summer	√	Excellent ground cover. Very vigorous. Evergreen leaves splashed with silver
Indefinite	Greenish	Summer		Very vigorous and spreading grass with white and green striped leaves. Makes good ground cover

Sloping sites

A sloping garden can certainly look more attractive than a perfectly flat site — but is not without its problems.

For instance, drainage of water from the soil can be too effective; moreover, if the soil is of a type to be naturally well drained — such as sand or gravel — then the garden may be very dry indeed. This is further accentuated if the site also faces the sun for much of the day.

Water of course drains to the bottom of any slope. If it cannot then escape — it may be blocked by the house if the garden slopes down to the house — then the ground is inevitably very wet and boggy. Such a damp spot can also become a frost pocket as cold air additionally drains down to the bottom and builds up. It is obviously not an appropriate site for a greenhouse, or for growing fruit trees.

If the garden slopes very steeply, there may well be the need to create some flatter areas. This can be achieved by terracing — either all or part of the garden, depending on the size of the plot — which involves building retaining walls and levelling the land between them.

Of course, conversely, there are advantages in a sloping site. If it faces the sun for much of the day, the soil warms up and dries out quickly in the spring, so that an early start can be made with sowing vegetables and flowers. And it is ideal for the building of a rock garden, which always looks far more natural when not built on a completely flat site.

Dealing with a wet patch

If constructing terraces is too energetic a means of dealing with a damp spot at the bottom of a slope, there are two other ways of approaching the problem. In the first instance, a line of clay land drain pipes (or the newer perforated plastic land drainage piping) could be laid across the plot from one side of the garden to the other at the bottom of the slope. The pipes should slope gently to a soakaway.

Alternatively, good use could be made of the wet area for growing bog and moisture-loving plants. A rock garden could perhaps be built just above it, and a natural looking pool and bog garden created in the wet area.

Creating level areas

Terracing creates a very pleasing feature in a

Informal steps in a rock garden setting form a natural link between levels on a sloping site.

garden. On a very steep site, however, some level terraces may actually be necessary in order to grow plants easily.

The type of terracing should suit the style of the house and garden. Near a modern house, for instance, the retaining walls for the terraces should be built of modern materials, such as concrete walling blocks, or perhaps of bricks that match those of the house.

On the other hand, next to a cottage in the country, more natural materials such as logs or tree sections are probably much more suitable. In a wild moorland area it may alternatively be appropriate to build dry-stone walls using local natural stone. The stones of such walls are not cemented together, although soil pockets can be made between some of them in which to grow trailing rock plants.

If they can be obtained, timber railway sleepers could be used to form the terraces; they can look good whether in a modern or old-style garden. Really, terraces are no more than a series of very wide 'steps', but the width of each step is determined by the gradient. On a very steep slope the retaining walls have to be much closer together than on a more gently sloping site.

Make a start with the terracing by moving soil around to form the outlines of the terraces — but before you start forming the terraces themselves, the topsoil should be removed and stacked in some convenient spot, so that it is not mixed up with the subsoil. After the terraces have been constructed the topsoil can then be replaced.

Brick, concrete or stone walls should be built on a solid foundation — a 15cm (6in) layer of well-rammed hardcore, topped with about

10cm (4in) of concrete that must be perfectly level across the width of the plot. Such horizontal flatness can be achieved by inserting a line of wooden pegs, and ensuring that the tops are parallel by means of a spirit-level and straight-edge board.

Make sure that any wall built with bricks, concrete walling blocks or stone, cemented together, does not block the natural flow of water through the soil, or wet areas will build up behind the walls. To prevent this, leave gaps at intervals between bricks or blocks or, better still, insert plastic tubes. Water can then pass freely through each wall. If still in doubt about drainage, then behind each wall fill in with rubble or stones, to about 30cm (12in) below the final soil level.

Remember that retaining walls should not be completely vertical, but should tilt back slightly into the slope to compensate for the weight of soil behind them. This applies especially to dry-stone walls.

A mountainscape
Basically, building a rock garden on a sloping site again involves constructing a set of terraces with level soil between them — but in this case, large and small pieces of natural rock are used, the idea being to simulate natural rock outcrops. Use the local rock of the area — if your garden is in a limy or chalky area, use limestone rock, which is whitish; if your garden is in a sandy area, then it is likely that honey-coloured sandstone is the natural rock. The accompanying drawing shows how a rock garden should be built, but before you start construction, study some examples in gardens open to the public.

The flat-topped flowerheads of *Achillea* cascade around the base of a fine specimen of *Corylopsis pauciflora* (**below**). This sunny sloping garden has low walls and clearly defined terraced areas.

Public gardens provide ideas for coping with difficult sites such as steeply sloping gardens. This bold rockery (**right**), planted with dwarf conifers and bulbs, features a series of interconnecting rock pools.

126

THE
HEALTHY
GARDEN

Planning and maintenance

Good health in the garden inevitably manifests itself as beauty, and is successfully achieved in two stages: correct initial planning, and proper maintenance thereafter. The maintenance involves not only the usual attention to feeding and protection but also includes the control of diseases and pests. All this care is made easier, and more effective, where the initial planning anticipates the eventual development of the mature garden.

Right from the start of the planning stage every need of each plant must be taken into account, including food, water, air, light and warmth. The soil on the site should also be analysed to determine its chemical nature. Most soils are either slightly acid or slightly the opposite (alkaline): there is no cause for alarm in a finding of either in reasonable degree. Only extremes of acidity or alkalinity create difficulties, particularly as to the choice of plants. The soil analysis also gives guidance on the type of fertilizers that may be required before planting; once that consideration is taken care of, the first on the list of a plant's basic needs — food — can be ticked off as reasonably secure.

The second need — water — is made easier by looking after the soil's moisture-holding capacity. Its physical condition should preferably be neither extremely light (sand) nor extremely heavy (clay), but should have enough fibre in it to hold moisture, and enough grit to drain freely. Whatever the soil is deficient in, however, can be added before planting. The natural supply of moisture depends on the weather, though, and it is wise not to rely exclusively on it. Hoses and watering-cans must be available to meet shortages.

Two other basic needs — air and light — require that the site is not overshadowed, and that the plants should not be so close to one another as to blind or choke each other. Nor should they be too close to a wall or fence. Spacing between plants must allow room for each plant to grow to maturity.

As for warmth, all that is wanted on a permanent outdoor site is a screen of some kind to protect plants from strong drying winds until they are fully established. Without such protection, growth may be checked.

Even when the garden has been carefully planned, the soil adequately prepared, and the planting carried out, the first stage cannot be reckoned as complete until the plants are settled in. Daily checking may help them to settle, perhaps treading the soil around some plants and giving others a drink.

The next stage in a healthy garden — maintenance — means much more than keeping out pests and diseases, although that is certainly important. Plants have to mature and

they need help to see that they grow up strong and healthy. They may need staking, tying, and removal of dead flowers; some want feeding, some pruning, and nearly all need weeding.

Weeding is one of the most important jobs in any garden but it is especially in a healthy garden, where tidiness means cleanliness. A weed is a plant in a place it is not wanted. As a plant, it is competing with the rest of the garden for a proportion of everything — all the available food, water, light and air; it is also a potential refuge for pests and diseases. That is why weeds must be removed before they reach maturity, long before they produce seed.

It helps plants to be surrounded by a healthy environment. The rest of the planted garden, and the paths, walls, fences, buildings, machines, equipment, tools and sundry items — all must be kept clean. The list is long, and includes even such garden features as heaps of stones, plant debris, and discarded pots and boxes each of which can harbour pests.

Greenhouses and garden frames need particular attention because they are full of plant material which becomes a potential source of infection when plants die or are discarded. Such structures also have cosy corners in which pests can nest. Paintwork must be maintained or cracks develop, to be avidly seized upon by harmful bacteria. Pots and boxes that have been used for plants must be cleaned immediately after use, and put away, so that they do not become contaminated.

Other buildings — toolshed, potting shed, or garage — which house any garden machines, tools or equipment need attention on similar lines. Even a handful of grass clippings left in the mower grass-box can go mouldy and create trouble.

Fences need an application of wood preservative put on in winter and brushed thoroughly into all the crevices. Soil must never be piled against woodwork or the wood rots. Walls are more easily kept free from plant pests and diseases, but fill in holes from which the mortar has fallen out, and keep them clear of debris and weeds.

When clearing away weeds and plant debris, never just dump it in a corner and call it a compost heap. Such a dump may well become a nuisance and is certainly a likely breeding-place for pests and diseases. Compost heaps must be carefully built up with the right mixture of materials so that they ferment in a controlled fashion. Woody material is slow to break down and it is usually better to burn it. But a bonfire can itself be a hazard, giving off fumes if burning slowly, so an incinerator is much better for disposing of such material. Any plant material known to contain pests or disease should of course be put on the incinerator and not on the compost heap.

Techniques and aids

Having planned and planted the garden, the essential is to start a routine of maintenance to keep it in good health. Today, there is a surprisingly wide range of techniques and equipment available to assist the gardener: certainly the modern garden-owner has things a lot easier than previous generations ever did — look back a little and consider the time when the gardener coped with all the problems without scientific aids. He would search his plants regularly for signs of pest damage — and knew just where to look for the insects. Caterpillars, grubs, slugs, earwigs — anything big enough to get hold of — he would pick off and drop into a jar containing salt. Smaller creatures, such as aphids, he would crush between his thumb-nail and the leaf on which he found them. On the soil near a plant salt would be placed to deter crawling pests; fresh soot could also be used in a similar way. So the gardener's only equipment for these techniques was the jar of salt... and that was optional.

One successful early pesticide that is still in use is derris dust, made by crushing the root of the plant of that name. From ancient times it was known that derris is poisonous to fish: pieces of root were thrown into the water to stupefy the fish so that they could be easily netted. Derris (active ingredient, rotatone) is

An annual border (**left**) glows with health at the height of summer, but only constant attention will keep pests and diseases away. Furtunately, many remedies are now available.

A clean well-ordered greenhouse set within a paved area (**above**) is an ideal arrangement for a healthy garden. Insect pests and infections can proliferate in untidy corners.

Perennial borders
(**left** and **below left**)
are a target for many
diseases and pests.
Keep a watch
for trouble.

used in horticulture both as a dust and as a liquid, for the control of aphids, caterpillars, red spider mite and thrips. It has the small drawback that sprayed food-crops must not be picked for at least 24 hours after treatment. And there is the added limitation in an ornamental garden that it must not be allowed to drift on to a garden pool where it could of course kill the fish.

Some of the most fearsome poisons were once popular garden pesticides: arsenic and cyanide, for instance. And even among modern, more sophisticated, garden chemicals there are still some which must not be used on food crops within two weeks of harvesting, although — unlike arsenic and cyanide — they may be considered safe in an ornamental garden.

Techniques have advanced from the primitive method of applying pest-killer dust by sprinkling it through the fingers to the modern dispenser — a disposable, cylindrical, pliable container operated simply by squeezing to puff out a cloud of dust.

One early method of applying insecticides in liquid form was to use a bulbous syringe, operated by simply squeezing the bulb. Today, popular sprays have a pump incorporated so as to pressurize the container and send out a fine spray through a plastic rubber tube and brass lance.

Even as designers were producing ever more efficient sprayers, scientists were searching not only for improved chemicals, but for a way of making them stay longer on the plant instead of running straight off. At one time, soft soap solution became a favourite because it is sticky enough to remain for a while on the leaves. Soft soap and quassia chips made a spray that was highly successful against greenfly on roses.

After soft soap came modern detergents to serve as what were called 'wetters' or 'spreaders' to help the pesticides and fungicides adhere to the plants. Spray chemicals are now sold complete with wetters.

A further scientific development has been the formulation of a type of spray called 'systemic', so called because it is absorbed into the plant's vesicular system (into its sap stream). It means that the pest does not even have to be on the plant at the time of spraying, for the plant remains lethal to pests for as long as the chemical is in its sap stream.

The first systemics stayed active in the sprayed plant for months, which meant that roses, for example, needed only one spray per season. Such a long period of residual toxicity, however, had its dangers, especially in that the insecticides used were poisonous to humans and had to be kept well away from food crops. New systemics were therefore developed that would stay in a plant long enough to knock out the pests, but not long enough to cause danger were they to drift on to a food crop.

There are still nevertheless a number of domestic garden chemicals, including systemics, which must not be used on food crops too close to the time at which the food is to be eaten. The fact that a spray is for use on a flower border does not mean that no precautions are needed: it is surprisingly all too easy for other plants to become contaminated through spray drift or spillage.

A typical warning on a spray can states that 'food crops must not be harvested for (so many) days after spraying'. Whatever the number of days specified is, try to avoid using any chemicals carrying such a warning altogether if there are food plants in your garden or your neighbour's garden, in case by accident some of the spray should get on to the wrong plant.

Problem Anticipation and Control

The old gardener's close inspection of every plant in his hunt for pests is no longer essential. Nor is his intimate knowledge of the pests, both insects and fungi, and their habits. Furthermore, it is now possible to keep the garden in a clean and healthy state with a minimum of plant inspection, and even to cut out the inspection almost entirely, exercising pest control by routine sprays aimed at keeping the whole garden protected. Caution, however, remains necessary.

Maintaining a look-out for garden pests and diseases is in any case not as difficult as it may seem, because in a clean, healthy garden any plant in trouble is conspicuous enough for most people to notice. It generally lacks the brightness of leaf colour and sturdiness of stem that it ought to have; it may even be droopy. There may be holes in leaves where they have been chewed, or the leaves may be distorted where the sap has been sucked out.

One good reason for watching for such signs is that whatever trouble they indicate is likely to spread to neighbouring plants. So when a damaged plant is found, all surrounding plants should also be checked. A caterpillar that hatches out on one plant and starts chewing then moves on to other plants. Spray immediately, and cover as much of the garden as is affected.

If the pest is in a rose-bed, spray the whole bed and any other roses. Spray the whole

Stunning displays of ornamental garden plants (**far left**, **left** and **below left**) rely on a host of preventative measures to keep them in full health. Decorative plants are often more susceptible to certain pests and diseases than their wild counterparts and may need special care to help them avoid or survive their ravages. When using garden chemicals be sure to do so in strict accordance with the instructions supplied with the particular product.

garden if there is doubt. You can spot any slugs or snails that are causing damage by the slimy trails they leave on the ground.

Once the specific source of the trouble is identified, choose a spray suitable for dealing with that individual problem. That is not difficult to do, particularly with advice, but if in doubt collect a permanent 'First-Aid Kit' of wide-spectrum items on hand to use.

Against pests, spray with fenitrothion;
Against fungi, use benomyl;
Against slugs and snails, use slug bait based on either metaldehyde or methiocarb.

It is neither sufficient nor wise to rely on just these few substances despite their general effectiveness, however, and your collection should also contain far more specific remedies to individual problems. There are two reasons for this. First, a specific remedy is one designed to cover a very small range of pests or diseases: there should be no need to protect a plant from something it may never suffer from anyway. Second, and more important, a remedy used constantly eventually ceases to be effective. This can happen when a pest escapes the full treatment and gets only a tiny dose which acts rather like an inoculation and renders the pest immune to further doses of the chemical. In the event of not being able to find a specific remedy and having to use the first-aid items frequently, the following advice on alternatives in both substance and technique may be useful.

As an alternative to fenitrothion, try derris;
As an alternative to benomyl, try a copper-based fungicide;
Alternate the two slug baits metaldehyde and methiocarb rather than keeping to one.

A further choice sometimes difficult to make is between dusts and liquid sprays. Given the choice, use whichever is the more convenient: chemically they are equally effective. In showery weather, however, dust may have the disadvantage of being washed off too quickly; it is also sometimes possible for a fine spray at high pressure to get into crevices that dusts cannot reach. But judge for yourself.

All garden chemicals should be handled with great care. Always wear rubber gloves, for even those substances recognized as safe and non-poisonous should not be allowed to get on to the skin or the clothing — or in fact anywhere except on to the plant for which they are intended (and the ground beneath it). If by accident any of these chemicals does get on to the hands, or worse still on to vulnerable places like the eyes or mouth, it must be washed off immediately. Furthermore, before using any chemical labelled as poison, be sure you know its antidote, and have it readily to hand.

Have a safe, locked cupboard, out of children's reach, in which to keep all the chemicals. As you put each chemical into the cupboard, read the label carefully so that you know what you are storing. Read it again when you take the chemical out to use it, in case you have forgotten a warning. Avoid spilling or splashing when mixing a spray.

Do not attempt to spray in windy weather. It is surprising how far a fine spray can be carried by the wind.

Do not spray in strong sunshine either, when plants could be scorched by sun striking the droplets.

Do not spray when bees are active; wait until dusk when they have gone back to their hives.

Never use the watering-can for chemicals other than plant foods. Nor should a sprayer that has been used for pesticides or fungicides be used for any other purpose, not even for weed-killers or for plain water. Conversely, residue after a can has been used for a weed-killer can also kill plants if water or a pesticide is later used from that can.

For that reason it is not enough simply to have separate cans or sprayers: it is essential that *all* equipment be thoroughly washed out immediately after use. The term 'immediately' may seem to suggest unnecessary haste, but it is vital that the washing is done before any chemical residue has time to dry. In fact, when using several cans or sprayers, each should be filled with clean water after use and then set down to await the full washing out. Accident reports prove all the same that mistakes are frequently made.

The following pages attempt to provide a clear guide to help you to identify your garden foes — pests and diseases — and select suitable remedies. When in doubt, however, use one of the 'First-Aid' treatments; these should be kept always in stock. With them keep a good sprayer, of the type which incorporates a pressure pump and hand lance, maintained always to be in good, clean, working order.

Propagation

Seed-sowing

Most plant-raising by do-it-yourself gardeners is done by seed-sowing, and most of the subjects are annuals. This reflects the fact that annuals are easy to raise from seed and that they bring quick and highly satisfactory results. Also, sowing usually produces plants more cheaply than other methods.

Where there are failures, they can be traced often to not reading the seedsman's directions printed on the packet, possibly through overconfidence engendered by familiarity with the task.

Hardy annual flower seed can be sown in early to mid-spring in the bed or border where the plants are to flower; it is seldom worth while sowing in an outdoor seedbed for later transplanting.

Half-hardy annuals, more sensitive to frost and low temperatures, are sown no earlier than mid-spring. The first of these sowings should be done under glass, later ones in a sheltered seedbed.

Tender annuals are sown under glass in mid to late spring and subsequently hardened off for planting out when frost risk is finished. Most of these annuals (all classes) present no problems — although sweet pea is an important exception — but there are several points to watch in order to ensure first-class results.

Soil or seed compost should be moist but not wet; seeds must never be overcrowded; the depth of sowing should equal the diameter of the seed; and there should be no drying out between sowing and germination. This latter restriction is easy to ensure indoors by sowing in seed trays and covering each tray with a sheet of glass to lock in moisture, and a sheet of dark paper to keep out light until germination.

Tough seeds

Sweet pea seeds need a little extra care because they have a tough skin. Soak them for 24 hours — those which swell in that time can be sown without further attention; those which fail to swell (probably mostly black seeds) may be classed as too tough for the seed-shoot to break through. Take a razor-blade or sharp knife and nick the skins of these tough ones, and then sow them like the rest. Note, however, that the skins of white, wrinkled, or brown seeds *must not* be nicked. Give these an extra day's soaking if they fail to swell in the first 24 hours. After that, sow them, because there is still a reasonable chance that the shoots will break out.

Not all seeds are quite as simple as the hardy annuals and it pays to examine them and decide which ones need special attention. For example, among trees and shrubs there are seeds even harder than the sweet pea, like those of the peach or the walnut, or of some of

Sow medium-sized seeds indoors or in the greenhouse (**above**) by scattering them thinly on moist seed compost in pots or trays. Cover them with their own depth of compost.

Place the pot or tray in a plastic bag (**above**) to conserve moisture. This will help to ensure germination. A sheet of glass will do the same job. Put the pot in a warm place.

Large or pelleted seeds (**above**) can be spaced out on the seed compost. This will save thinning out later on. As well as covering seed containers with plastic or glass, place dark paper over them until germination occurs.

Many flower seeds are extremely fine. To help ensure an even distribution mix them with sand and sprinkle the mixture across the compost. Such fine seeds hardly need covering at all, just the merest dusting of compost.

the forest trees such as oak; roses are another good example.

These and hard seeds from various shrubs do not respond to soaking. Instead, they require a spell of moist, cold treatment. Mix them with moist peat and put them in a domestic refrigerator at a temperature of about 4°C (just under 40°F) for eight weeks before sowing. They should then be sown in seed compost in a greenhouse at a temperature anywhere between 7°C (45°F) and 15°C (60°F). Another cold method, especially if larger quantities are involved, is to put the seeds in a plant pot containing a mixture comprising half peat and half sand and bury them outdoors in late autumn or early winter. Among horticulturalists this process is

described as a form of 'stratification'.

Examine the seeds in early to mid-spring and take out (for sowing) any that have split open. Those that have not split after six months should be buried again and left for another whole year.

Seeds which have undergone this cold treatment should be sown in any recognized seed compost in small pots indoors. Following such chilling, seeds should respond quickly to the greenhouse warmth — anything from 7°C (45°F) to 15°C (60°F) — but not warmer.

Slightly modified forms of these stratification treatments can be given to nearly all seeds of hardy shrubs and trees. They can be sown in small pots of seed compost immediately after gathering in autumn. The pots should then be

Successful germination will produce trays or pots bursting with tiny seedlings. These must be pricked out to another container of compost to enable them to develop into individual plants. This new compost should have more 'body' to it and a trace of fertilizer. Tease out clumps of seedlings (**right**) and carefully remove individual seedlings by holding the leaves (not the stems). Transfer the seedlings to the new container of compost, spacing them out to allow for future growth. Before pricking out it is advisable to spray the seedlings with a suitable fungicide to prevent the development of a fungal disease called 'damping off'; this causes the tiny seedlings to collapse.

plunged outdoors in cool, moist conditions and left till spring, then brought indoors where they normally germinate in a few weeks.

Other types of seed
Besides hard skin, there are other characteristics that differentiate some seeds. They can be like dust (such as begonia), or perhaps oily (like the castor oil plant), or winged (like ash), or plumed (like scabious).

Dust-like seeds should be sown in a seed-tray, on the surface of the compost. They should be lightly pressed into the surface but not covered. Seed of this sort soon loses its viability and ought to be sown as soon after gathering as possible, or stored in a sealed, moisture-proof container.

Oily seeds, perhaps surprisingly, have the same fault as dusty ones in rapidly losing their viability; these too should therefore be sown as soon as possible.

Winged seeds should have their wings removed before sowing.

Plumed seeds should be sown individually, leaving the plume visible above the surface.

Herbaceous perennials form an important group of plant seeds. Although they survive for years — the top growth dying off in autumn and growing again in spring — they vary in length of useful life and tend to deteriorate. The lover of this category of plant has thus continually to be culling and replacing them. Replacements can be raised from cuttings (see below) or from seed.

Sowings can be carried out in spring at the same time as shrubs which have been stratified.

Plants raised in this way can be flowered in the same year. This may be inconvenient where reserve space is limited, in that the plants may be ready for their permanent positions before those positions have been vacated. To avoid such inconvenience, sow herbaceous perennials on a seedbed in early to mid summer. Seedlings from this sowing can be planted in their permanent positions in either autumn or the following spring.

The advice provided here on the sowing of perennials applies equally to the sowing of seeds of alpines and those of rock garden plants.

Seeds and heat

Most seed-sowing routines so far described can be modified by using equipment to raise the temperature at sowing time and for a period immediately after germination. Outdoor sowings, for example, may take place about two weeks earlier if cloches are used before the sowing to get the ground warmed. Even more time can be gained by sowing in cold frames which have brick side-walls. Further time still can be gained by putting soil-warming cables laid below the soil surface in the cold frames.

More warmth is afforded by a greenhouse with sufficient heat to allow for spring sowings of annuals, and stratified shrubs and trees, as already described. In fact, full heating can be provided from mid winter, although it is expensive. It depends on how highly the gardener values the crop.

Where tender plants are wanted from seed for a greenhouse summer display, the cost can be trimmed by using a heated propagating frame — in effect a mini-greenhouse — as a seed-raiser. Propagators are available electrically heated or paraffin-heated, and are not expensive either to buy or to run. To the greenhouse enthusiast they are indispensable. Note, however, that seedlings raised in this way need a heated greenhouse when they come out of the propagator.

Other and newer methods of seed-sowing include a practice called fluid sowing, which can stand on its own or can incorporate the technique of pre-germination.

For raising seeds and cuttings a gentle warmth can be a great bonus. Rather than heating the whole room or greenhouse it is more efficient to use electric thermostatically controlled propagators (**top** and **above**).

Modern sowing methods

Fluid sowing involves stirring a quantity of seed into a plastic bag of wallpaper paste, snipping off a corner of the bag, and squeezing ribbons of the mixture into seed drills. The drills are then lightly covered with soil as might be done in normal sowing.

The advantage is that each seed gets a better chance of germinating through having the protection of the paste. Germination should also be fairly even.

A slightly more sophisticated method of following this system is to use a syringe of the type made for icing cakes. Some doubt remains, though, whether these methods actually gain enough normal bare-seed sowing to justify the extra process.

When pre-germination (a useful technique for which is fully described below) is incorporated with the technique, there is definitely a useful bonus. Germination is achieved much more quickly, and is usually near 100 per cent. The secret is in the control of moisture and temperature during the short time the seeds take to sprout.

In other methods of sowing, one aim is to see that the temperature does not drop below a set minimum. Heated propagators are designed to achieve that, but they do not prevent fluctuations. Seeds sown in the open without any help may encounter substantial variations in temperature and moisture, which interrupt the effort to germinate.

The aim of a good pre-germination technique is to avoid both those fluctuations. A shallow box with a secure lid is needed for the first stage. (Suitable types of box are commonly used in home freezers.) A layer or two of soft paper tissue is laid in the bottom, and then a sheet of firm notepaper. Enough water is poured in to get all the paper thoroughly wet, and the surplus is poured off. Seeds are sprinkled on to the paper; care should be taken to ensure that they do not end up touching each other. Finally, the lid is put on securely to prevent moisture loss.

The box must then be placed in a constant temperature: if in doubt aim at between 15° and 18°C (60° and 65°F) — but the seed packet or the seedsman's catalogue usually gives some indication. Avoid going too high, or the seed may be killed. One way of maintaining a constant temperature is to put the box in a closed room that receives no direct sunlight but that has a steady source of heat, night and day, such as a radiator. Tests with a maximum and minimum thermometer should establish the best position in the room for the required temperature.

Another means is to use a cool room and put in a heated propagator. If the propagator's thermostat is set for the minimum required, the fluctuations should be passably small, unless of course the room temperature itself rises above the figure set for the propagator.

Check the box at least once a day. Some of the seed may start sprouting in two or three

Pre-germinate seeds on a moist (but firm) surface in a suitable container (**top**) This usually takes a week.

The sprouted seeds can be sown in a 'carrier medium' of wallpaper paste (**above**) to give them a good start.

days; most of it should within a week. As soon as the seeds have made shoots 5mm (one fifth of an inch) long, put them into wallpaper paste mixed at half the strength used actually for wallpapering. The paste must not contain any fungicide.

A glass jug is useful in which to mix the paste, in that it shows how well the seed is distributed when put in. If the seeds fall straight to the bottom, the paste is too thin; if they float on the surface, it is too stiff. Correct as needed.

Some people wash the sprouted seed out of the box; others prefer to scrape it gently off the sheet of notepaper on which it has sprouted. Either way, it is at this point that it becomes apparent that had the seed been sprouted on the soft tissue it would have been difficult to get out at all.

For sowing outdoors, use the icing syringe or plastic bag in the way described. Temperature at this stage does not have to be normal sowing temperature but only what the plant needs when in growth.

If sowing is being done indoors in a seed tray or pot, the mixture can be poured straight from the jug. Always cover with a sprinkling of soil and keep this moist so that the paste does not set firm, or the seed sprout may not be able to push through.

It may take a week for green growth to appear through the surface.

Cuttings

Although seed-sowing is the only method of sexual propagation, there are various asexual or vegetative methods. Because seed (or the embryo in it) is a product of the union of male pollen and female ovule, illicit mating can occur when insects or winds bring in alien pollen. The progeny of such unions can be very different from what is required by the gardener and so, in seeking to reproduce any plant identically, it is necessary to practise vegetative propagation. Perhaps this is one reason that the rooting of stem cuttings comes second only to seed-sowing in popularity as a means of plant increase.

The three chief classes of stem cuttings are soft, half-ripe, and hard. Cuttings of the soft new shoots of spring quickly go limp when severed. Persuading them to root involves getting the cut to heal (callus) quickly, before the cutting collapses. The essential is to maintain temperature and keep the atmosphere moist to avoid water loss through the leaves. Commercial growers use mist (a constant fog of moisture) plus soil heating. A few keen amateurs do it with cuttings of fuchsia, chrysanthemum, dahlia, pelargonium, and two or three more favourites.

In general, however, amateurs wait for half-ripe cuttings, which are ready from late spring in the greenhouse to summer outdoors, and include both trees and shrubs. A suitable cutting should bend without snapping and straighten itself; 7.5 to 10cm (three or four inches) is a useful length. Trim to just below a node (a leaf-joint); remove leaves from the lower half; dip the end in a rooting powder; and insert the cutting into a pot to half its length in a half-sand half-peat mixture. Put a plastic bag over pot and cuttings, leaving a large volume of air space inside, and secure the bag to the pot with an elastic band. Keep it out of direct sunlight.

Hardwood cuttings are ready from late autumn and can be 15 to 20cm (six to eight inches) long; no pots are required — they can root in a cold frame. Trickle coarse sand into the hole for each cutting. Close the frame tight.

Many hardwood cuttings are taken in winter and set to root in open ground in a sheltered border. Some rose cuttings do extremely well this way if cut 25 to 30cm (10 to 12 inches) long. Make a slit with the spade, put plenty of coarse sand into the slit, and set each cutting two-thirds its own length in the slit. Make firm with your foot. Signs of rooting appear in mid spring, but the cutting should be left undisturbed until autumn.

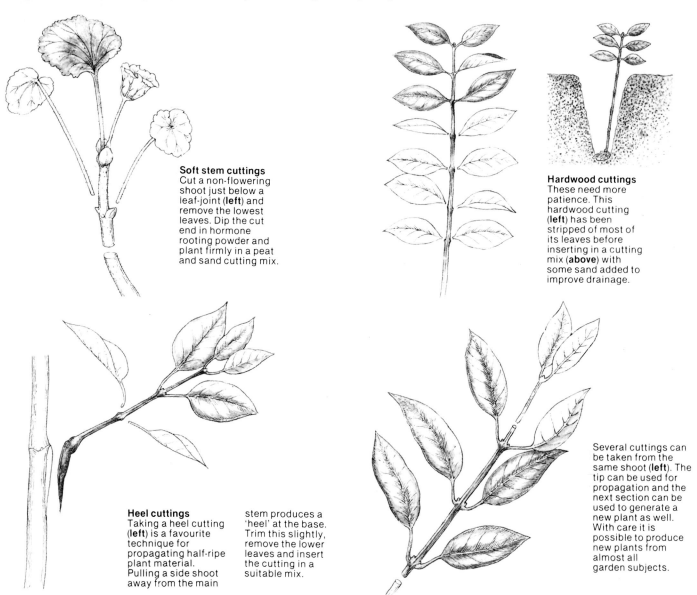

Soft stem cuttings
Cut a non-flowering shoot just below a leaf-joint (**left**) and remove the lowest leaves. Dip the cut end in hormone rooting powder and plant firmly in a peat and sand cutting mix.

Hardwood cuttings
These need more patience. This hardwood cutting (**left**) has been stripped of most of its leaves before inserting in a cutting mix (**above**) with some sand added to improve drainage.

Heel cuttings
Taking a heel cutting (**left**) is a favourite technique for propagating half-ripe plant material. Pulling a side shoot away from the main stem produces a 'heel' at the base. Trim this slightly, remove the lower leaves and insert the cutting in a suitable mix.

Several cuttings can be taken from the same shoot (**left**). The tip can be used for propagation and the next section can be used to generate a new plant as well. With care it is possible to produce new plants from almost all garden subjects.

Root division

The simplest of all methods of propagating is by root division, which is practised in every garden. It is not very productive, the object often being not so much to increase stock as to relieve overcrowded growth. On light sandy soil this division is better done in autumn; on heavy soil it is better done in spring.

A well-established herbaceous perennial plant when dug up and examined may be found to have become three or more plants clustered together. These can be pulled apart by hand and replanted separately. Sometimes the old root needs to be cut or chopped.

Iris germanica has thick rhizomatous roots which produce sucker shoots, and is easy to cut into separate plants. This is best done just after flowering finishes in early summer.

The dahlia has a tuberous root normally stored for the winter. Division can be made either at lifting time or at planting time, but must be done carefully. The dahlia root is not actually a tuber like the potato. Any root broken off dies unless it already has a shoot growing from it.

With bulbs and corms, 'dividing' the root, means removing some immature bulbs or corms and growing them on for two or three years until they attain flowering size. In gladioli, the corm dug up at the end of the season has clusters of tiny cormlets (like grains of rice) around the bases. With a tulip, you might find small bulbs around the base of the parent.

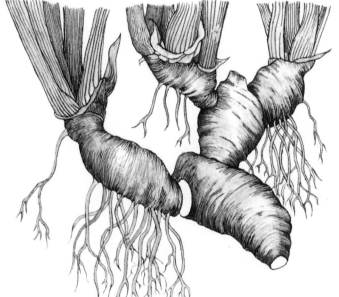

The simplest way to propagate dahlias is to cut the tuberous roots (**left**). Do this carefully with a clean sharp knife, ensuring that each divided section has a shoot arising from it. Cut the root either in the autumn before storing for the winter or in the spring just before planting.

Many herbaceous perennials grow from thick rhizomes — underground stems from which shoots arise. It is fairly easy to cut these (**left**) into separate pieces about 7.5cm (3in) long, each with an obvious growing point. Planted separately, these pieces should develop healthy new growth. It is wise to discard any old pieces of rhizome and only replant the youngest sections.

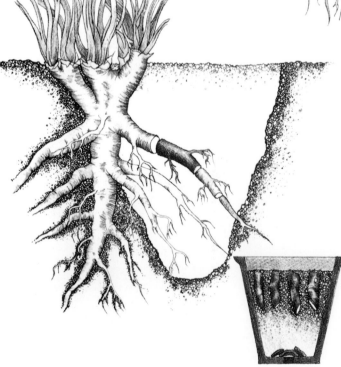

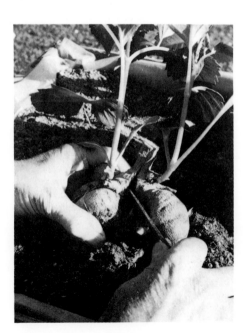

Taking root cuttings (**left**) is a fairly straightforward way of generating new plants for the garden. Herbaceous perennials and woody plants with thick fleshy roots are the best ones to try. Cut sections of root up to 15cm (6in) long and 12mm (½in) in diameter from lifted plants during autumn or winter. Trim the base of each piece with a sloping cut and insert them in a mix of peat, sand and loam with a layer of sand over the top. All being well, new shoots should appear in the spring. Cutting dahlia roots (**right**) needs a steady hand and a sharp clean blade for success.

Layering (**left**) is yet another technique for increasing garden plants. It is especially suitable for shrubby plants with low branches. It involves pegging down a shoot against the soil to encourage roots to develop. This process is aided by partly cutting through the stem at a leaf-joint.

Carnations are ideal subjects for layering. Select a vigorous side shoot and remove the lower leaves. Make a partial cut through the stem (**below**) at a leaf-joint so that a 'tongue' is formed that can be kept open while in contact with the soil. Roots will develop at this point on the stem.

Carefully bend the side shoot down and peg it firmly to the soil (**bottom**) so that the tongue cut in the stem is kept open. Dusting the cut with hormone rooting powder will speed the formation of roots. These should develop in about six weeks, when the new plant can be severed.

Layering

Layering is another easy method suited only to small-scale propagation. It involves pegging a branch to the ground, heaping soil over the pegged spot, and leaving it to form roots there. The new roots support the outer portion of stem, which ultimately can be severed from the parent and planted separately.

Before pegging down, a tongue is cut in the stem, and this cut is kept open with a matchstick to help it callus and make roots. Autumn is a good time for this, on suitable shrubby plants which have branches low enough and flexible enough. It may take between a year and 18 months before the new plant can be moved.

A few herbaceous plants have stems tough enough for layering (carnations, for example), but in the main herbaceous plants are better raised by division, cuttings or seed.

Air layering is a process of making a plant produce roots and shoots from an upright stem. It is not an easy method. A tongue is cut in the stem and part of the stem is encased in damp moss and sealed with polythene. The rubber plant *(Ficus robusta)* is a suitable indoor subject for this treatment.

Other methods

Some trees and shrubs send up shoots at points along their outstretched roots. These shoots, called 'suckers', can be dug up with a portion of root and transplanted.

Grafting and budding are popular with commercial growers and nurserymen. The aim is to give the subject a root system that influences its growth. Apples, for instance, may take ten to twenty years to mature and fruit, when grown on their own roots. But an apple stem grafted on to a dwarfer subject makes a small tree that begins to fruit in only three or four years.

Budding is a form of grafting, using an eye (dormant growth point) instead of a whole shoot, and is popular with rose tree and apple tree raisers. It is economical because the portion of stem needed for one normal graft may have seven or more eyes, each capable of producing a tree.

INDEX

soil, garden 11
Solanum 20
Solidago 12, 57
 'Goldenmosa' **57**
Solomon's seal **109**
Sorbus aria **78**, 81, 88
 S. aucuparia 88
 S. cashmiriana 88
 S. esserteauana 88
 S. hupehensis 88
 S. vilmorinii 88
sorrel tree 87
sowing methods,
 modern 134
Spartium junceaum 57,
 114, 114-115
spindle, evergreen 106,
 107
spiraea 106, **107**
 blue 67
Spiraea 69
 S. arguta 46, 106
 S. japonica 61, 72
 S. prunifolia 'Plena'
 75
spurge 40, 56, 58, 114-
 115
Stachys lanata **70**, 71,
 71
steps **24-25**
 brick **25**
 log **25**
 paving **25**
 wooden **25**
steps in a rock garden
 124
steps with mixed annual
 24-25
Sternbergia lutea 57
Stewartia koreana 88
 S. sinensis 88
stock, Brompton 13
 East Lothian 13, 60
stonecrop 33, 40, 114-
 115
strawberry tree 89
Styrax japonica 88
sumach, stag's horn
 121, 122
 Venetian 73
summerhouse, mock
 Tudor **26**
 pavilion style **27**
 simple wooden **26**,
 27
summerhouses 26-27,

26-27
sunlight in the garden
 11
sunroom extension **27**
swamp cypress 96
sweet box 40
sweet pea 13, 46, 104
sycamore 84
Symphoricarpus albus
 122
Symphytum
 grandiflorum 40, 41
Syringa 46, 64
 'Louis van Hout' **47**
 S. ×josiflexa 88
 S. microphylla **64**
 S. velutina
 palibiniana 88

T

Tagetes 20, 33, 57, 59
 'Lemon Queen' **56**
 T. erecta 'Orange
 Jubilee' **58**, 59
 T. patula **119**
Taxodium distichum 96,
 116-117
Taxus baccata 73, 106
 'Semperaurea' **72**,
 73
teasel, 48, 49
temperature in the
 garden 11
terraces 24-25, 125
 timber deck **24, 25**
 timber windbreak for
 24
 traditional **25**
Teucrium fruticans 71
thistle, globe 67, 114-
 115
thrift 33
Thuja occidentalis
 plicata 106
thyme 42
 creeping 40, 114-115
 wooly 31
 Thymus **21**
 T. pseudo-
 lanuginosus 31
 T. serpyllum 40, 114-
 115
Tiarelle cordifolia 40
Tilia 93
 T. petiolaris **93**, 95

T. tomentosa **93**, 95
Tithonia speciosa 59
tobacco, sweet 57
topiary 110, **110**, 111
 peacock **111**
 yew 100
Trachicarpus fortunei
 119
traveller's joy 49
Tree of Heaven 94
tree poppy, Californian
 71
tree shapes, conical **81**
 fastigiate **81**
 spreading **81**
 weeping **81**
trees, fastigiate 12
 large 94
 planting 82, 83 **83**
 small deciduous 84
 small evergreen 89
trees and shrubs 11-12,
 14-15
 value of 79
Trollius 56, 58
 T. europaeus 36
tulip 20, 56, 58, 60, 62,
 64, 68, 120
twiners 13

U

Ulex europaeus
 'Plenus' 114-115

V

valerian 72
Valeriana phu 'Aurea'
 72, 73
verbascum 12, 48
Verbascum
 bombyciferum 71,
 71
Verbascum hybrids
 114-115
Verbena 33, 61, 120
veronica 40, 61
Veronica gentianoides
 66
 V. incana 71
Versailles baskets,
 wooden 21
Viburnum 46, 69, 88
 V. betulifolium 88
 V. ×bodnantense 88
 V. ×burkwoodii 46, 93
 V. carlesii 46, 88, 93

V. davidii 40, 93
V. farreri 46
V. opulus 88
 'Compactum' 88
V. plicatum 88
V. rigidum 93
V.tinus **92**, 93, 106
V. tomentosum
 'Mariessii' 69
Vinca 75
 V. major 40, 41, 75
 'Variegata' 41
 V. minor 40, 41, **110**
 'Alba' 41
 'Azurea Flore Pleno'
 41
 'Bowles Variety' 41
 'Gertrude Jekyll' 41
 'Variegata' 41
vine, glory 23
 mile-a-minute 105
 Russian 18, 105
Viola 60, 64
 V. cornuta 68
violet 68
Virginia creeper 104,
 120
Vitis coignetiae 23

W

wallflower 13, 20, 49,
 56, 120
 Siberian 46
walls 101, **101**
 covered in climbing
 plants **104**
 making them more
 beautiful 104-106
waxbell 36
weeping willow, golden
 12, 72, 116-117
Weigela 61, **75**
 'Bristol Ruby' **61**
 W. florida 75, **75**
Welsh poppy 58
wet and flooded areas
 116-117
wet patches 124
willow, scarlet 116-117
 white 72
windbreaks and
 screens, tall 110
winter sweet 44
wisteria 13, **104**, 105

Wisteria floribunda
 'Macrobotrys' **66**
witch hazel 45, 87
wormwood 31, 114-115

Y

yew 73, 79
 Irish 12
Yucca filamentosa 106,
 118, **119**
 'Variegata' 118
 Y. flaccida 'Ivory' 118
 Y. gloriosa 118

Z

Zantedeschia
 aethiopica 116-117
 'Crowborough' **116**
Zelkova carpinifolia **93**,
 95
 Z. serrata **93**, 95
 Z. sinjica **93**, 95
Zinnia 47, 57, 59
 'Pacific Gold **57**
 'Peter Pan Orange'
 59